Sport and Disability

Inclusion is primarily discussed in education. With the increasing number of member states of the United Nations ratifying the Convention on the Rights of Persons with Disabilities, academics have vividly discussed inclusion in the context of other areas of life, such as the community at large, as 'social inclusion' in the context of work and employment, and with regard to the aspects addressed by Article 30.5 of the Convention, namely cultural life, recreation, leisure, and sport. This volume is organised around the topic inclusion in sport and has a particular focus on the participation of people with disabilities in sport. Typical barriers for people with disabilities to participate in sport include lack of awareness on the part of people without disabilities as to how to involve them in teams adequately, lack of opportunities and programmes for training and competition, too few accessible facilities due to physical barriers, and limited information on and access to resources. The chapters attribute central importance to the processes and mechanisms of inclusion that operate within sporting environments and to the question of either what happens or could happen to persons with disabilities who enter the playing field.

The chapters were originally published in a special issue of *Sport in Society*.

Florian Kiuppis, formerly Chairholder of UNESCO Chair in Inclusive Physical Education, Sport, Fitness and Recreation at the Institute of Technology, Tralee (Ireland) and currently Professor of Inclusive Education at the Catholic University of Applied Sciences Freiburg (Germany) and Inland University of Applied Sciences – INN University, Lillehammer (Norway).

Sport in the Global Society: Contemporary Perspectives
Series Editor: Boria Majumdar, *University of Central Lancashire, UK*

The social, cultural (including media) and political study of sport is an expanding area of scholarship and related research. While this area has been well served by the *Sport in the Global Society* series, the surge in quality scholarship over the last few years has necessitated the creation of *Sport in the Global Society: Contemporary Perspectives*. The series will publish the work of leading scholars in fields as diverse as sociology, cultural studies, media studies, gender studies, cultural geography and history, political science and political economy. If the social and cultural study of sport is to receive the scholarly attention and readership it warrants, a cross-disciplinary series dedicated to taking sport beyond the narrow confines of physical education and sport science academic domains is necessary. *Sport in the Global Society: Contemporary Perspectives* will answer this need.

Recent titles in the series include:

The State of the Field
Ideologies, Identities and Initiatives
Edited by David Kilpatrick

Global and Transnational Sport
Ambiguous Borders, Connected Domains
Edited by Souvik Naha

New Perspectives on Association Football in Irish History
Going beyond the "Garrison Game"
Edited by Conor Curran and David Toms

Major Sporting Events
Beyond the big two
Edited by John Harris, Fiona Skillen and Matthew McDowell

Research Methodologies and Sports Scholarship
Edited by James Skinner and Terry Engelberg

Sport and Disability
From Integration Continuum to Inclusion Spectrum
Edited by Florian Kiuppis

For a complete list of titles in this series, please visit https://www.routledge.com/series/SGSC

Sport and Disability
From Integration Continuum to Inclusion Spectrum

***Edited by*
Florian Kiuppis**

LONDON AND NEW YORK

First published 2018
by Routledge

2 Park Square, Milton Park, Abingdon, Oxfordshire OX14 4RN
52 Vanderbilt Avenue, New York, NY 10017

Routledge is an imprint of the Taylor & Francis Group, an informa business

First issued in paperback 2020

Copyright © 2018 Taylor & Francis or SOCIETY

All rights reserved. No part of this book may be reprinted or reproduced or utilised in any form or by any electronic, mechanical, or other means, now known or hereafter invented, including photocopying and recording, or in any information storage or retrieval system, without permission in writing from the publishers.

Notice:
Product or corporate names may be trademarks or registered trademarks, and are used only for identification and explanation without intent to infringe.

British Library Cataloguing-in-Publication Data
A catalogue record for this book is available from the British Library

ISBN13: 978-1-138-58538-6 (hbk)
ISBN13: 978-0-367-58931-8 (pbk)

Typeset in Minion Pro
by codeMantra

Publisher's Note
The publisher accepts responsibility for any inconsistencies that may have arisen during the conversion of this book from journal articles to book chapters, namely the possible inclusion of journal terminology.

Disclaimer
Every effort has been made to contact copyright holders for their permission to reprint material in this book. The publishers would be grateful to hear from any copyright holder who is not here acknowledged and will undertake to rectify any errors or omissions in future editions of this book.

For Ute, Teresa, Rolf and Danny

Contents

Citation Information	ix
Notes on Contributors	xii
Prologue	xiv
Florian Kiuppis	

Preface	1
Eli A. Wolff and Mary A. Hums	

1 Inclusion in sport: disability and participation   4
Florian Kiuppis

2 Hard bodies: exploring historical and cultural factors in disabled people's
participation in exercise; applying critical disability theory   22
Marsha Saxton

3 Making the right real! A case study on the implementation of the right to
sport for persons with disabilities in Ethiopia   40
Mina C. Mojtahedi and Hisayo Katsui

4 The relationship between physical activity and self-efficacy in children with
disabilities   50
Kim Wickman, Madelene Nordlund and Christina Holm

5 A global perspective on disparity of gender and disability for deaf female athletes   64
Becky Clark and Johanna Mesch

6 The outcomes of running a sport camp for children and youth with visual
impairments on faculty members' teaching, research, and service activities:
a case study   76
Otávio L. P. C. Furtado, Lauren J. Lieberman and Gustavo L. Gutierrez

7 Sense of belonging: is inclusion the answer?   91
Melissa H. D'Eloia and Pollie Price

CONTENTS

8 Between a rock and a hard place: the impact of the professionalization of the role of the teaching assistant in mainstream school physical education in the United Kingdom 106
Jackie Farr

9 The fiddle of using the Paralympic Games as a vehicle for expanding [dis]ability sport participation 125
P. David Howe and Carla Filomena Silva

10 About inclusive participation in sport: cultural desirability and technical obstacles 137
Alexy Valet

11 Forgotten bodies – an examination of physical education from the perspective of ableism 152
Martin Giese and Sebastian Ruin

12 Social participation of people with disabilities in boxing and capoeira: a comparative ethnographic multi-sited focus 166
Martial Meziani

Epilogue 179
Cheri A. Blauwet
Index 181

Citation Information

The chapters in this book were originally published in *Sport in Society*, volume 21, issue 1 (January 2018). When citing this material, please use the original page numbering for each article, as follows:

Preface

Preface
Eli A. Wolff and Mary A. Hums
Sport in Society, volume 21, issue 1 (January 2018) pp. 1–3

Chapter 1

Inclusion in sport: disability and participation
Florian Kiuppis
Sport in Society, volume 21, issue 1 (January 2018) pp. 4–21

Chapter 2

Hard bodies: exploring historical and cultural factors in disabled people's participation in exercise; applying critical disability theory
Marsha Saxton
Sport in Society, volume 21, issue 1 (January 2018) pp. 22–39

Chapter 3

Making the right real! A case study on the implementation of the right to sport for persons with disabilities in Ethiopia
Mina C. Mojtahedi and Hisayo Katsui
Sport in Society, volume 21, issue 1 (January 2018) pp. 40–49

Chapter 4

The relationship between physical activity and self-efficacy in children with disabilities
Kim Wickman, Madelene Nordlund and Christina Holm
Sport in Society, volume 21, issue 1 (January 2018) pp. 50–63

CITATION INFORMATION

Chapter 5

A global perspective on disparity of gender and disability for deaf female athletes
Becky Clark and Johanna Mesch
Sport in Society, volume 21, issue 1 (January 2018) pp. 64–75

Chapter 6

The outcomes of running a sport camp for children and youth with visual impairments on faculty members' teaching, research, and service activities: a case study
Otávio L. P. C. Furtado, Lauren J. Lieberman and Gustavo L. Gutierrez
Sport in Society, volume 21, issue 1 (January 2018) pp. 76–90

Chapter 7

Sense of belonging: is inclusion the answer?
Melissa H. D'Eloia and Pollie Price
Sport in Society, volume 21, issue 1 (January 2018) pp. 91–105

Chapter 8

Between a rock and a hard place: the impact of the professionalization of the role of the teaching assistant in mainstream school physical education in the United Kingdom
Jackie Farr
Sport in Society, volume 21, issue 1 (January 2018) pp. 106–124

Chapter 9

The fiddle of using the Paralympic Games as a vehicle for expanding [dis]ability sport participation
P. David Howe and Carla Filomena Silva
Sport in Society, volume 21, issue 1 (January 2018) pp. 125–136

Chapter 10

About inclusive participation in sport: cultural desirability and technical obstacles
Alexy Valet
Sport in Society, volume 21, issue 1 (January 2018) pp. 137–151

Chapter 11

Forgotten bodies – an examination of physical education from the perspective of ableism
Martin Giese and Sebastian Ruin
Sport in Society, volume 21, issue 1 (January 2018) pp. 152–165

CITATION INFORMATION

Chapter 12

Social participation of people with disabilities in boxing and capoeira: a comparative ethnographic multi-sited focus
Martial Meziani
Sport in Society, volume 21, issue 1 (January 2018) pp. 166–178

For any permission-related enquiries please visit:
http://www.tandfonline.com/page/help/permissions

Notes on Contributors

Cheri A. Blauwet is an Assistant Professor of Physical Medicine and Rehabilitation, Harvard Medical School, USA.

Becky Clark is an Independent Scholar based in the USA.

Melissa H. D'Eloia is based in the Department of Health and Human Development, Western Washington University, Bellingham, USA.

Jackie Farr is a Lecturer in the Faculty of Education and Health, University of Greenwich, London, UK.

Otávio Luis PC Furtado is a Post-doctoral fellow at the University of São Paulo, Brazil.

Martin Giese is based at the Institut für Rehabilitationswissenschaften, Blinden-und Sehbehindertenpädagogik, Humboldt-Universität zu Berlin, Germany.

Gustavo L. Gutierrez is based at the Department of Adapted Physical Activity, Physical Education College, State University of Campinas, Brazil.

Christina Holm holds a Master degree in Social Science with a major in Sport Education from Umeå University, Sweden. For the past twenty years she has worked as Special Sports Teacher at the Habilitation Center for children with disabilities in Halmstad, Sweden.

P. David Howe is a Reader in the Social Anthropology of Sport at the School of Sport, Exercise and Health Sciences, Loughborough, UK.

Mary A. Hums is a Professor of Sport Administration at the University of Louisville, Louisville, Kentucky, USA.

Hisayo Katsui is an Adjunct Professor in Disability Studies at the University of Helsinki and Research and Development Manager at Abilis Foundation, Finland.

Florian Kiuppis is a Professor of Inclusive Education at the Catholic University of Applied Sciences Freiburg, Germany, and Inland University of Applied Sciences – INN University, Lillehammer, Norway.

Lauren J. Lieberman is based at the Department of Kinesiology, Sport Studies, and Physical Education, The College at Brockport, State University of New York, USA.

Johanna Mesch is an Associate Professor of Sign Language at the Department of Linguistics, Stockholm University, Sweden.

NOTES ON CONTRIBUTORS

Martial Meziani is part of the Research Group on disability, accessibility and educational practices (Grhapes, EA 7287) at the National Higher Education Institute for Teacher Training and Research for Special Needs Education (INS HEA), Suresnes, France.

Mina C. Mojtahedi is based at the Threshold Association, Helsinki, Finland.

Madelene Nordlund is Senior Lecturer and Associate Professor at the Department of Sociology, Umeå University, Sweden.

Pollie Price is Program Director of the Post Professional Occupational Therapy Department Program and Associate Professor at the Department of Occupational and Recreational Therapies, University of Utah, Salt Lake City, USA.

Sebastian Ruin works as postdoc at the German Sport University Cologne (Institute of Sport Didactics and School Sport), Germany.

Marsha Saxton is Director of Research and Training at the World Institute of Disability, Berkeley, USA.

Carla Filomena Silva is a Senior Lecturer at the School of Science and Technology, Nottingham Trent University, UK.

Alexy Valet is an Associate Researcher in Social Sciences and Humanities at the Laboratory on Vulnerabilities and Innovation in Sport (L-ViS, EA7428) at the Université de Lyon, France.

Kim Wickman is an Associate Professor of Education at the Department of Education, Umeå University, Sweden.

Eli A. Wolff is based at the Brown University and Institute for Human Centered Design, Boston, USA.

Prologue[1]

Florian Kiuppis

This volume is organised around the topic of inclusion in sport and has a particular focus on the question how the *participation of people with disabilities* in sport can be guaranteed once access has been secured. The chapters go beyond questions of who has or should have access to sport, or who makes achievements in joint physical activities, and instead move towards consideration of various terms of inclusion. Participation is understood as the process between access for all in the true sense of the word, namely covering the whole range of different target groups and all age groups, and achievement in sport experiences – eventually involving Personal Assistance Services (PAS). The goal is full enjoyment without discrimination, as outlined in the Convention on the Rights of Persons with Disabilities (CRPD) – adopted in the year 2006 at the United Nations Headquarters in New York – that provides a framework for addressing a rights-based approach to the inclusion of people with disabilities in sport. For the process of inclusion in sport, this means that all participants of a shared sport experience should be valued by the others through – what Alexy Valet calls – "the real recognition of their participation" therein (see Chapter 10). In other words, through the taken-for-grantedness that persons with disabilities are in the thick of the experience or – how Cheri Blauwet illustrates it with reference to a concept borrowed from Eli Wolff – by letting team members with disabilities merge into a "desired form of 'invisibility'" (see Epilogue), then the above stated goal is reached.

The ideational centrepiece of the book is the "Inclusion Spectrum," published in 1996 by Ken Black (who was at that time Inclusive Sport Officer at the Youth Sport Trust, UK), that consists of five modalities that cover the spectrum of opportunities for people with disabilities, ranging from 'inclusion within mainstream settings' to 'inclusion within disability-specific opportunities' (see Preface).

What remains at stake – and here Article 30.5 of the CRPD gets the focus of our attention – how to enable persons with disabilities to participate on an equal basis with others in sporting activities of their choice. Since it is individual preferences and wishes of people with disabilities that determine which sporting activity out of a variety of separate activities for persons with disabilities and modified activities designed for all is appropriate to set-up inclusively, "disability sport" appears to be a term that attributes each approach equal importance and validity, given that persons with disabilities can participate therein in full consideration of their individual autonomy and independence (compare CRPD, Preamble). That is why this volume contains not only articles about options of sporting activities for people with disabilities together with non-disabled peers and competitors but also contributions that emphasise disability sport in segregated settings – as the cover picture indicates: a whole variety of different forms, intersecting shapes, and overlapping colours.

PROLOGUE

Note

1 The following chapters were originally published in *Sport in Society*, volume 21, issue 1 [Special Issue "Inclusion in Sport – Disability and Participation"], in January 2018. This Prologue and the Epilogue have been added as complements to the articles (including the Preface). For Acknowledgements see the end of Chapter 1.

Preface

Eli A. Wolff and Mary A. Hums

The Convention on the Rights of Persons with Disabilities (CRPD), through Article 30.5, provides the world with a framework for addressing a rights-based approach to the inclusion and integration of people with disabilities in sport, recreation and leisure activities. Article 30.5 utilizes a universal design approach and covers the spectrum of opportunities for people with disabilities: inclusion within mainstream settings as well as inclusion within disability-specific opportunities. The CRPD's language also enables opportunities for people with and without disabilities to participate and compete together through unified sports and reverse integration settings. Additionally Article 30.5 covers inclusion in venues, activities in school settings, and inclusion and access to services provided to all.

Article 30.5 is a significant contribution to the CRPD as it reinforces the vital contribution of sport, recreation and leisure to human rights and the human condition. The CRPD reinforces a paradigm shift from a medical model to a social model of disability, including the domain of sport and recreation. Article 30.5 indicates the need for people with disabilities to become full members of the sporting world with rights and dignity. People with disabilities are stakeholders at all levels of sport, recreation, physical activity, physical education and leisure and as such must be in the room as meaningfully involved and engaged participants, competitors, administrators and officials.

The CRPD has served as a catalyst for international organizations, some of which we do not typically associate with sport, to begin to adopt language inclusive of people with disabilities. Organizations such as the United Nations Office of Sport for Development and Peace (UNOSDP), the International Disability Alliance (IDA), and UNESCO now recognize disability in their public discourses and updated policies.

The UNOSDP includes people with disabilities as a priority area and focus of their office. UNOSDP has integrated a focus on 'Sport and Persons with Disabilities' through their Thematic Working Group of the Sport for Development and Peace International Working Group (SDP IWG) co-chaired by the Republic of Korea and the People's Republic of China. The Working Group focuses on the following three Strategic Priority Areas: (a) Independence and Sport Participation, (b) Using Sport to Empower Persons with Disabilities, and (c) Inclusion of Persons with Disabilities within Sport.

In 2015, IDA issued a statement titled, 'Calling for the Global Sport Community to Promote the Rights of Persons with Disabilities in Accordance with the CRPD'. IDA articulates,

To ensure full and effective implementation of the Convention on the Rights of Persons with Disabilities (CRPD), IDA calls upon the entire global sport community, including Governmental and Non-Governmental actors, to acknowledge and promote the rights of persons with disabilities to participate in all forms of sport and recreation. This includes, but is not limited to, organized and non-formal sport, physical education, physical activity and fitness, recreation and play. The promotion of the rights of persons with disabilities to participate in sport and recreation must be consistent with the principles of the CRPD and must likewise reflect the social model understanding of disability.

In 2015, UNESCO completed its work on the revised UNESCO Charter on Physical Education, Physical Activity and Sport, and in so doing, included disability as a part of the new language.

The adoption of the revised Charter should mark a shift away from words towards action, from policy intent to implementation. It sets the tone for a new international sport policy debate, which should now focus on the exchange of good practice, education and training programmes, capacity development, and advocacy. This is also a strong recognition of physical education as a driver for promoting gender equality, social inclusion, non-discrimination and sustained dialogue in our societies,

said UNESCO Director-General, Irina Bokova.

At the time of the adoption of the revised UNESCO charter, the authors provided this statement:

The updated Charter represents a milestone in the global sporting environment, calling for people with disabilities to be at the table and visible, with a voice, at the center and within physical education, physical activity and sport. People with disabilities can no longer be on the sidelines, no longer objects of charity and pity. The new Charter reflects the paradigm shift as indicated in the Convention on the Rights of Persons with Disabilities, moving toward empowerment, dignity, universal design and full inclusion.

The CRPD also relates to the Olympic Movement. The Olympic Movement's reach includes athletes with disabilities on several levels – competitors with disabilities in the Olympic Games, as well as athletes of the Paralympic Games, Special Olympics and Deaflympics. The CRPD reaffirms that athletes with disabilities in the Olympic Movement receive equal treatment and equal protection in the Olympic Games as well as the Paralympic Games, Special Olympics and Deaflympics. The CRPD does not call for the creation of one Games for all, but it does call for all athletes with disabilities within the Olympic Movement to be respected and valued as athletes first – all athletes are equally Olympians. While the non-discrimination language in Principle 6 of the IOC's Olympic Charter does not currently address disability, it is being recommended to the IOC to add the word 'disability' into Principle 6 to align with the CRPD. As Hudson Taylor of Athlete Ally states,

If the IOC believes the practice of sport is a human right, then they should amend Principle 6 of the Olympic Charter to include people with disabilities. Without this language, people with disabilities at the Olympic, Paralympic, Special Olympic and Deaflympic Games will not be valued, protected and respected as they deserve.

A book such as this one, with contributions from a cadre of respected authors, guides the reader via a well-laid out map to discover the scope and influence of the CRPD as it relates to sport and physical activity. As the first United Nations civil rights convention of the twenty-first century, the global footprint of the CRPD is becoming more evident. Yes, work remains to be done to level the playing field, but at least now the international rulebook has expanded and its pages, once silent on disability, have become more inclusive.

Voices of disability are being heard and valued, and the CRPD, specifically Article 30.5, has played a critical role in this new-found presence and visibility of people with disabilities in sport. Article 30.5 is a powerful tool for promoting and ensuring equality and inclusion of people with disabilities in all aspects and levels of sport, recreation, physical activity, physical education and leisure. We hope each chapter in this book will help readers to realize and understand how the power of sport empowers people with disabilities.

Inclusion in sport: disability and participation

Florian Kiuppis

ABSTRACT

For the last couple of decades UNESCO has aimed to achieve to a far extent the implementation of the guiding principle of inclusion at all levels in education systems worldwide. The idea that countries 'should ensure an inclusive education system at all levels' is also a central objective of the UN Convention on the Rights of Persons with Disabilities. This Introduction to the Special Issue explores what participation as an aspect of inclusion means in general, and realistically can mean in sport and quality physical education in particular. Sport is introduced as a context in which, unlike in education, the individual choice of a sporting activity on a spectrum ranging from separate activities for persons with disabilities to modified activities designed for all makes it necessary to attribute each approach equal importance and validity instead of discrediting segregated structures and glorifying supposedly inclusive ones.

For the last couple of decades, while following up the World Conference on Special Needs Education that was held in Salamanca in 1994, UNESCO and its collaborators have aimed to achieve to a far extent the implementation of the guiding principle of *inclusion* at all levels of education systems worldwide (Kiuppis and Hausstätter 2014). In context of the most recent International Conference on Education, held in Geneva in 2008 and hosted by the International Bureau of Education (IBE), UNESCO stated:

> [I]t has now been several decades since the international community provided itself with significant legal instruments which, by stressing the right of ALL children to benefit from an education without discrimination, express – implicitly or explicitly – the concept of 'Inclusive Education'. (UNESCO 2008, 3)

Inclusion is primarily discussed in education, as is apparent from just a quick search of the term on the Internet. However, with the increasing number of UN member states ratifying the Convention on the Rights of Persons with Disabilities (CRPD) (UN 2006),[1] politicians and academics have vividly discussed inclusion in the context of other areas of life, such as the community at large (Milner and Kelly 2009), as 'social inclusion' in the context of work and employment (Hall and Wilton 2011), and with regard to the aspects addressed by Article 30.5 of the CRPD, namely cultural life and leisure (Singleton and Darcy 2013), recreation (Gray, Zimmerman, and Rimmer 2012) and sport (e.g. Thomas and Smith 2008; Kiuppis and Kurzke-Maasmeier 2012).

What does 'Inclusion in Sport' mean?

This volume is organized around the topic *inclusion* in sport and has a particular focus on the *participation of people with disabilities* in sport once their access has been secured.[2] This Introduction deals in particular with the point that research is clearly indicating, namely that sport is an area of life in which people with disabilities arguably have less favourable experiences than their non-disabled peers and competitors (Stevenson 2009). Typical barriers for people with disabilities to participate in sport include lack of awareness on the part of people without disabilities as to how to involve them in teams adequately; lack of opportunities and programmes for training and competition; too few accessible facilities due to physical barriers; and limited information on and access to resources (DePauw and Gavron 2005). Central importance is attributed to the processes and mechanisms of *inclusion* that operate within sporting environments and to the question of either what happens or could happen to persons with disabilities who enter the playing field (cf. Spaaij, Magee, and Jeanes 2014).

Let us begin with the basic premise – originally formulated by German-American sociologist Reinhard Bendix (and post-mortem published by his son John Bendix) – that the use of a term (in this case 'inclusion') in different social contexts is itself a worthwhile subject of comparative analysis (Bendix 1998, 310). Accordingly, as a rhetorical starting point for this Introduction I chose the question: Does *inclusion* in sport mean the same as *inclusion* in education? In other words, when the word 'inclusion' is used in the context of sport, do we actually associate the same theories, concepts and methods as in Inclusive Education (IE)? For the purpose of finding a preliminary answer, the work from the later phase of Austrian British philosopher Ludwig Wittgenstein (1889–1951) appears useful, since it states that 'in general, the meaning of a word is its use in language' (Wittgenstein [1936–1946] 2001, 22). While Wittgenstein specified this statement by arguing that 'a meaning of a word is one kind of its use in language', he left open the difference between 'a general use' and, for example, 'two kinds of use' of a word. However, according to Wittgenstein's understanding, one could find out about meanings of 'inclusion' in sport and education by considering the use of the word in language as the 'the hinge of investigation' (cf. Biletzki and Matar 2011).

As a person who has been academically trained in comparative education and whose scholarly work encompasses for the most part studies on institutions and knowledge, analysing shifts in meanings, I am sure that what we know about one context does not automatically apply to another context. For an initial understanding of the use of the word 'inclusion' in different contexts (here, I will not go so far as to conduct a comparative analysis), I am wondering about functional equivalents between debates relating to *inclusion* in education and in sport. For both contexts, the following holds true: *inclusion* is 'about the participation of *all* children and young people and the removal of *all* forms of exclusionary practice' (Len Barton, as quoted in Armstrong 2003, 3).

When thinking about differences between sport and education, the first argument supporting the answer 'no' to the question about the same meaning of *inclusion* in sport and education is that sport is a context, which, with the exception of compulsory Physical Education (PE), is more or less voluntary. So, unlike in education, the provision of opportunities and structures for doing sport seems to be generally much more oriented towards the *choice* of those who decide to do sport. Accordingly, as Spaaij, Magee, and Jeanes (2014) illustrate it, when dealing with inclusion in sport it is important to keep in mind that non-participation does not equal social exclusion, as this occurs when people want to participate but cannot. Indeed, not everyone, regardless of whether they have disabilities, wants to take part in sport.

In front of this backdrop it is better to understand why this volume titled 'Inclusion in Sport: Disability and Participation' contains not only articles about options of sporting activities for people with disabilities together with non-disabled peers and competitors (e.g. the papers from Valet; Meziani), but also contributions that emphasize Disability Sport in segregated settings (e.g. the papers from Saxton; Mojtahedi and Katsui). Also, the Preface of this volume makes perfect sense now, informing the reader about that through Article 30.5 the CRPD provides a framework for addressing a rights-based approach to the inclusion and *integration* of disabled people in sport and covers the spectrum of opportunities for people with disabilities, ranging from 'inclusion within mainstream settings' to '*inclusion within disability-specific opportunities*' (emphases added). Accordingly, in connection with the Olympic Movement Wolff and Hums outline that the CRPD does not call for the creation of one Games for all, but for all athletes with disabilities within the Olympic Movement to be respected and valued as athletes first, since all athletes are equally Olympians.

This Introduction deals with various scenarios of people with disabilities involved in sport and quality physical education (QPE). Due to my background in education and knowledge of the variety of meanings attributed to *inclusion*, I chose to focus particularly on the aspect of *participation* as part of processes of *inclusion of people with disabilities in sport* and QPE. I follow the basic assumption borrowed from studies of fairness, justice, equity and equality of opportunity in education, that inclusive approaches can be characterized by 'ensuring a basic minimum standard […] for all' (Ainscow 2012, 290), in our case a minimum standard of *sport for all*. Hence, my focus is on the question of the interrelations between *inclusion* in sport and QPE, *disability* and *participation*, which is the reason why I want to go beyond questions of *who* has or should have access to sport, or *who* achieves in joint physical activities, and instead move towards consideration of various 'terms of inclusion' (Ramirez 2006, 434).

The issue of different wording: 'disabled people'/'people with disabilities'

In the Disability Studies and IE literature there is tension over the basic terms of 'disabled people' versus 'people with disabilities' (e.g. Le Clair 2011). The issue of the different wording is controversial (Kiuppis 2013). 'People First' language, named after an organization in the US, emerged in the 1980s as a way to counteract objectifying language (such as '*the* disabled') and foregrounds the notion that this population is *people* first and that the personhood is of foremost importance. Such thinking is in line with the 'person-first' terminology used by international organizations such as the UN (e.g. UN 2006) and their respective suborganizations (e.g. WHO 2001; UNICEF 2016), which allows individuals to be the primary focus of attention and relegates the disability issue to a position of secondary importance. This is a way of framing that arguably dates back to the UN Decade of Disabled Persons (1983–1992), of which one outcome was the publication of the Standard Rules on the Equalization of Opportunities for Persons with Disabilities (UN 1993). However, Disability Studies in the UK have traditionally relied on the British 'Social Model', according to which disability is not an attributable feature of individuals but is imposed by society's oppression of people who are physically impaired (Finkelstein 1996). Understood in this way, the limitations of people who are considered 'disabled' result either primarily or – in a more radical understanding of the social model – *only* from their societal context (see Kiuppis and Soorenian, forthcoming). Accordingly, participation restrictions should be understood as mainly caused by barriers (not only physical ones, but also, for example, attitudinal ones) imposed by the social environment. Somewhat contrarily, members of the Disability Studies community in the US, such as those of the Society for Disability Studies, prefer to talk about 'people with disabilities' from a human rights based perspective, seeing the use of the term disability as a way to remove the stigma linked to disease, illness and impairment by both implying that some of those conditions cannot be explained by biological science and that disability is determined by social, political, cultural and economic factors.

From the above, readers may understand why I chose to vary my use of wording, depending on the context when referring to the group in focus in this Introduction. I decided to point out this variation, rather than to prioritize consistency.[3]

Structure of the Introduction

In the following, I introduce the key definitions on which this volume is based. Thereafter, I illustrate the *inclusion* debates in education as the main reference context for relatively more recent *inclusion* debates in sport. In this context I contrast the discourses of *inclusion* in education and in sport and discuss what equivalence the debate about the conceptual development from special education, via education in integrated settings, to IE has in the world of sport.

In the main part of the Introduction, I deal with major 'shifts in the positioning and meaning of international disability sport' (Le Clair 2011, 1075) in three stages. First, I identify the position I take on a *Sports Development Continuum* as conceptualized by Spaaij, Magee, and Jeanes (2014). Second, I introduce the *Integration Continuum for Sport Participation* developed in the US (Winnick 1987), which, according to the author, builds upon those developed for provision of special education services (Reynolds 1962; Deno 1970) and PE services (Winnick 1987, 160).[4] Third, I provide an overview of the processes of the various revisions of the *Integration Continuum* carried out in the UK in connection with the development of the *Inclusion Spectrum,* a model that has been reworked into a practical tool (Black and Stevenson 2011)[5] and that, like the *Index for Inclusion* that is well known in the IE literature (Booth, Ainscow, and Kingston 2002), can be used to support practitioners to think when planning and delivering activities in sport (Stevenson 2009). The main part culminates in a summary of the five modalities of the Inclusion Spectrum and the introduction of a model known as 'STEP' or 'TREE'. At the end of the Introduction, I provide a conclusion.

Basic definitions

The three key defining factors of the UNESCO Chair in Inclusive Physical Education, Sport, Fitness and Recreation at the Institute of Technology (IT) in Tralee (Ireland) are 'sport', 'disability' and 'QPE' and 'physical literacy' as a central aspect of QPE (UNESCO Chair at IT Tralee 2015, 8). I rely here on slightly different definitions than other works on *inclusion* in sport, particularly those on which me and my team members based our UNESCO Chair's work.

Sport

The UNESCO Chair at IT, Tralee understands sport as 'all forms of physical activity that contribute to physical fitness, mental well-being and social interaction, such as play, recreation, organized or competitive sport, and indigenous sports and games' (UN Inter-Agency Task Force 2003).

Disability

Disability is commonly associated with functional limitations. Le Clair (2011, 1078) states: 'Disability is often equated with inferiority and deficiency rather than a neutral difference that may require some adaptation'. However, the meaning of 'disability' we rely on is borrowed from the World Health Organization (WHO), according to which 'disability',

> is an umbrella term, covering impairments, activity limitations and participation restrictions. An impairment is a problem in body function or structure; an activity limitation is a difficulty encountered by an individual in executing a task or action; while a participation restriction is a problem experienced by an individual in involvement in life situations. (WHO 2016)

This definition is in line with the bio-psychosocial model of disability, which is connected with WHO's classification of the components of health, namely the International Classification of Functioning, Disability and Health (ICF) (WHO 2001), which is a conceptual 'pentagon' containing the following components that are used to conceptualize disability, starting with a health condition: (1) activity, (2) body structures and functions, (3) participation, (4) environmental factors and (5) personal factors (see Kiuppis 2013). The ICF is an integrated model that describes a continuum of more to less 'functioning' and 'disability' and uses arrows between the different components to indicate how they are connected. In context of the ICF, a change in one component means a shift in the whole fabric of components, which makes the model applicable for the assessment and interpretation of sport dynamics. To give an example: (1) a person experiences an impairment in their body structures and functions (e.g. blindness); (2) that impairment causes a limitation in their activity (e.g. their ability to see a ball in a game); (3) that limitation in turn leads to a restriction in the person's participation (e.g. their exclusion from a team); (4) the latter restriction potentially has consequences in terms of environmental factors (e.g. mobilization of extra support); and (5) all of the components together have an impact on personal factors, such as the person's coping styles and level of involvement in sport (for the use of this example in education, see, e.g. Hollenweger and Moretti 2012).

Quality physical education

ur understanding of QPE relates to guidelines for policy-makers published by UNESCO 15), which are in line with the International Charter for Physical Education, Physical vity and Sport that was recently revised and in its new form adopted by the UNESCO ber states.[6] Section 3.1 (on 'Ensuring an Inclusive Approach') of the QPE guidelines licy makers highlights the UNESCO Chair's work on the project European Inclusive l Education Training (EIPET), which was officially acknowledged by UNESCO as udy for instituting inclusion (UNESCO 2015, 37). EIPET, launched in 2009, was nternationally by many higher education teacher-training institutions and by many allied professionals for in-service training or lifelong learning (UNESCO Chair at IT Tralee 2016). UNESCO (2015) describes QPE as not only the entry point for lifelong physical activity, but also as improving health awareness, enhancing civic engagement and contributing to social inclusion. UNESCO's QPE policy identifies the UN's Post-2015 Development Agenda as outlining how sustainable development begins with healthy, safe, active, well-educated children. However, UNESCO highlights 'inclusion', 'equality' and 'physical literacy' as central tenants of QPE (see UNESCO Chair at IT Tralee 2015, 8).

Physical literacy

UNESCO (2015) promotes the concept of physical literacy, which was originally defined by Physical and Health Education Canada, as a part of their programme for physical and health educators, Passport for Life, as the ability to move,

> with competence and confidence in a wide variety of physical activities in multiple environments that benefit the healthy development of the whole person. Competent movers tend to be more successful academically and socially. They understand how to be active for life and are able to transfer competence from one area to another. Physically literate individuals have the skills and confidence to move any way they want. They can show their skills and confidence in lots of different physical activities and environments; and use their skills and confidence to be active and healthy.[7]

Physical and Health Education Canada (2016) describes physical literacy as follows:

> Individuals who are physically literate move with competence and confidence in a wide variety of physical activities in multiple environments that benefit the healthy development of the whole person.

- Physically literate individuals consistently develop the motivation and ability to understand, communicate, apply and analyse different forms of movement.
- They are able to demonstrate a variety of movements confidently, competently, creatively and strategically across a wide range of health-related physical activities.
- These skills enable individuals to make healthy, active choices that are both beneficial to and respectful of their whole self, others and their environment.[8]

While conducting a literature search I found that physical literacy is mostly dealt with in PE journals, such as the *European Journal of Physical Education, Physical and Health Education Journal, British Journal of Teaching Physical Education, Journal of Physical Education, Recreation and Dance* and *Physical Education Matters*. Colin Lankshear's (1997, 1998) account of the meanings of 'literacy' in reform conceptions may be a useful analytical tool for (further) research, since Lankshear focuses on meanings at the level of policy proposals in education. Framed with his approach, one could argue that physical literacy spans a spectrum of different meanings, of which 'some remain close to its earlier connotative and denotative associations, while others stretch to encompass sophisticated levels of analysis, abstraction, symbol manipulation, and theoretical knowledge and application' (Lankshear 1998, 356). Following this line of reasoning, we would have to ask how the meanings of physical literacy could be seen to encode values that define physical literacy as an ideal to be realized in both sporting and educational practice, establish the bases of its perceived worth and set parameters for what counts as physical literacy and engagement in it as social idea (Lankshear 1998). According to Lankshear, documents reflect different 'types' of the concept under study, different 'physical literacies', of which some are oriented closer to earlier 'associations' than others. The different types of physical literacy appear to have a common denominator, as 'they share more or less in common a number of features that are important and contentious from a normative perspective' (Lankshear 1998, 357).

Inclusion debates in education as the main reference context for inclusion debates in sport

The main reference context of debates on inclusion in various areas of life still remains education, which arguably is the reason why 'sport', 'disability' and 'participation' are often discussed in connection with Inclusive PE (Goodwin 2009; Coates and Vickerman 2010). What IE in general and Inclusive PE in particular means, what is the main target population and how teacher education and school reform could and should be organized accordingly, have all been subject to academic discussions (Connor et al. 2008; Elliott 2008; Flintoff, Fitzgerald, and Scraton 2008), particularly since the most recent International Conference on Education, held in Geneva in 2008 (Kiuppis 2015a, 6). At that conference, UNESCO stated:

> [I]t has now been several decades since the international community provided itself with significant legal instruments which, by stressing the right of ALL children to benefit from an education without discrimination, express – implicitly or explicitly – the concept of 'Inclusive Education'. (UNESCO 2008, 3)

While some authors understood IE as primarily concerned with people with disabilities, in the sense of education in integrated settings (Sharma, Forlin, and Loreman 2008), others interpreted and still interpret it as an objective to widen the focus of special needs education in terms of the target group by reaching out to the heterogeneity of learners in 'schools for all' and taking diversity as a starting point for educational theory and practice (Kiuppis 2014a).

It is common sense that the Salamanca Statement and Framework for Action (UNESCO 1994) adopted at the World Conference on Special Needs Education in 1994, connected the emerging principle of *inclusion* with the idea of overcoming the divide between regular and segregated provision of education for people with special needs. From a comparative inclusive (physical) education point of view,

> the question we have to answer is to what extent and how the principle of inclusion can be translated to the activities of sport, because obviously education and sport cannot be easily compared, they are not functionally equivalent. So, in other words, what inclusion in education means is something else than what inclusion in sports means. (Kiuppis 2015b)

The relevance of clarity when defining IE becomes clear in UNESCO's Guidelines for Inclusion, a manual designed to 'assist countries in making National Plans for Education more inclusive' (UNESCO 2005, 3), in order to ensure full access to education for all in the true sense of the word, covering the whole range of different target groups and all age groups, and not only guaranteeing access to education, but also tackling active participation and achievement (Whitehead 1995). UNESCO considers its Guidelines for Inclusion to be 'a first step in seeking to foster dialogue on the quality of educational provision and the allocation of resources, providing a policy tool for revising and formulating Education for All plans, and also raising awareness about a broadened concept of inclusive education' (UNESCO 2008, 31), which – following a recommendation at the East Asia Workshop on IE, held in Hangzhou (China) in 2007 – has been called 'New Inclusive Education' (Kiuppis 2015a, 11).

As outlined above, this volume has its focus on *disability* because I assembled the articles in my role as the Head of the UNESCO Chair with the official title 'Transforming the Lives of People with Disabilities, Their Families and Communities, Through Physical Education, Sport, Recreation and Fitness'. We understand inclusion in PE and sport as encompassing the levels of 'access, participation and achievement' (Slee 2006). Instead of focusing just on the question of placement, which is how to make sure that people with disabilities have the chance or become enabled to do sport, the more process-oriented understanding of *inclusion* draws from ideals of empowerment of persons with disabilities and their communities and aims at activating civic society and the various communities therein to become inclusive.[9]

Arguably, the main difference between inclusion debates fuelled by the CRPD in both education and sport is that in sport disability-specific activities are accepted as part of what in the sport and PE literature is commonly called the 'inclusion spectrum', but not in education, in which inclusion debates commonly deal with positive aspects of education in segregated settings and especially with negative aspects of education in such settings. As I show in the following, sport is a context in which special, integrative and inclusive structures are co-existing non-hierarchically.

However, since sport is associated not only with *social inclusion*, but also with physical well-being and the enhancement of self-esteem, it is crucial to understand it as a right and to consider *access* and *participation* in sport – unlike in education – as a question about *individual choice* of a sporting activity across a continuum of segregated, integrated and inclusive approaches, rather than about placement in a context chosen by professionals. Thus, as Wolff and Hums indicate in the Preface, participation of people with disabilities in disability-specific sporting activities is – again, unlike in education – to be considered part of an *inclusion spectrum* (see next section). In a sporting context, the goal is to assist people with disabilities in making their 'independent' choice to participate in sport in the way that they want to and with whom they want to participate (see Misener 2014, 3–4). Hence, inclusion debates in sport are not about how to substitute special structures with integrative ones, and those in turn with inclusive ones, but are characterized by giving each approach equal importance and validity.

Major conceptual shifts in the positioning and meaning of international disability sport

Spaaij, Magee, and Jeanes (2014) edited a volume in which they deal with social exclusion as a phenomenon that can occur or be challenged at any level of sporting competition. In this connection, they introduce different levels as parts of what they refer to as a *sports development continuum*, which ranges from the foundation/participation levels through to the performance/excellence levels. In this connection they refer to this continuum as 'a logical progression from learning the basic skills at foundation level to performing as an elite performer at the excellence level' (Spaaij, Magee, and Jeanes [2014, 3], see also Enoch [2010, 46]; as quoted). The *sports development continuum* suggests that elite competitive sport is as much part of 'sport for all' (ie the promotion of access to sport) as the provision of community opportunities for participation (Houlihan and White 2002). As such, the continuum seeks to reconcile some of the historical tension between those promoting elite sport and those promoting grass roots participation by suggesting that these dual goals are inextricably interdependent (Bloyce and Smith 2010). The *sports development continuum* is described as instructive for conceptualizing the relationship between sport and social exclusion (Spaaij, Magee, and Jeanes 2014).

Spaaij, Magee, and Jeanes (2014, 7) state: '[E]xclusionary processes can be found at any level of sporting competition, and the different levels are often interdependent in terms of the experiences, causes and consequences of social exclusion', to which I would add social inclusion. For this reason, I decided to assemble articles that focus both on the foundation and participation end of the continuum (e.g. the papers by Valet; Wickman, Nordlund and Holm) and on the performance and excellence end (e.g. the papers by Howe and Silva; Saxton).

Integration continuum for sport participation

The *integration continuum for sport participation* is a conceptual framework on the provision of sport opportunities for 'individuals with handicapping conditions' (Winnick 1987).[10] This framework was published as a 'Viewpoint' article in the *Adapted Physical Activity Quarterly* and reflects alternative 'settings' of sport for people with disabilities, ranging from regular sport with no modifications to segregated sport (Winnick 1987, 157–158). The settings are distinguished on the basis of the 'degree of integration' and 'sport type' (Winnick 1987, 160). The continuum ranges from the least restrictive setting possible (1. Regular Sport), which is described as 'most normal/integrated', to the most restrictive segregated one (5. Adapted Sport Segregated). The other settings located between those two poles are: '2. Regular Sport with Accommodation', which is described as necessarily 'reasonable and [should] allow individuals with handicapping conditions equal opportunities to gain the same benefits or results from participation in a particular activity' (Winnick 1987, 159); '3. Regular and Adapted Sport'; and '4. Adapted Sport Integrated'.

For each of the five settings, Winnick offered various 'scenarios' and examples, such as the following respective ones:

(1) 'A mentally retarded[11] athlete [participating in] his school's track team because of his performance in the high jump' (157).
(2) 'A blind bowler competing in regular sport competition with only the accommodation of a guide rail' (159).
(3) '[A] handicapped athlete participating from a wheelchair (adapted sport) may compete against all runners in a marathon including able-bodied and handicapped athletes. Able-bodied athletes run the marathon (regular sport)' (159).
(4) '[B]oth able-bodied and handicapped athletes participate in an adapted version of the sport in an integrated setting. [...] One example of level 4 is when both able-bodied and handicapped athletes use wheelchairs in their competition against wheelchair-confined opponents in wheelchair tennis' (159).
(5) '[H]andicapped athletes participate in adapted sport in a totally segregated setting. A mentally retarded athlete participating in the Special Olympics program is an example. Also, two teams of blind youngsters competing in goal ball exemplifies level 5' (160).

Despite the wording, although the model might seem accurate and up to date for researchers and practitioners outside the field of sport, it arguably appears outdated for those familiar with *inclusion* debates in sport. As outlined above, the CRPD covers the spectrum of opportunities for people with disabilities: inclusion within mainstream settings, as well as inclusion within disability-specific opportunities, depending on the independent individual choice of persons with disabilities themselves. While Winnick acknowledged that '[a]lthough level 5 is most restrictive, it should not be inferred that experiences at these levels are not beneficial and should be minimized' (Winnick 1987, 160), his model clearly privileges participation of persons with disabilities in regular sport, eventually with accommodations, rather than in segregated settings. Winnick suggested greater involvement of persons with disabilities on levels on which arguably they are underrepresented: levels 3 and 4. When critically reading his text in connection with the continuum of the five settings, it becomes clear that his personal main goal was to serve as many people with disabilities as possible (level of access) in settings ideally located on one extreme of the continuum (1. Regular Sport) rather than on the other extreme (5. Adapted Sport Segregated). This tendency is also expressed in the following quotation:

> It is hoped this sport continuum will broaden perspectives in regard to integration in sport. It should help include into sport more persons with handicapping conditions and encourage involvement at levels that are least restrictive and most appropriate. (Winnick 1987)

In sum, Winnick's structure is a hierarchical one suggesting that inclusive activity is the programme pinnacle, and the other approaches he described are adaptations or modifications leading to this goal. However, from an IE perspective, it might seem appropriate to declare hierarchically level 1 the most ideal and level 5 the least ideal. However, for the context of sport it appears to be outdated that the preferences of the individuals described in the scenarios and examples are not given any consideration. Sport appears here as a context, in which what is regarded as relevant is not the *individual's independent choice* of a setting on the continuum from special to inclusive, but rather the *replacement* of special offers by integrative ones.

Subsequent revisions of the integration continuum for sport participation

In this section, I provide an overview of the process of various revisions of the integration continuum that have been carried out in the UK, and which were connected with the development of the Inclusion Spectrum (see Valet 2013). In context of the conceptual framework for the provision of sport opportunities for people with disabilities developed by Winnick (1987), scholars and practitioners considered it necessary 'to arrange the format of the continuum to give each approach equal validity and importance within the overall programme' (Black and Williamson 2011, 203).

A first version of an *Inclusion Spectrum* was introduced in 1996 by Ken Black (at that time Inclusive Sport Officer at the Youth Sport Trust, UK), who changed Winnick's model of a hierarchical order and instead introduced different strategies for participation that could be adopted without one strategy being considered superior to another. In contrast to the *Integration Continuum*, this first revision demonstrated how varying degrees, rather than levels, of participation can be thought of in the sporting environment. In this view, inclusion was more about accepting responsibility for the provision of sporting opportunities for people with disabilities and taking the necessary steps to ensure that everyone is given equal chance and choice to participate (Misener 2014). According to Pam Stevenson (2009), Black refined Winnick's model in a chapter of a handbook titled *Including Young Disabled People* (Youth Sport Trust 1996), '[arranging] the format of the continuum in a manner that gave each strategy equal importance' (Youth Sport Trust 1996, 123). Aiming for an inclusive approach was only considered legitimate if professionals oriented their thinking, decision-making and action on the preferences of individuals with disabilities and their respective independent choices. 'Regular sport activities' were no longer considered the ultimate aim and segregated ones were not, in Winnick's terms per se, considered 'more restrictive'. According to Black and Williamson (2011, 203), '[t]his amended Winnick's hierarchical structure that suggested that inclusive activity was the programme pinnacle, and the other approaches he described were adaptations or modifications leading to this goal'. They provided an informative description of efforts made mostly by practitioners with great impact on the emergence of practical programme designs that addressed inclusion in sport.

One difficulty facing those who started to work on revisions of Winnick's model was the underlying dilemma of *inclusive* approaches: 'How does one include without excluding or further marginalising in the process?' (Kiuppis 2015a, 13). To some extent, and with reference to John Rawls' 'egalitarian difference principle', a perspective that takes into consideration both the differences between persons as well as their equal rights might have been helpful here (Rawls 2003 [1921]). Accordingly, specific measures that are necessary to accelerate or achieve equality among athletes (regardless of the extent of their participation) do not necessarily need to be considered discriminative, marginalizing or excluding (cf. UN 2006, Article 5). Rather, exclusive concentration on different development potentialities, abilities, characteristics and expectations should be understood as a prerequisite of inclusive approaches in any heterogeneous group of people doing sport together.

However, slightly deviating from Winnick's five levels, developers of early forms of the *Inclusion Spectrum* subdivided physical activity into five types: separate activity (e.g. Paralympic sports); parallel activity (e.g. sport for all with separated subcontexts); reverse integration activity (e.g. wheelchair basketball); open activity (e.g. Capoeira);[12] and modified activity (e.g. Baskin).[13] Black's version of an *Inclusion Spectrum* published in 1996 was developed further by him in cooperation with David Tillotson (at that time an advisory teacher of PE in Birmingham). Stevenson used that model then in her practical work with students and teachers, and subsequently the model became a tool for practitioners.

Summary of the five modalities of the inclusion spectrum

The inclusion spectrum proposed five distinct modalities of practice, which according to Stevenson (2009) overlap in principle and methodology. Black and Williamson (2011) presented a graph showing an oval containing the following categories:

(1) Separate Activity: Special activities, specially thought for and proposed for people with disability and practised in different times and spaces, such as skate soccer in Ghana.

(2) Parallel Activity: Disabled athletes may need to train separately with disabled peers to prepare for a competition, such as a wheelchair basketball group included in a local basketball club (see Black and Williamson 2011, 210).

(3) Disability Sport Activity: Reverse integration whereby non-disabled children and adults are included in disability sport together with disabled peers, such as using the Paralympic sports goalball, boccia or sitting volleyball as a basis for an inclusive game.

(4) Open (inclusive) Activity: 'Everyone does the same activity with minimal or no adaptations to the environment or equipment; open activities are by their nature inclusive so that the activity suits every participant. For example, warm-up or cool down, and cooperative or unstructured movement games (like collecting games, play canopy games, or actions songs and activities)' (Black and Williamson 2011, 207).

(5) Modified Activity Activities designed for all, with specific adaptations to space, tasks, equipment and people's teaching (e.g. Baskin, Unified Sports program).

Black and Stevenson's version of the Inclusion Spectrum published in 2006 was broadly considered 'definite' (see Black and Williamson 2011, 206). Black and Stevenson then cooperated to develop an inclusion workshop for the English Federation of Disability Sport (Stevenson 2009; Black 2011; Black and Williamson 2011, 203). In 2007, a further refinement was made by placing the 'reverse integration activity' strand, which was also considered 'disability sport activity' at the centre of the spectrum of settings. The reason for that move was to express that 'reverse integration' activities can be used as the basis for open, modified, parallel or separate activities (Black and Williamson 2011, 207). This arguably opened up the *Inclusion Spectrum* towards approaches that do not associate *inclusion* only with disability, but also connect this guiding principle with an all-embracing approach allowing for ways of sport activity in heterogeneous teams without the group being imagined as divided into people with or without disabilities. To date, reverse integration has been understood as:

> a descriptor for those approaches to sport which turn around the philosophy of integrating the needs of people with disabilities into mainstream society by adapting the functioning of athletes without disabilities to those with disabilities, e.g. when playing wheelchair basketball. (Ogden 2016)

The STEP/TREE model

The STEP or TREE model resulted from the conceptual shifts in the positioning and meaning of international disability sport. It provides a useful way for practitioners to structure changes to sporting activities, and it should be used as a complement to the Inclusion Spectrum.

STEP is an acronym derived from the word 'Space', 'Task', 'Equipment' and 'People'. STEP was developed in Youth Sport Trust resource material as a simple means of assisting teachers, coaches and community sport deliverers in differentiation (ie changing activities in order to provide suitable entry points across the ability range). As a structure, STEP can be used to ensure that participants with different abilities can be included in physical activities. Changes in the way an activity is delivered can be made in one or more of the STEP areas (Black and Williamson 2011, 212). For each word represented by the letters of the acronym, the authors offer the following examples:

> Space – Increase or decrease the size of the playing area; vary the distances to be covered in practices to suit different abilities or mobility levels; use zoning, for example where players are matched by ability and therefore have more opportunity to participate. (213)

> Task – Ensure that everyone has equal opportunity to participate, for example in a ball game, all the players have the chance to carry/dribble, pass, shoot, etc.; break down complex skills into smaller component parts if this helps players to more easily develop skills; ensure there

is adequate opportunity for players to practice skills or components individually or with a partner before including in a small-sided team game.

Equipment – In ball games, increase or decrease the size of the ball to suit the ability or age range of the players, or depending on the kind of skill being practiced; provide options that enable people to send or receive a ball in different ways, for example using a chute or gutter to send, a catching mitt to receive; the use of bell or rattle balls can assist the inclusion of some players.

People – Match players of similar ability in small-sided or close marking activities; balance team numbers according to the overall ability of the group, that is, it may be preferable to play with teams of unequal numbers to facilitate inclusion of some players and maximize participation of others.

TREE is an acronym derived from the text or words 'Teaching or coaching style', 'Rules and regulations', 'Equipment' and 'Environment'. This slight variation from STEP was developed by the *Disability Sport unit* of the Australian Sports Commission. The advantage of introducing the 'T' is that attention is given to the actions of the teacher or coach (Black and Williamson 2011, 213).

Conclusion

This Introduction to the volume on *inclusion* in sport started with the claim that the questions of what *inclusion* in sport means and which steps need to be taken in order to ensure *inclusion* in sport at all levels has to be answered differently in the context of sport than in education, which is the context primarily known for debates on 'inclusion'. Borrowing from Wittgenstein, who stated that 'in general, the meaning of a word is its use in language' ([1936–1946] 2001, 22), I have dealt with the meaning of *inclusion* in sport, and have contrasted the use of the word 'inclusion' in sport with its use in the reference context, education.

The Introduction clarifies that, unlike the context of education, in which the CRPD demands that countries 'should ensure an inclusive education system at all levels', through Article 30.5 the CRPD has provided a framework for addressing a rights-based approach to the inclusion and *integration* of people with disability in sport and covers the spectrum of opportunities for people with disabilities: inclusion within mainstream settings as well as *inclusion within disability-specific opportunities*. Thus, a preliminary answer to the question of how the participation of people with disabilities in sport can be guaranteed is simple: in accordance with their individual preferences, wishes and choices.

The idea behind the aim to shed light on 'the issues related to disability in sport and physical activity in different cultural settings intersected by gender, race and ethnicity, class and age' (Le Clair 2011, 1072) is that inclusion in sport is to be considered more than guaranteeing access. Moreover, the guiding principle of inclusion requires approaches to improve participation, beyond the question of 'who', in the process-oriented sense and in accordance with the fundamental right to participate in physical education and sport, as proclaimed in UNESCO's International Charter of Physical Education and Sport. In other words, the 'how' is of central importance here, as Article 30.5 of the CRPD covers the spectrum of opportunities for people with disabilities: inclusion within mainstream settings as well as inclusion within disability-specific opportunities (see Wolff and Hums in this volume).

In sport, the view embedded in the CRPD's text, 'to enable persons with disabilities to participate on an equal basis with others' (UN 2006, Art. 30.5) does not per se favour approaches that take diversity and/or heterogeneity as a starting point but allows for segregated contexts in which persons with disabilities can be physically active together with their peers and competitors who have a similar level of functioning. In the beginning of the Introduction I have argued the case for why, unlike in education, where inclusion debates typically discredit segregated structures and glorify supposedly inclusive ones, in sport the individual should be able to choose an activity on a spectrum ranging from separate activities for persons with disabilities to modified activities designed for all.

This volume is the result of my intention to contribute to a 'terms of inclusion' debate in sport with a focus on participation, rather than merely to an 'access for all' debate (Gold and Gold 2007), and throughout it has reflected the 'discursive simultaneity' (Kiuppis 2014b) of different ideas on the question of how the relation between 'sport' and 'disability' could be thought of and ideally put into practice when thinking about 'participation' in the context that most readers of this journal are more familiar with, namely inclusion in education.

Notes

1. Since its adoption in 2006, the CRPD has been ratified by 166 countries.
2. *Inclusion* does not necessarily relate to people with disabilities (Kiuppis 2014a, forthcoming). However, I focus here on people with disabilities in sport because in my role as the Head of the UNESCO Chair at the Institute of Technology (IT), Tralee (in Ireland), since February 2015, I have been continuously engaged in questions relating to sport, inclusive Physical Education, recreation and fitness with a focus on people with disabilities.
3. I thank Marsha Saxton (World Institute on Disability, Berkeley, CA) who encouraged me to make these decisions. For further clarification regarding the definition of disability see below.
4. Since these frameworks that fuelled the development of the *Integration Continuum* did not precisely or directly apply to sport settings but rather to special education, I do not describe them in detail here. For further details see Fait and Dunn (1984) and Sherrill (1986).
5. See Fitzgerald (2012).
6. For information on the revision see http://unesdoc.unesco.org/images/0023/002,338/233885e. pdf.
7. See http://www.unesco.org/new/en/social-and-human-sciences/themes/physical-education-and-sport/sv14/news/physical_education_for_healthier_happier_longer_and_more_productive_living/#.Vt3fLRgVhE4.
8. See http://www.phecanada.ca/programs/physical-literacy/what-physical-literacy.
9. One of the main goals of the UNESCO Chair at IT, Tralee is to '[p]romote empowerment and active participation of people with disabilities in physical activity contexts' (UNESCO Chair at IT Tralee 2015, 6).
10. The wording has to be understood in its historical context. While today in the Anglo-American context it is common to use the descriptor 'people with disabilities' or 'disabled people' when, for example, talking about Paralympic athletes, and to use 'people with intellectual disabilities' when referring to Special Olympics athletes, between the 1960s and 1980s the former were typically referred to as 'with handicaps' or 'the handicapped', and the latter as 'mentally retarded'. In context of education, the group of 'exceptional children' was imagined as subdivided into 'the handicapped' and 'the gifted' (cf. Ross 1964; Kirk 1962). For historical shifts in the use of terminology in context of the Deaflympics see Clark and Mesch in this volume.
11. See the previous footnote.
12. See Meziani in this volume.
13. See Valet in this volume.

Acknowledgements

I edited this volume in the role I played since February 2015 as Chairholder of the UNESCO Chair in Inclusive Physical Education, Sport, Fitness and Recreation at the Institute of Technology, in Ireland. For their support I would like to thank in particular the members of my team in the Chairgroup: Catherine Carty (UNESCO Chair Manager), Therese Conway (Postdoctoral Researcher), Shauna Kearney (Social Media), Ann O'Connor (International Development and Research), Katharina Schlüter (Sport and Development), Aisling Sugrue (Resource Development); the Vice President of the Institute: Brid McElligott; the 'Strand Leaders' of the UNESCO Chair: Tomas Aylward (Outdoors), Ursula Barrett (Adapted Physical Activity), Edel Randles (Civic Engagement), Eileen Sayers (Aquatics), and Karen Weekes (Physical Education); all our numerous partners, including our partner on campus: the CARA Centre; my valuable Chairholder colleagues, particularly Pat Dolan (NUI Galway, Ireland), Mark Brennan (PennState University, USA) and Bernhard Streitwieser (George Washington University, USA), who followed my invitation to a panel titled 'Bridges between international organizations, academic communities, and practice: UNESCO Chairs at the forefront of ensuring inclusive approaches in education' in context of the Annual Conference of the Comparative and International Education Society, in March 2016 in Vancouver (Canada), and Alan Smith (University of Ulster, Northern Ireland). Moreover, I am very grateful to the contributors of this volume; the peer reviewers; and not least to the Editor Boria Majumdar; the production editor Carolyn Haynes; and Shathipriya Ganesan from the FCSS production team.

Disclosure statement

No potential conflict of interest was reported by the author.

References

Ainscow, M. 2012. "Moving Knowledge around: Strategies for Fostering Equity within Educational Systems." *Journal of Educational Change* 13 (3): 289–310. doi:10.1007/s10833-012-9182-5.

Armstrong, F. 2003. "Researching the Practices and Processes of Policy Making." Chap. 1 in *Spaced out: Policy, Difference and the Challenge of Inclusive Education*, edited by F. Armstrong, 1–8. New York: Kluwer Academic.

Bendix, J. 1998. "Comparison in the Work of Reinhard Bendix." *Sociological Theory* 16 (3): 302–312. doi:10.1111/0735-2751.00060.

Biletzki, A., and A. Matar. 2011. "Ludwig Wittgenstein." In *The Stanford Encyclopedia of Philosophy*. Summer Edition. http://plato.stanford.edu/archives/sum2011/entries/wittgenstein/.

Black, K. 2011. "Coaching Disabled Children." In *Coaching Children in Sport*, edited by Ian Stafford, 197–212. London: Routledge.

Black, K., and P. Stevenson. 2011. *The Inclusion Spectrum*. http://www.sportdevelopment.info/index.php/browse-all-documents/748-the-inclusion-spectrum.

Black, K., and D. Williamson. 2011. "Designing Inclusive Physical Activities and Games." In *Design for Sport*, edited by A. Cereijo-Roibas, E. Stamatakis and K. Black, 195–224. Farnham: Gower.

Bloyce, D., and A. Smith. 2010. "Elite sports development: promoting international success." *Sport policy and development: An introduction* 132–156.

Booth, T., M. Ainscow, and D. Kingston. 2002. *Index for Inclusion: Developing Play, Learning and Participation in Early Years and Childcare*. Bristol: Centre for Studies on Inclusive Education. http://www.eenet.org.uk/resources/docs/Index%20EY%20English.pdf.

Coates, J., and P. Vickerman. 2010. "Empowering Children with Special Educational Needs to Speak up: Experiences of Inclusive Physical Education." *Disability and Rehabilitation* 32 (18): 1517–1526. doi:10.3109/09638288.2010.497037.

Connor, D. J., S. L. Gabel, D. J. Gallagher, and M. Morton. 2008. "Disability Studies and Inclusive Education: Implications for Theory, Research, and Practice." *International Journal of Inclusive Education* 12 (5–6): 441–457. doi:10.1080/13603110802377482.

Deno, E. 1970. "Forum: Special Education as Developmental Capital." *Exceptional Children* 37 (3): 229–237.

DePauw, K. P., and S. J. Gavron. 2005. *Disability and Sport.* Champaign, IL: Human Kinetics.

Elliott, S. 2008. "The Effect of Teachers' Attitude toward Inclusion on the Practice and Success Levels of Children with and without Disabilities in Physical Education." *International Journal of Special Education* 23 (3): 48–55.

Enoch, N. 2010. "Towards a Contemporary National Structure for Youth Sport in England." In *Examining Sports Development*, edited by M. Collins, 45–71. London: Routledge.

Fait, H. F., and J. M. Dunn. 1984. *Special Physical Education: Adapted, Individualized, and Developmental.* Virginia, VA: Saunders College.

Finkelstein, V. 1996. "The Disability Movement Has Run out of Steam." *Disability Now*, 11.

Fitzgerald, H. 2012. "'Drawing' on Disabled Students' Experiences of Physical Education and Stakeholder Responses." *Sport, Education and Society* 17 (4): 443–462.

Flintoff, A., H. Fitzgerald, and S. Scraton. 2008. "The Challenges of Intersectionality: Researching Difference in Physical Education." *International Studies in Sociology of Education* 18 (2): 73–85.

Gold, J. R., and M. M. Gold. 2007. "Access for All: The Rise of the Paralympic Games." *The Journal of the Royal Society for the Promotion of Health* 127 (3): 133–141.

Goodwin, D. 2009. "The Voices of Students with Disabilities: Are They Informing Inclusive Physical Education Practice." In *Disability and Youth Sport*, edited by H. Fitzgerald, 53–75. London: Routledge.

Gray, J. A., J. L. Zimmerman, and J. H. Rimmer. 2012. "Built Environment Instruments for Walkability, Bikeability, and Recreation: Disability and Universal Design Relevant?" *Disability and Health Journal* 5 (2): 87–101.

Hall, E., and R. Wilton. 2011. "Alternative Spaces of 'Work' and Inclusion for Disabled People." *Disability & Society* 26 (7): 867–880.

Hollenweger, J., and M. Moretti. 2012. "Using the International Classification of Functioning, Disability and Health Children and Youth Version in Education Systems: A New Approach to Eligibility." *American Journal of Physical Medicine & Rehabilitation* 91 (13): 97–102.

Houlihan, B., and A. White. 2002. *The Politics of Sports Development.* Abingdon: Routledge.

Kirk, S. A. 1962. *The Intellectually Gifted Child. In: Educating Exceptional Children.* Boston: Houghton Mifflin Company.

Kiuppis, F. 2013. "'Pedagogikkens Pentagon' Revis(It)Ed – Considerations on Emancipation from a Disability Studies and Inclusive Education Perspective." In *Pedagogikk under Livets Tre* [Education under Life's Tree], edited by J. Steinnes and S. Dobson, 147–160. Trondheim: Akademika.

Kiuppis, F. 2014a. "Why (Not) Associate the Principle of Inclusion with Disability? Tracing Connections from the Start of the 'Salamanca Process'." *International Journal of Inclusive Education* 18 (7): 746–761.

Kiuppis, F. 2014b. "Risiko Oder Gefahr, Bedarfe Oder Bedürfnisse? Zur Diskursiven Gleichzeitigkeit Von Sich Widersprechenden Grundideen Bei Der Entwicklung Bildungspolitischer Projekte Im Kontext Internationaler Organisationen." [At Risk or in Danger, in Need or with Requirements? On the discursive simultaneity of contradictory ideas in the course of the development of educational projects in context of International Organizations.] *Schweizerische Zeitschrift Für Bildungswissenschaften* 36 (2): 243–264.

Kiuppis, F. 2015a. "'Friendly but Demanding'? On Different Meanings of Inclusive Education as an Imagined Concept in National Reform Planning." *Opuscula Sociologica* 1: 5–21.

Kiuppis, F. 2015b. Inaugural Address as UNESCO Chairholder, Presented at the Launch of the UNESCO Chair IT Tralee 'Transforming the Lives of People with Disabilities, Their Families and Communities, through Physical Education, Sport, Recreation and Fitness', Tralee, February 23. http://tinyurl.com/jjnxxgu.

Kiuppis, F. Forthcoming. "From Special Education, via Integration, to Inclusion: Continuity and Change in UNESCO's Agenda Setting." *Zeitschrift Für Internationale Bildungsforschung Und Entwicklungspädagogik – ZEP* 2016 (3).

Kiuppis, F., and R. S. Hausstätter, eds. 2014. *Inclusive Education 20 Years after Salamanca.* New York: Peter Lang.

Kiuppis, F., and S. Kurzke-Maasmeier, eds. 2012. *Sport Im Spiegel Der UN- Behindertenrechtskonvention [Sports Reflected in the UN-Convention on the Rights of Persons with Disabilities – Interdisciplinary Approaches and Political Positions]*. Stuttgart: Kohlhammer.

Kiuppis, F., and A. Soorenian. Forthcoming. "Bridging Continents, Cultures, and Crip Theories: Teaching Comparative and International Disability Studies in Sociology and Education." *Scandinavian Journal of Disability Research*.

Lankshear, C. 1997. *Changing Literacies*. Buckingham: Open University Press.

Lankshear, C. 1998. "Meanings of Literacy in Contemporary Educational Reform Proposals." *Educational Theory* 48 (3): 351–372.

Le Clair, J. M. 2011. "Global Organizational Change in Sport and the Shifting Meaning of Disability." *Sport in Society* 14 (9): 1072–1093.

Milner, P., and B. Kelly. 2009. "Community Participation and Inclusion: People with Disabilities Defining Their Place." *Disability & Society* 24 (1): 47–62.

Misener, L. 2014. "Managing Disability Sport: From Athletes with Disabilities to Inclusive Organisational Perspectives." *Sport Management Review* 17: 1–7.

Ogden, L. E. 2016. *Reverse Integration – Doing Disability Sport Differently*. Inclusion Club, Episode 63. http://theinclusionclub.com/reverse-integration/.

Physical and Health Education Canada. 2016. "What is Physical Literacy?". http://www.phecanada. ca/programs/physical-literacy/what-physical-literacy.

Ramirez, F. O. 2006. "Beyond Attainment and Achievement Studies – Revitalizing a Comparative Sociology of Education." *Comparative Education* 42 (3): 431–449.

Rawls, J. 2003 [1921]. *The Principles of Justice. In: A Theory of Justice*. edited by J. Rawls, 47–101. Harvard: Harvard University Press.

Reynolds, M. C. 1962. "A Framework for Considering Some Issues in Special Education." *Exceptional Children* 28 (7): 367–370.

Ross, A. O. 1964. *The exceptional child in the family*. Oxford: Grune & Stratton.

Sharma, U., C. Forlin, and T. Loreman. 2008. "Impact of Training on Pre-service Teachers' Attitudes and Concerns about Inclusive Education and Sentiments about Persons with Disabilities." *Disability & Society* 23 (7): 773–785.

Sherrill, C. 1986. *Adapted Physical Education and Recreation: A Multidisciplinary Approach*. Dubuque, IA: William C. Brown.

Singleton, J., and S. Darcy. 2013. "'Cultural Life', Disability, Inclusion and Citizenship: Moving beyond Leisure in Isolation." *Annals of Leisure Research* 16 (3): 183–192.

Slee, R. 2006. "Teacher Education, Government and Inclusive Schooling: The Politics of the Faustian Waltz." In *Inclusion, Participation and Democracy: What is the Purpose?*, edited by J. Allen, 207–223. New York: Kluwer Academic.

Spaaij, R., J. Magee, and R. Jeanes. 2014. *Sport and Social Exclusion in Global Society*. Abingdon: Routledge.

Stevenson, P. 2009. "The Pedagogy of Inclusive Youth Sport: Working towards Real Solutions." In *Disability and Youth Sport*, edited by H. Fitzgerald, 119–131. London: Routledge.

Thomas, N., and A. Smith. 2008. *Disability, Sport and Society: An Introduction*. London: Routledge.

UN (United Nations). 1993. *Standard Rules on the Equalization of Opportunities for Persons with Disabilites*. New York: United Nations.

UN (United Nations). 2006. *Convention on the Rights of Persons with Disabilities*. New York: United Nations.

UN Inter-Agency Task Force on Sport for Development and Peace. 2003. *Why Sport?*. Paris: UNESCO. http://www.un.org/wcm/content/site/sport/home/sport.

UNESCO (United Nations Educational, Scientific and Cultural Organization). 1994. *The Salamanca Statement and Framework for Action*. Paris: UNESCO. http://www.unesco.org/education/pdf/ SALAMA_E.PDF.

UNESCO (United Nations Educational, Scientific and Cultural Organization). 2005. *UNESCO Guidelines for Inclusion: Ensuring Access to Education for All*. Paris: UNESCO. http://unesdoc. unesco.org/images/0014/001402/140224e.pdf.

UNESCO (United Nations Educational, Scientific and Cultural Organization). 2008. *Inclusive Education: The Way of the Future. General Presentation of the 48th Session of the ICE.* Paris: UNESCO. http://www.ibe.unesco.org/fileadmin/user_upload/Policy_Dialogue/48th_ICE/General_Presentation-48CIE-English.pdf.

UNESCO (United Nations Educational, Scientific and Cultural Organization). 2015. *Quality Physical Education: Guidelines for Policy Makers.* Paris: UNESCO. http://unesdoc.unesco.org/images/0023/002311/231101E.pdf.

UNESCO Chair at IT Tralee. 2015. *A Blueprint for Action.* Tralee: UNESCO Chair. http://unescoittralee.com/wp-content/uploads/2015/03/A-Blueprint-for-Action.pdf.

UNESCO Chair at IT Tralee. 2016. *European Inclusive Physical Education Training.* Tralee: UNESCO Chair. http://unescoittralee.com/european-inclusive-physical-education-training/.

UNICEF (The United Nations Children's Fund). 2016. *The State of the World's Children* [Report on Children with Disabilities]. New York: UNICEF. http://www.unicef.org/sowc2016/.

Valet, A. 2013. "Sport, Inclusion, Innovation. Le Cas Italien Du Baskin (2001-2013)." [Sport, Inclusion, Innovation. The Italian Case of Baskin (2001–2013).] Doctoral diss., Université Claude Bernard Lyon 1. December 9. http://www.theses.fr/2013LYO10318.

Whitehead, J. 1995. "Multiple Achievement Orientations and Participation in Youth Sport: A Cultural and Developmental Perspective." *International Journal of Sport Psychology* 26 (4): 431–452.

WHO (World Health Organization). 2001. *International Classification of Functioning, Disability and Health.* Geneva: WHO.

WHO (World Health Organization). 2016. *Health Topics: Disability.* Geneva: WHO. http://www.who.int/topics/disabilities/en/.

Winnick, J. P. 1987. "An Integration Continuum for Sport Participation." *Adapted Physical Activity Quarterly* 4 (3): 157–161.

Wittgenstein, L. (1936–1946) 2001. "Philosophische Untersuchungen. [Philosophical Investigations]" In *Philosophische Untersuchungen*, edited by J. Schulte, 7–34. Frankfurt am Main: Suhrkamp.

Youth Sport Trust. 1996. *Including young disabled people: a handbook to support TOP Play and BT TOP Sport.* Loughborough: Youth Sport Trust.

Hard bodies: exploring historical and cultural factors in disabled people's participation in exercise; applying critical disability theory

Marsha Saxton

ABSTRACT

The popularity of the Paralympics co-exists with persistent exclusion of disabled youth and adults in community sport and recreation programmes around the world. This study explored the experiences of disabled people in sport, fitness and dance, drawing upon a range of participants' perspectives from Paralympic athletes and professional dancers, to those who'd never engaged in physical activities. We asked participants about the range of psycho-social factors that intervene between a disabled person and a workable, enjoyable fitness regimen. Insights emerged into factors that encourage enjoyable physical movement for some, and factors that discourage or prohibit this for others. Analytic tools of *Critical Disability Theory* were applied to penetrate stereotyped conceptualizations of disabled people, taking a long view into the history of disability discrimination and exclusion. An example is the concept and (English) word, 'fitness' used during the Eugenics Movement to dismiss the worth of disabled people. Along with other marginalized populations, the 'unfit' were systematically targeted with elimination. We addressed these archaic attitudes, in concert with the present era's intrusions of architectural, programmatic and attitudinal barriers, which may become *internalized* as resistance to physical activities. Participants offered strategies to support others in the world of movement, along with encouragement to Disability Studies scholars to expand research in this arena.

In our research about exercise and disability, a participant in our focus groups commented, 'Fitness? My body is hard enough to live in without having to make it fit into someone's fitness regimen.'[1] Another joked, 'We all have hard bodies!' We laughed at the irony of our 'hard bodies', also a term in the popular vernacular for the culture's ideal of a buff, abled physique. These comments led us to a deeper focus into the world of 'fitness' and how this is experienced by disabled people.

The qualitative study presented here offers key analytic tools of Disability Studies as a timely resource in exploring this diverse population's relationship to exercise, sport and dance. It is hoped that these Disability Studies concepts and tools, also referred to as Critical Disability Theory (CDT) by Meekosha and Shuttleworth (2009) will enable our analysis to penetrate traditional stereotyped conceptualizations of disabled people. Using these tools, we ask: what are the range of psycho-social factors that intervene between a disabled person and a workable, enjoyable fitness regimen? And beyond 'exercise' for health, what might further enable or interfere with a disabled individual envisioning and becoming an athlete or dancer?

As is true with the non-disabled population, only a small portion of disabled people have found their way to an enjoyable and active fitness regimen. Some excel and become athletes or dancers. Others struggle continuously or may not even try. The idea that people with disabilities *can exercise, enjoy movement, and become athletes and dancers* is still surprising to the general public, as well as to many people with disabilities, their families, and even their health providers.

That 'fitness' is a complex concept for disabled people is no surprise. Stereotypes of this population include notions of passivity, incapacity and burden (Longmore and Umansky 2001). The often unattainable models of 'fit bodies' offered via the media, reflecting the diet and fitness industries, can masquerade as 'motivation' to move and exercise; they often become a confounding hindrance to moving just for the sake of enjoyment and well-being. Understandably, the cultural ideals of 'body beautiful' may hit people with disabilities especially hard in confronting and achieving a fitness mindset and exercise practice (Hahn 1984).

Disability rights and inclusion

The Disability Rights Movement has successfully fought for inclusion in many fields, such as architecture, access to transportation and telecommunications, employment opportunities, integration into education at all levels, the arts and media, provision of personal assistance and access to the full range of public accommodations like restaurants and retail stores (Longmore and Umansky 2001). Each of these arenas once served as a bastion of disability exclusion. The increasing visibility of disabled people's participation in athletics and dance is testimony to the community's success in gaining and enjoying inclusion.

Clearly, participation in sport and movement has benefits for people with disabilities in many realms of life experience beyond physical health and well-being (Van Rheenen, 2016). Sport scholar Derek Van Rheenan states, in describing the value of the sport goalball, which was created to allow blind and sighted players to play together,

> The somatic experience of learning the sport itself [goalball] brings home the idea, the 'ah ha moment' among blind and sighted players and spectators that blind people can and must actively engage in the community and in dynamic relationships with each other and others – challenging the blindness stereotype of passivity and being cast simply as 'recipients of service.'[2]

The Paralympics and Special Olympics have become visible to viewers around the world. The gradually increasing availability of inclusive facilities and programmes in community services like the YMCAs, and Parks and Recreation Services is expanding the options for the disability community. Popular documentary films have emerged in the past decade that attest to the success of sport for disabled athletes and serve to reframe the limits of disability. Garland-Thomson describes the documentary film introducing the public to *quad rugby*.[3] *Murderball*,[4] she states, 'invites us to relish along with the players how adaptability and innovation produces a new sport – quad rugby – to which their new bodies are perfectly suited'. Further, she adds,

The film is a guy story about exuberant flourishing made possible because of, rather than in spite of, disability. What *Murderball* captures is the counterintuitive idea that disability can provide a meaningful life in which one thrives rather than languishes'.(Garland-Thomson 2007)

This is good news, but many challenges remain for full inclusion in the world of fitness, sport and movement for people with disabilities.

A disability studies perspective on sport and fitness

Disability Studies has emerged in the past 30 years to address the complex social factors that operate with these marginalized populations. CDT grew out of several other theoretical interdisciplinary fields such as Feminism and Ethnic studies to examine the social construction of disability (Meekosha and Shuttleworth 2009). CDT explores the complex interplay of social power dynamics, normalization, inclusion/exclusion, accessibility, mobility, identity politics, intersectionality and privilege (Titchkowsky 2011). Key perspectives and analytic tools developed by CDT and explored in this chapter include a focus on key historical elements, notably Eugenic ideology; the Medical/Social Model distinction; the use of language and terminology about disability; intersectionality; internalized oppression; and the disability community-derived concept of the 'super-crip'.

Eugenics and the concept of 'fitness'

Understanding the values and practices of Eugenics ideology and its historical influence on public policy has become an essential focus of Disability Studies and critical theory. Eugenics drew upon the notion of the *able body* as a cultural signifier of not only beauty and function but also of traits of 'human goodness', such as acceptability, normality and worthiness (Baynton 2001).

As a result, those with disabled bodies have been made to feel unwelcome, incapable, burdensome, unattractive, despised and unworthy even of life itself. This phenomenon has been documented since earliest times in writings and artwork. For example, the Greeks and Romans celebrated abled-bodiedness; disabled beings from infancy through old age were ostracized, marginalized, vilified or killed. Garland-Thomson asserts that functionality, attractiveness and *normality* itself are defined in our culture on the basis of boundaries set by aberrant bodies (Garland-Thomson 1997).

In the 1890s, the Eugenics Movement, initiated primarily in Britain and the US, then spread throughout the Western world, sought to control human breeding in order to eliminate the 'unfit'. The category of 'unfit' included people with disabilities, people of a wide range of ethnicities – essentially, 'people of difference', distinct from the dominant culture of white, non-disabled, middle and upper class people (Baynton 2001).

The Eugenics movement targeted people with disabilities, as well as immigrants, people of color, and other 'undesirables', through public campaigns that included both institutionalization and systematic sterilization, affecting over 70,000 people in the US (Kevles 1985).

The movement reached the popular culture of the era. Archived photos of county fairs show contests for 'Fitter Families' (white, able-bodied people) receiving blue ribbons at the county fair for their 'good genes', apparently revealed by their adherence to and appearance of normalcy (Kevles 1985).

The belief that disabled people should not procreate to reproduce more of themselves was not new in the 1800s. Indeed, it was already expressed in the writings of Aristotle. The dramatic shift to pseudo-scientific justification came with the distortions of Darwinian Theory. 'Science' could now be employed to validate ancient values, resulting in aggressive sterilization programmes between the late 1800s and into the 1970s (Baynton 2001). An operant assumption in this period was that undesirable social traits could be eliminated through selective breeding (Hubbard and Wald 1993).

The notion that even criminality and pauperism are heritable is typically considered poor social science now. But Eugenic thinking regarding disability has persisted into the current era – in public policy, service delivery and fundamental cultural notions about what bodies and which humans are acceptable and worthwhile (Kevles 1985). Thus, the very term 'fitness' has a uniquely charged cultural history for the disability community.

Medical/social model distinction

CDT draws a distinction between two fundamental perspectives on the circumstances of disabled people. This distinction helps expose the complex *social construction* of disability beyond the simplistic notion that one's impairment is the only locus or problem to be addressed regarding disabled people. This analytic tool helps *deconstruct* disability.

The *Medical Model*, also referred to as the *Deficit Model* (Pfeiffer 2002) operates on the assumption that an individual's bodily limitations, their 'impairments',[5] are the locus and cause of their difficulties in achieving social, financial or personal success. A resulting assumption is that medical intervention and subsequent cure is the amelioration of such difficulties. In contrast, the *Social Model* looks to *society*, to socially imposed restrictions, such as discriminatory attitudes, architectural barriers and exclusionary policies, as the *crucial source of difficulties*. Various remedies emerge from this model, such as community education, advocacy, legislative change and the restructuring of the built environment to facilitate participation in the community and to transcend low socio-economic status associated with disability (Longmore and Umansky 2001). While disabled individuals would, of course, still experience the bodily limitations of their physiologically based impairments, their inclusion into the mainstream life of the community would be enabled by the welcoming resources of society, which would override the socially imposed and thus, unnecessary exclusions.

The Medical/Social Model distinction is an important tool in addressing our research questions. In Disability Studies, we seek to challenge the placing of the responsibility, indeed 'blame', on the physical bodies of disabled individuals as the source of their difficulties. Instead, we look to the larger society as the arena where exclusion can operate.

Terminology of disability

Languages reflect and reinforce beliefs and values inherent in different cultures. Disability Studies have explored the use of terminology regarding disability. The words *crippled* and *retarded*, for example, carry the stigma of disability discrimination and are thought to invalidate people with mobility and intellectual impairments. The word *invalid* as a descriptor of a person, clearly reveals the historic notion that disabled people are to be devalued as human beings (Linton 1998). These terms are now widely considered outdated and to be avoided ([wid] 2001). The term *able-bodied*, implies the *opposite* of *disabled*. Used to describe people who are specifically *not disabled*, the term connotes physical prowess associated with active *men*, competent and attractively 'fit' to do work or go to war.[6] Disabled people across most, if not all, categories of impairment are thought to be excused from or considered *un*able to perform these roles.

The term *disabled* has been questioned as inappropriate in our (English-speaking) culture because of concern that 'dis' reinforces negative attitudes (Linton 1998). Alternatives have been offered, including 'other-abled' and terms with unique spellings, such as 'dis-ABLED'.

Euphemistic terms in popular culture, employed to avoid the negative connotation of *disabled,* suggest a curious connection to sport. The term *physically challenged* can be interpreted to suggest that people with mobility impairments are seeking or are forced with an opportunity to exceed the physical limits of their impairments through athleticism. The term 'other-abled' suggests that individuals may have some extra abilities to compensate for impaired functions. This reflects the admiration (further discussed below) many hold for disabled people as 'courageous' or 'inspirational' in doing activities that those in the public don't generally expect disabled people to be able to do. This leads to the disability community's joking description of this population as 'the euphemistically challenged'.

Internalized oppression

Internalized Oppression is an insidious effect of any oppression. Oppressed people, including people with disabilities, are targeted with a lifetime of discriminatory attitudes and practices, ranging from negative messaging to blatant exclusion to threats or actual violence, perhaps resulting in death. This experience is often referred to as the 'stigma' of disability discrimination.

Internalized oppression arises when individuals within a marginalized constituency are led to accept the values of the dominant culture, thereby becoming complicit in their own marginalization (Collins 2000). Internalization is a collective experience of a population of people that has been targeted with the systematic messaging of discriminatory attitudes and social practices. Individuals with disabilities as a *community* may come to internalize certain values, meaning 'feeling' and 'believing' that they may not, should not, or cannot participate or succeed in activities available to non-disabled people (Kevles 1985). In *Right to Play*, in an international focus on disability and sports, internalization of stigma is addressed:

> Stigma is not only an external barrier, preventing persons with disabilities from accessing social, economic, and political rights, but it is often an internal barrier, causing persons with disabilities to question their own worth in society. For example, most landmine victims participating in the Cambodian Volleyball League report that they contemplated suicide when they first lost a limb. (Right to Play (International Platform on Sport and Development) 2016, 78)

Sport can play a role on the road to recovering a positive sense of self and identity (Huang and Brittain 2006). This may be considered a way to grapple with internalized oppression. These disabled people may be perceived by the public as having 'overcome' their disabilities (Hahn 1984). Michael Rembris writes about disabled athletes finding in the status of athlete a way to 'pass' by achieving a role more laudable and acceptable to the public (Rembris 2013). Disabled athletes can raise their social status from membership in the marginalized identity of *disabled* to that of 'over-comer'. But Rembris explores whether 'passing' is actually challenging the oppression or actually colluding with it.

As oppressive assumptions can be conveyed by authority figures, including parents, educators and community leaders, it is extremely difficult to resist, particularly when conveyed to young people. Recognition of this phenomenon is essential in moving an oppressed community towards resistance of the oppression. This key concept is an important part of our discussion and analysis of our participants' comments about exercise.

Critiquing the 'super crip'

A component of resistance to internalized oppression comes in the form of a uniquely disability community-created concept, the 'super-crip'.[7] Disabled athletes, such as those who participate in the Paralympics, are often considered by the public to be *heroes*, celebrated for 'overcoming' their disabilities (Hardin and Hardin 2004). These successful disabled individuals are often acclaimed in conversations among the public and in the media, framed in such phrases as: 'Isn't that amazing?' 'What courage!' or 'Such an inspiration'.

Disability advocates, such as Marilyn Golden,[8] argue that 'Isn't that amazing?' reveals a hidden insult: extremely low expectations held by those surprised by achievements of disabled people. Media attention to a few uniquely successful disabled individuals gives the impression that only selected few can be successful in this way. This tends not to help question the general public's understanding of the impact of *disability discrimination*.

Golden states,

> When a whole society has low expectations of you, how likely are you to have confidence in yourself? When you don't succeed under such conditions, it says a lot more about self-fulfilling social expectations than about any inherent limitation posed by your disability'.

This perspective evokes our concept of internalized oppression. Stereotyped attitudes framed as 'compliments' still target individuals with invalidation. It is difficult not to submit to these stereotypes as 'truths', rather than recognizing them as part of the oppression.

People with disabilities, like others in marginalized constituencies, will try to counteract discrimination and internalized oppression through humour and irony. This slang term and concept of 'super-crip' illustrates the disability community's grappling with the stereotype that disabled people should strive to 'overcome' disability. The term derives from the common experience for many disabled persons who have, at some point, been told directly, by insinuation, or through the media, that if one *just tried harder*, one would succeed and transcend the limitations of his/her disability, ultimately as if he/she could somehow function as non-disabled (Linton 1998).

But of greater concern to disability rights advocates like Golden is the fact that the elevation of a few high achievers as inspirational to all or as role models to other disabled people implies that all what is needed to succeed as a disabled person is 'drive and spirit'. Thus, there would be no need to enact civil rights protection that would remove social barriers to inclusion; or education to change the way society treats disabled people.

Intersectionality

In considering the barriers to physical exercise for any individual with a disability, we must, of course, regard the *whole person's* full range of social characteristics as they interact with disability. Intersectionality addresses an analytic focus on the interplay of social characteristics of marginalized categories of individuals and groups. Stigmatized traits, such as disability, race, gender and sexual orientation, interact or combine to further increase marginalization and disenfranchisement of the 'other' – the 'different one'. Black feminist sociologists, including Patricia Collins (2000) and Kimberlé Crenshaw (1991) introduced the concept intersectionality into the social analysis of biological and social categories of people targeted with social exclusion. Individuals may experience increasing oppression as a result of membership in multiple categories of marginalized constituencies.

The emerging priority of *diversity* has alerted institutions, organizations and services to challenge their own limiting practices, which may prioritize some and exclude other populations and communities. Many, including Davis (2011) assert that the disability community has yet to make it to the list of the diversity imperative in current discourse about marginalized constituencies.

Intersectionality is important to address with any marginalized constituency. Oppressive assumptions often tend to reduce individuals in the minds of those who stigmatize as if 'those people' have lost their other human qualities, such as gender, race, age and so forth, foregrounding their unfamiliar or problematic uniqueness as the chief characteristics. Disability Studies, with the tools of DCT, seek to appreciate all aspects of the disabled individual's full range of constituency identities.

Methodology

The research project this paper is drawn from is based on a collaborative project between three organizations that promote exercise, dance and sport for people with disabilities. Our team, the WID, AXIS Dance Company, and Bay Area Outreach & Recreation Programme conducted a series of focus groups and interviews with people with disabilities about physical exercise, sports and dance. All researchers were disabled people working for disability services and/or advocacy organizations located at the Ed Roberts Campus in Berkeley, CA. The author of this chapter teaches Disability Studies at the University of California, Berkeley.

Our participant population consisted of 67 adults, aged 19 to 78, including those self-described as 'athletes' and 'dancers' with disabilities; disabled students and teachers of fitness classes; and disabled persons not currently engaged in any formal or informal exercise activities. Impairments of participants included spinal cord injury, spina bifida, spinal muscular atrophy, stroke, osteogenesis imperfecta, visual and hearing impairments, rheumatoid arthritis, Multiple Sclerosis, Post-polio Syndrome and developmental disabilities. Participants' racial and ethnic backgrounds included approximately 49% Caucasian, 17% Asian heritage, 14% Hispanic, 8% African heritage, 2% Native American, 4% Pacific Islander, 3% mixed heritage and 3% reported as 'other'. Of these, 65% per cent (41) were female. We built eight groups with up to 12 participants per group. Group meetings were facilitated by two investigators and lasted 60 to 90 min each. Fourteen participants were interviewed individually. Sessions were recorded and transcribed verbatim without names for confidentiality. Formal written consents were obtained with clear explanation about the purpose and use of participants' ideas and comments. Refreshments were served; honoraria for participation was made in the form of $20 gift cards.

Initial questions posed by interviewers were, 'What helps or hinders your participation in these kinds of activities?' (then, listed and described) and, 'What is your experience-what is it like for you, in relation to these kinds of activities?' We asked participants to share stories and offer insights about their relationship to exercise. Open-ended questions were employed such as 'What else should we ask?' to expand discussion. Participants contributed richly to stimulate the range of issues and questions posed. To initiate analysis, focus group and individual interview data was coded using constant comparative procedures (Lincoln and Guba 1985).

Findings and discussion

This section will present our research findings, offer illustrative quotes from participants and apply the analytic tools of CDT. Researchers were particularly interested in how socially constructed barriers may limit disabled people and how these social factors may interact with the presence of physiologically based impairments.

Eugenics lurks in barriers to inclusion

Barriers to inclusion are constructed over time and within culture. History proffered the attitudes and practices still with us. Many participants repeatedly voiced the notion of 'disconnect' between *disability* and *fitness,* as if fundamentally an oxymoron. Titchkowsky asserts that disability is 'essentially excludable' (Titchkowsky 2011). This reflects the Eugenics-influenced notion that disabled bodies are legitimately marginalized and don't qualify as valued humans. One participant said,

> When a person becomes disabled, there's a new rule: I'm not included in that kind of activity. That's especially true of sports.

Within the Medical Model of disability, the distorted logical assumption is that one must be cured of disability in order to attain a 'fit' body (Pfeiffer 2002). Fitness advice, abundant in popular media, virtually ignores disabled people. The exception is advice on recovery from temporary injuries for those expected to return to able-bodiedness. The non-disabled public is rarely offered educational resources about disability issues, let alone options for recreation and fitness for children or adults with disabilities. When disability occurs at any age, there is little knowledge for considering fitness as a factor in the life of a disabled child, adult or senior. This will likely become internalized by the disabled person, as voiced by this participant:

> After my accident, I just sat still for about six years because I had no idea what to do in a disabled body.

One of our participants, a medal-winning Paralympic athlete and rehabilitation trainer to peers and professionals, spoke of assumptions communicated to her following her spinal cord injury:

> It was assumed that I was staying at home, sedentary, not even interacting socially.

Reinforcement of the assumption of social isolation comes from Hollywood movies. Reflecting the blue-ribbon 'fitter families' of the earlier Eugenics era, attractive able-bodied people in movies are shown physically active, working out at the gym, jogging, biking, mountain climbing and so forth. Disabled people in film are typically portrayed as passive, dependent and pitiful – metaphorically representing negative stereotypes. Classic film examples include the 1937 movie *Heidi,* starring Shirley Temple, whose character, with her cheerful encouragement, enables the disabled character, Clara, to walk. The more recent

Academy Award winning film, *Million Dollar Baby,* expresses the sentiment that suicide is the solution to the problem of disability for a formerly athletic woman. This character was portrayed as working class, her sport a source of upward social/financial mobility, revealing of the complex intersectionality of gender and class in her relationship to becoming disabled. This dichotomy in film, *the super-abled* and *the pathetic-disabled,* has long been critiqued by Disability Studies scholars (Zola 1985). While Hollywood has begun to incorporate more positive images of disability in recent years, there are, as yet, few portrayals of disabled characters as athletes or as people simply engaged in exercise, again 'essentially excludable'. As one participant put it,

> We're symbolically annihilated from media representation, either seen as medicalized and helpless – or as super athletes. Two extremes, nothing in the middle.

Medical system barriers

In the purview of CDT, the Medical Model has misinformed health providers about disabled people's relationship to exercise. People with mobility impairments have the highest rates of secondary conditions, due to relative inactivity. Intervention studies with secondary conditions, such as heart disease, joint problems, diabetes, obesity, osteoporosis and hypertension, demonstrate the health benefits of movement for our diverse populations of disabled people (Saxton 2016).

Cindy Chang, University of California, Berkeley staff physician and Paralympic team physician, agreed with our participants that most physicians have little idea how to prescribe exercise for patients with disabilities. She stated, 'As a healthcare provider, I think it is vitally important to understand and acknowledge our disabled patients' need to exercise'.

Ironically, those with significant mobility impairments could be considered as having *greater need* for organized and assisted fitness resources than people without mobility impairments. Non-disabled people can find some degree of weight-bearing exercise through the ordinary actions of walking or biking to work or school, house cleaning, etc. Yet medical providers typically lag behind in grasping these issues with disabled patients. Chang spoke with frustration about her physician colleagues:

> The training for most physicians does not allocate time to discuss patients with physical or mental impairments. But then, there is also not a good emphasis on inclusive fitness in our society. Unfortunately, in the U.S. we lag behind. ([WID] 2015)

Many chronic illnesses are considered the direct result of inactivity. Yet, for many providers, the connection appears not to be made between 'preventing illness with exercise' and ameliorating secondary conditions with exercise for those with disabilities. Disability stereotypes seemingly cancel out medical knowledge that moving helps disabled people as it does non-disabled people. As one participant stated,

> I told my doctor that the local YMCA has adaptive classes and a lift for the pool. She was actually surprised.

Communication between provider and patient can be significant for developing healthy perspectives about exercise (Saxton 2016). For one of our disabled participants, her provider encouraged her continuing her fitness; she explained to the group, 'My primary care doctor told me to get back to yoga after my surgery'. This doctor's encouragement was sadly atypical. Most participants said their physicians had never asked about or mentioned exercise. One participant said, 'If individuals are referred to rehabilitation, they will likely get encouragement to strengthen their bodies as central to their recovery'. But beyond rehab, this messaging is negligible (Saxton 2016). One participant commented,

> You know the stacks of brochures about 'health options in the community' in clinic waiting rooms? I never see anything about disabled kids or adults and athletics.

Another described a pamphlet she received from an HMO,

> My health plan sent out a brochure titled, 'Walking, A Step in the Right Direction' with little charts to motivate you. I looked for something mentioning that not everyone can walk. Nothing. They could have one sentence saying, 'For disabled people who don't walk, you could swim or do chair dancing.' Or link to a website. In their minds, I guess people like me don't exist or else don't need to exercise.

Therapeutic exercises may help regain function, but our participants reflected that medically prescribed exercises are rarely interesting or motivating. As one participant complained, 'Go home and do these ten boring exercises by yourself. Then, they worry about "poor compliance"'. The Medical Model intervenes here to offer cure or recovery but falls short of encouraging social inclusion or fun.

Chang stated that when parents are initially told of their child's disability, the focus is often on limitations, and not on positive options and resources ([WID] 2015). One of our participants, a yoga instructor, herself a senior with a disability, told of the birth of her grandson, born with severe clubfoot. His obstetrician commented off-handedly, 'He'll never play sports'. Our participant continued, 'My son said to this doctor, "Excuse me, but my mother is a yoga teacher and works in the disability community. There are many options for children with disabilities to become athletes"'. Our participant reported that this child is now active in sports in his school.

Impairment-based or socially constructed disability?

The public enjoys the Paralympics and Special Olympics and admires disabled athletes. Many in the public likely assume that the *physical impairment* is the crucial challenge, and they may have little understanding of the social and attitudinal barriers these athletes confront (Right to Play (International Platform on Sport and Development) 2016; Rimmer et al. 2008).

Disabled athletes entering sports now have role models in the media and may have mentors and coaches in established sports; many succeed and greatly enjoy their sport. This is the visible part of disability athletics that 'inspires' the public. But the majority of disabled persons in their own locale have little or no access to formal resources and must make do in a world with little support to do so (Kevles 1985).

There are, of course, real challenges to addressing impairments in the world of physical exercise. These include finding or creating adaptations; obtaining necessary assistance and appropriate equipment; and addressing safety considerations. Scheduling in fitness time may be complicated by the timing of disability self-care – with or without personal assistance. The extra time it may take to get showered, dressed and to prepare meals can be lengthier than for non-disabled people. Even if fitness centres were fully in compliance with disability law, the Public Accommodations section of the Americans with Disabilities Act, for example, other types of access barriers may intervene. A clear example of a socially constructed barrier is inaccessible transportation for mobility and visually impaired individuals.

The financial costs of fitness

Financial barriers present another complex challenge. Many of our participants identified financial barriers as significant to engaging in fitness. Even discounted or marginal fees can be prohibitive (Ipsen et al. 2006). They spoke of employment discrimination perpetuating low-income status. Many live on fixed incomes or incur the additional expenses of personal assistance and extra healthcare costs, all of which may remove any disposable income that could be spent on recreation or fitness classes. The cost of adapted equipment, such as a hand or adapted cycle may be prohibitive. Very few communities, perhaps a dozen in the US for example, have rental (or no fee) centres with adaptive bikes. A participant commented,

> Compared to a regular bike from the local shop, what, a few hundred bucks? Disability-adapted bikes cost thousands of dollars.

Several participants asked why the classes at supposedly disability-friendly fitness or adaptive sports centers charged fees. There seemed to be an agreement among our participants that exercise classes should be free for the disability community, as this participant indicated,

> I wish I had an extra $10 or $20 a week for a yoga or dance class. That money has to go for food and my co-pay for my meds.

Another participant reflected on her disabled peers' financial practices, noticing the disabled community hasn't yet begun to consider budgeting for the cost of exercise, even when it's subsidized:

> Yes, we're often strapped for money. And I notice my disabled friends, even on limited incomes, can afford a movie now and then or a latte but will say, 'I can't afford $5 for a fitness class.' It's not on their radar to figure in.

This insight illustrates the interactions and tensions between the socially constructed barriers of financial limitation from imposed disability-related poverty and the internalized disability–oppression-related values that may operate to keep fitness for this community's 'hard bodies' a low priority. Many marginalized communities have limited financial resource to pay for exercise resources, but because of both social exclusion and physical impairment, this community has fewer options to 'do it on your own'.

Impairment factors: severity phases, safety, re-injury, equipment 'fit'

Impairments raise many real challenges that interact complexly with social factors. Are these social or impairment-based concerns? The Medical Model mindset intervenes to confuse the issues of safety and to impede creative solutions in the realm of social reconstruction. Several participants revealed struggling with 'over-concern' for safety, facing a patronizing unwillingness among sports instructors and/or family members to allow disabled persons the same right to injury-risk that all must take in sports. Here are examples of these dilemmas:

An established 'routine' isn't workable for all. Severity of impairments can vary over short and longer range, as described by one participant:

> I have different needs, depending on the phase I'm in. I have MS [Multiple sclerosis] and have had a hip replacement. This makes it complicated to plan exercise.

Some impairments have an increased vulnerability to injury, which compromises safety. One participant stated,

> I am afraid of injuries, of transferring, because of broken bones. I have osteogenesis imperfecta. But I need to improve my fitness; I've had a heart attack and need to learn how I can get cardio.

Another said,

> For me, wheelchair sports are too rough, like that movie, *Murder Ball*. I'm in this [disabled body] for the long haul. I like to preserve what I am already working with.

Others were willing to risk injury for success and facing the consequences:

> I did wheelchair sports for five years ... representing the country. In the hundred yard dash, I broke every finger on this hand – my fingers got stuck in the spokes. But I won the race. I had to do reconstruction of my hand. In the cold weather, I feel it.

Participants spoke recognizing that many standard fitness practices are inherently unwelcoming despite good intentions of instructors, which could prevent inclusive classes with mixed impairments. One problematic technique was the relaxation meditation of 'scanning' bodies, tensing and relaxing muscles, foot to head. One participant explained,

> This just points out my pain and puts attention on what I can't do. You wouldn't believe the number of times they've used this, clueless that it doesn't work for me.

Many revealed a lack of confidence that instructors could grasp participants' limitations, let alone address their needs in a class. Several participants with post-polio were concerned about being pressured to exceed their capacity. Several participants mentioned fear of the 'no pain, no gain' mentality:

> I know I have a mental block about this. I can't imagine any sports teacher being able to think about me at all and would really rather I didn't show up.

Another spoke of seeking adaptive equipment in our still-limited world,

> The equipment doesn't fit you. You can't find a vendor. At *Abilities Expos*[9] adaptive equipment is mostly tailored for spinal cord injury, very little for people with my kind of bodies [short stature].

Facing discouragement in the challenges of inclusion

Internalized oppression results from repeated insult, exclusion and negative messaging. Well-meaning programme leaders may hope to offer inclusion, but without grounded knowledge of disability access needs, efforts may end up alienating and ultimately excluding. One participant shared this story:

> I went to fitness class that advertised 'disabled welcome.' The teacher kept saying, 'Just keep up with what you can.' She was clueless how to help me feel included but still needed to feel like the expert. She seemed to think I wasn't trying hard enough. Like I had a bad attitude. I left in tears.

This reveals the patronizing and Eugenics-based notion that disabled people are incompetent and incapable, even of knowing about their own needs. Insights from the Independent Living Movement reveal how this population must be included in all aspects of programme development, must offer input, indeed be encouraged to lead, if activities are to become inclusive, inciting the popular phrase in the disability community, 'Nothing about Us without Us'.

Several of our participants described feeling like a 'public spectacle', while working out or in a fitness class or locker room even before they ventured into activities. Others spoke of low confidence that 'I could do it', not just the physical activities but also explaining one's unique needs. Many spoke of dreading feeling like a burden in asking for help or requesting an accommodation. Many anticipated feeling (or actually being) patronized by instructors and the anticipation of encountering others' intrusive questions. One participant said,

> I've lived my whole life expecting the next person to ask me, 'What happened to you?!' I wish I had the nerve to say, 'None of your damn business.' Do I really need to deal with this again when I'm just trying to get some ordinary exercise?

As sometimes can happen in focus groups, collective insights can emerge. Several of our participants noticed in listening to each other that certain requests revealed unrealistic hopes for access in a world that is just 'not there yet'. Participants heard each other complain: we need a class at *specifically* this time of day; an instructor with expertise in a *specific impairment or condition*. The desire for deep understanding is legitimate, as one participant indicated,

> No one can understand what post-polio is like unless you have it. I don't think I would trust anyone with my body except someone who's been through it or at least close.

Another said,

> Why aren't there more instructors with disabilities? They should have classes that match the students' disabilities with the teacher's disability.

Another retorted quickly,

> *They* should? *They who*? What planet are you on that there are disabled teachers like that?

Long lists of criteria emerged in each of our groups, criteria that might make fitness classes more appealing to individuals' needs but that, realistically, would be difficult to achieve in even the most disability-friendly programmes. Some of our participants spoke of facing up to an uneasy realization that whatever activity they might consider, it wouldn't feel worth the risk or effort. As participants and researchers together began to formulate an emerging insight, one burst out with,

> Look! What do you expect?! It's been years of exclusion, humiliation. These things mount up to make you think, either it's gotta' be perfect or why bother?

Several participants reflected that, not surprisingly, fitness barriers are analogous and painfully reminiscent of other social barriers, barriers to employment, education, quality health care; to community access, sexuality and parenting. Experiences of exclusion accumulate over time for the individual and can result in deep discouragement, even despair, when confronting the realities of our society. This is the internalized oppression that interferes, understandably with a persistent willingness to always to speak up and battle for change in the face of ignorance and entrenched barriers, even among well-intentioned, would-be allies.

A participant's striking statement raised a ruckus in one of the groups. The researchers offered the prompt: 'Share thoughts about barriers to your own motivation to exercise'. This participant replied, 'Fitness isn't cool in Independent Living!' Some group members laughingly nodded. Another protested, 'That's sour grapes!' Researchers queried, 'Say more'. The group debated, only concluding that 'finding motivation' is painfully fraught with discouragement. The provocative comment about 'cool' reveals how disability internalized oppression can transform a reaction to blatant exclusion into a self-protective disability cultural value: 'uncool', meaning, 'Okay, since we are excluded, we don't want it'. Is this 'sour grapes'? While there is a 'health cost', (lack of exercise), perhaps such self-protective coping mechanisms enable marginalized individuals and communities to find ways to enjoy their lives as best they can within imposed limits.

Language: 'overcoming', 'fitness' and the 'super-crip'

Our use in the chapter title of a participant's term, 'hard bodies', gives an example of how language can expose exclusion. Language also enables those targeted with discrimination to reframe oppression, as well as counter-internalized oppression. One participant quipped, 'Fitness doesn't fit us'. Many of our participants used the word 'fitness' with an ironic tone, consciously or unconsciously reflecting the word's charged history of Eugenic ideology.

Speech and writing invite opportunities for word play, reclaiming and reframing oppressive terms. The phrase 'super-crip' engages with this process. 'Crippled' and 'crip', rejected in past years, have since been reclaimed by some as terms of proud affinity with the disability community. Our participants mentioned the term 'super-crip' employed ironically to name those disabled people who have striven to exceed the culture's low expectations of disabled people. One participant reflected,

> Sometimes I'm afraid of even trying because I will fall so short of the super-crips in the Paralympics. Why risk looking like a dork with those amazing athletic guys all muscled and buff? Even though they are crips like us, they are in a whole other league.

Another reflected thoughtfully, in response,

> They somehow didn't get hit with the same stuff the rest of us did, didn't get the same message. They got more encouragement or help in overcoming the stigma.

This participant's phrase, 'overcoming the stigma', pivots on the stereotyped notion of 'overcoming one's disability'. This reframes the lifelong dual task of addressing the *physical challenges* of embodied impairment and the equally or perhaps greater *emotional challenges* of confronting discrimination and resisting internalizing it. This again evokes Michael Rembris' exploration of efforts at *passing* through disability athletics, in the quest to achieve acceptance by hiding or minimizing the impact of disability in one's life (Rembris 2013). This, the addition of the *insult to injury* of disability social exclusion, offers the true challenge of 'overcoming' disability.

What works? facilitating success factors

Our focus groups queried disabled people already active in sport, dance, or fitness programs. Many responses resonated across our divergent categories of professional athletes, serious amateurs and those engaged primarily for enjoyment and health. We asked, 'With all the barriers, why and how can some disabled people make their way to enjoying and/or excelling in these activities?' Many spoke of supportive factors that engaged them in physical movement. A few had gotten encouragement by friends or family, some from childhood, others after they had acquired adulthood disability. Some spoke of using sport as a way to gain confidence, satisfy a competitive spirit or enjoy being on a team. Several told of seeking socializing for fun through sport or fitness. One spoke of sport as a path to resilience:

> I got into sports at the young age of five. Sports helped me to be my own person and prevented things like bullying to get in the way.

Several joined physical activities as a way to recover a sense of physical and/or emotional well-being from an injury. One participant said,

> Since my motorcycle injury eight years ago, I felt like I had to start over again with a new body. With dance, I felt I won't know the limits until I try it.

Another said,

> Prior to my injury, I was a professional dancer. I believe that my dance training all of those years became a gateway to regain a lot of my function, from paralysis to 'move as much as I can.'

Some participants felt that dance and fitness was a path to self-expression; the 'sheer enjoyment of movement'; an 'emotional release'; a way to 'obtain the after-glow of exertion'. One participant addressed intersectionality of gender and disability in wanting to positively reinforce a gender role that he felt had been compromised by his disability:

> An athletic sport develops the parts of the body that you use for that sport. In basketball, the arms; wheelchair marathons or sprint, the arms. Able-bodied or not, sport says a lot about self image. For disabled men, I think it's a way to get back their manliness and compete with other men.

Reflecting on the function of sport for gender role reinforcement, again regarding the film, *Murderball*, Garland Thomson states, 'The shared experience, which underpins the masculine community, partakes of the dominant sport model of cooperation among peers in coalition against a common competitor' (Garland-Thomson 2007, 116).

The challenge of gender stereotyping operates with women as well. One participant told of wanting to resist the stereotype that disabled women are passive,

> I had played sport a bit in high school but wasn't a jock. After my injury, I saw the stereotype of disabled women as helpless and motionless. I knew I had to challenge that.

Favourable factors included architecturally accessible, funded (no fee or discounted) classes, local opportunities, role models, parental involvement, well-trained instructors and formal and informal education about options. Somehow, a *door was opened* that invited individuals in. Age of onset of disability was mentioned as a factor. Younger people with disabilities are increasingly included in school athletic programmes, though still limited throughout the US and around the world, as this comment revealed,

> My high school had nothing to offer, but community college opened a whole new world of sport. My life totally changed.

One participant told of making personal connection as a success factor in outreach and follow through,

> There's a lot of loneliness especially among disabled seniors. Follow-up with students is very important ... for a sense of community – the idea that we're 'thinking of you.'

Bringing fitness classes to people already connected in community has proven extremely effective. Where an affinity group had already formed, exercise might be added more readily than efforts to recruit a group of strangers. Such existing groups could include Senior Centers, Independent Living Centers, disability or illness-specific support groups, advocacy groups and sub-communities of people also marginalized in other ways than disability.

Positive, relevant messaging

Different populations and individuals better respond to tailored 'messaging' to attract attention and reassure participants of accessibility and sensitivity. Our yoga instructor participant said,

> Some need to hear that you can have fun while being active. It's all about belonging. Others are worried about looking good. You have to ask, 'What will penetrate this wall?' 'Arthritis stretch class' may be more welcoming to some than a title with the word 'disability' in it. Not everyone will see herself as an *athlete*, so avoid that word; for others *tai chi* is completely mysterious.

Many emphasized that outreach materials must take into account age categories, gender, sub-culture, language of origin and all other social characteristics. Multiple oppressions add up to increased exclusion. These are the 'intersectional issues' to which programmes must become highly attuned for successful inclusion of marginalized groups and individuals.

Conclusion

Disability Studies, as the scholarly wing of the Disability Rights Movement and CDT, the associated set of analytic tools, seek to research, document, contextualize and ameliorate limits to full inclusion of this population in order to support legal, programmatic and technological interventions. Our participants revealed that success factors that counteract exclusion and engender inclusion include: challenging stereotypes and discriminatory practices; using appropriate, relevant language and messaging; and opening doors to connection, belonging and fun with one's disabled body just the way it is.

Disabled people's lives operate within the broad context of society, history, family of origin and community values. Applying CDT reveals that fitness programmes must take into account this broad context in developing approaches to inclusion. As with other realms of exclusion, such as barriers to employment and educational opportunities, numerous historical, cultural, psychological and logistical barriers intrude into the daily lives of disabled people in the realm of physical exercise. Barriers to exercising may seem even more daunting than in these other areas, in that barriers to physical movement brightly illuminate *the bodily reasons for exclusion*. This is difficult not to internalize, not to take personally, as there is nothing more personal than one's own body. Internalized oppression is understandably a confusing factor in hindering participation in exercise of all kinds. These barriers must be addressed with creative, innovative and supportive approaches, welcoming disabled individuals to join, enjoy, excel and lead.

Notes

1. Quoted comments are from original qualitative research funded by the National Institute on Disability, Independent Living, and Rehabilitation Research and Kaiser, conducted by a collaboration of three organizations described in the Methodology section of this article.
2. Personal communiqué, October 29, 2015, paraphrased from Van Rheenen, 'Blind Leading the Blind'.
3. Quad rugby, created for quadriplegic and paraplegic wheelchair users engages full contact in competitive rugby, using rules only somewhat altered to accommodate disability.
4. *Murderball* is a 2005 American documentary film directed by Henry Alex Rubin and Dana Adam Shapiro, and produced by Jeffrey V. Mandel and Dana Adam Shapiro. www.murderballmovie.com.

5. Impairment is the term employed by Disability Studies to describe the physically-based components of a physical condition as opposed to societal factors that may impose limits (Linton 1998).
6. Cambridge Dictionary Online, s.v. 'able-bodied'.
7. From the Urban Dictionary of slang, the term 'supercrip' is a proper word used by people studying disabled narratives to describe someone who is disabled but has some sort of genius or other skill.
8. Golden, Marilyn (1992), East Bay Guardian, 24 June, quoted from a letter written to Brian Wilson, who lost both his legs under a train in a protest against US policies in Central America, and who considered a cross-country protest walk across the US, but decided against it after receiving feedback from the disability community.
9. Abilities Expos bring products and services together in a community venue of people with disabilities, their families, caregivers, seniors, and healthcare professionals. See http://www.abilities.com/expos/.

Disclosure statement

No potential conflict of interest was reported by the author.

References

Abilities Expo. 2016. "Abilities Expo: Inspirational, Unforgettable, and Coming Your Way." http://www.abilities.com/expos/.
Baynton, D. 2001. "Disability and Justification of Inequality in American History." In *The New Disability History: American Perspectives*, edited by P. K. Longmore and L. Umansky, 33–57. New York: New York University Press.
Cambridge Dictionary Online. 2016. "Able-bodied." http://dictionary.cambridge.org/us/dictionary/english/able-bodied.
Collins, P. H. 2000. "Gender, Black Feminism, and Black Political Economy." *The ANNALS of the American Academy of Political and Social Science* 568: 41–53.
Crenshaw, K. W. 1991. "Mapping the Margins: Intersectionality, Identity Politics, and Violence against Women of Color." *Stanford Law Review* 43 (6): 1241–1299.
Davis, L. 2011. "Why is Disability Missing from the Discourse on Diversity?" *Chronicle Of Higher Education*. http://chronicle.com/article/Why-Is-Disability-Missing-From/129088/.
Garland-Thomson, R. 1997. *Extraordinary Bodies: Figuring Physical Disability in American Culture and Literature*. New York: Columbia University Press.
Garland-Thomson, R. 2007. "Shape Structures Story: Fresh and Feisty Stories about Disability." *Narrative* 15 (1): 113–123.
Hahn, H. 1984. "Sport and the Political Movement of Disabled Persons: Examining Non-disabled Social Values." *Arena Review* 18 (1): 1–15.
Hardin, B., and M. M. Hardin. 2004. "The 'Supercrip' in Sport Media: Wheelchair Athletes Discuss Hegemony's Disabled Hero." *Sociology of Sport Online* 7 (1). http://physed.otago.ac.nz/sosol/v7i1/v7i1_1.html.
Huang, C.-J., and I. Brittain. 2006. "Negotiating Identities through Disability Sport." *Sociology of Sport Journal* 23 (4): 352–375.
Hubbard, R., and E. Wald. 1993. *Exploding the Gene Myth*. Boston, MA: Beacon Press.
Ipsen, C., C. Ravesloot, T. Seekins, and S. Seninger. 2006. "A Financial Cost – Benefit Analysis of a Health Promotion Program for Individuals with Mobility Impairments." *Journal of Disability Policy Studies* 16 (4): 220–228.
Kevles, D. J. 1985. *In the Name of Eugenics: Genetics and the Uses of Human Heredity*. New York: Knopf.
Lincoln, Y. S., and E. G. Guba. 1985. *Naturalistic Inquiry*. Beverly Hills, CA: Sage.
Linton, S. 1998. *Claiming Disability: Knowledge and Identity*. New York: New York University Press.

Longmore, P. K., and L. Umansky, eds. 2001. *The New Disability History: American Perspectives*. New York: New York University Press.

Meekosha, H., and R. Shuttleworth. 2009. "What's So 'Critical' about Critical Disability Studies?" *Australian Journal of Human Rights* 15 (1): 47–75.

Pfeiffer, D. 2002. "The Philosophical Foundations of Disability Studies." *Disability Studies Quarterly* 22 (2).

Rembris, M. 2013. "Athlete First: A Note on Passing, Disability, and Sport." In *Disability and Passing: Blurring the Lines of Identity*, edited by J. A.Bruneand D. J., Wilson, 111–141. Philadelphia: Temple University Press.

Right to Play (International Platform on Sport and Development). 2016. "Sport and Persons With Disabilities: Fostering Inclusion and Well-being." http://www.sportanddev.org/.

Rimmer, J. H., B. Ainsworth, D. R. Young, and M. La Monte. 2008. "President's Council on Physical Fitness and Sports: Research Digest-promoting Inclusive Physical Activity Communities for People with Disabilities." *PsycEXTRA Dataset* 9 (2): 1–8.

Saxton, M. 2016. "Access to Care: The Heart of Equity in Healthcare." In *Eliminating Inequities for Women With Disabilities: An Agenda for Health and Wellness*, edited by Shari Miles-Cohen. Washington, DC: American Psychological Association.

Titchkowsky, T. 2011. *The Question of Access: Disability, Space, Meaning*. Toronto: University of Toronto Press.

Van Rheenen, D. 2016. "Blind Leading the Blind." In *Journal of Postsecondary Education and Disability*. Huntersville, NC: Association on Higher Education and Disability.

WID (World Institute on Disability). 2001. "Language Guidelines." 2001. http://www.wid.org.

WID (World Institute on Disability). 2015. *Physical Exercise and Disability (Film)*. http://wid.org/access-to-health-care/health-access-and-long-term-services/new-door/physical-exercise-and-disability.

Zola, I. K. 1985. "Depictions of Disability-metaphor, Message and Medium: A Research and Political Agenda." *Social Science Journal* 22 (4): 5–18.

Making the right real! A case study on the implementation of the right to sport for persons with disabilities in Ethiopia

Mina C. Mojtahedi and Hisayo Katsui

ABSTRACT

Even though the right to participate in sport, recreation and play is stipulated in the United Nations' Convention on the Rights of Persons with Disabilities as a stand-alone provision, it is often treated as a 'second class right'. This paper critically investigates challenges of realizing this right in the context of Ethiopia. Findings are based on wheelchair basketball trainings held in Ethiopia for persons with physical disabilities in 2015 as a case study and from follow-up data to assess the impact of the trainings. Firstly, inequalities in structures related to disability sports between the Global North and South are described. Secondly, examples of discrimination between groups within disability communities are shown. Lastly, the complex nature of realizing the rights of persons with disabilities is examined in the context of accessibility and sports. In conclusion, we summarize the key components for genuine implementation of 'Sports for all'.

In international development programmes sport is most often used as a tool for social benefit, such as empowerment (Kay 2009; Wedgwood 2014) and integration (Wilson and Khoo 2013), for the realization of human rights through sports and for the realization of rights of specific groups such as women or persons with disabilities (Donnelly 2008). There is a wide range of international programmes focused on sport as a tool for advancing social inclusion and empowering persons with disabilities. In fact, the Sport for Development and Peace International Working Group provides a broad set of recommendations to governments on how to use sport for development and what the benefits are to persons with disabilities (SDP and IWG 2008). For example, using sports as a communication platform to improve access to health information and education, for women with disabilities (SDP and IWG 2008). Another example is reducing stigma associated with disability that prevents children with disabilities from attending school (SDP and IWG 2008).

However, access to and participation in sport is also a right in itself. One of the fundamental principles of the Olympic Charter (IOC 2015) is that the practice of sport is a human right. Several international conventions and declarations state the right to leisure, cultural life and sports, including, most importantly, the Universal Declaration of Human Rights

(UN 1948) in which is included the right to rest and leisure. The Convention on the Rights of Persons with Disabilities (CRPD) (UN 2006) is a human rights convention with the purpose of 'promoting, protecting and ensuring the full and equal enjoyment of all human rights and fundamental freedoms by all persons with disabilities'. The CRPD Article 30 is a stand-alone article on the rights for persons and in particular children with disabilities to participate on an equal basis in cultural life, recreation, leisure and sport.

Barriers to making the right to sport real in the Global South

Although persons with disabilities form 15% of the world's population and 80% of persons with disabilities live in the Global South (WHO and The World Bank 2011) persons with disabilities in the Global South have very few opportunities to do sport. The fact that the Sustainable Development Goals (SDGs) include 13 mentions on education in its goals and targets, while no mention is given to sports, implies that all rights are not equally paid attention to in reality today. Also the disabled activists' movement prioritizes equality in education, employment, health, housing and transportation and there is an apparent lack of interest in the right to sport for persons with disabilities (Braye, Dixon, and Gibbons 2013). 'The principle of 'progressive realization' recognizes that some rights may have to be given priority over others, because not all rights can be fulfilled at the same time or at the same place' (OHCHR 2006). 'Leaving no one behind' is a global slogan for the SDGs which pay great attention to human rights principles such as non-discrimination and equality. However, there are many risks that persons with disabilities in the Global South will be, once again, left behind in the global discourse on human rights and development in general, and it seems that the right to participate in recreational activities and sports will receive very little attention.

Contradictory to the concept of 'Sport for All', many marginalized groups are excluded from this right. There are often sports opportunities for 'either able or disabled' (Carter et al. 2014) in the Global North, and thus one of the mainstream discourses on disability and sports today is to promote inclusive sports. When it comes to the right to sport of persons with disabilities in the Global South, it has not been paid sufficient attention to (Wilson and Khoo 2013), especially in comparison to other rights, such as the right to education. Also, as access of persons with disabilities to sports is severely limited in the Global South, provision of inclusive sport is not yet on the agenda in most countries. A study found that Kenyan wheelchair basketball players faced many challenges such as negative attitudes towards persons with disabilities, transportation, and lack of financial resources (Crawford and Stodolska 2008). Similarly, Malaysian athletes with disabilities faced attitudinal difficulties such as lack of commitment and poor understanding of disability among coaches, and also structural barriers such as inaccessible sports facilities, lack of adaptive sports equipment and lack of funding for disability sport (Wilson and Khoo 2013). Inclusive sports is far from a reality in many parts of the Global South where one of the first steps still would be to make efforts to secure access to sport for persons with disabilities.

The gap between disabled and non-disabled populations is growing in many sectors. For instance, while many governments of low-income countries, including Ethiopian, have succeeded in dramatically increasing the net enrolment rate in primary education to over 90% for both boys and girls over the last two decades, the progress observed with respect to children with disabilities is minimal (Katsui et al. 2014). In fact, in Ethiopia, 97% of children with disabilities do not attend school (Ministry of Education of Ethiopia 2012). In the Global North, inclusion of children with disabilities into physical education activities within schools is one of the steps towards inclusive sports (Carter et al. 2014). In the Global South, however, most children with disabilities are not even in schools and thus miss the opportunity of sport altogether. When intersection of gender, age, ethnicity, religion and so forth is taken into account, root causes of inequalities including poverty and stigma are intertwined and multi-layered. Considering such inequalities exist in the education sector, which is often a primary focus of development efforts, and that the right to sport does not receive much attention, it is no wonder that very little information is available on the realization of the right of persons with disabilities living in the Global South to participate in recreational activities and sport.

Access to sport in the Ethiopian context

This paper elaborates on the right to sport for persons with disabilities in low-income countries, specifically in Ethiopia, using wheelchair basketball trainings held in 2015 as a case study. The following sections describe the trainings and follow-up data collection, the issues underlying the challenges to realizing the right to sport as well as access to sport of persons with disabilities and the benefits to persons with disabilities reported in this study.

Ethiopia has a long tradition of organized sport and in particular in basketball. The Ethiopian Basketball Federation has been a member of the International Basketball Federation (FIBA) since 1949. The Sport Policy of the Federal Democratic Republic of Ethiopia (1998) states under section 3 on 'Methods for the Execution of the Policy', that the government should 'ensure the participation of the disabled in sports activities at their locality, educational institutions and working places and to also ascertain their equal sharing of the benefits'. Regarding disability sports, the Ethiopian National Paralympic Committee is the primary organized disability sport representative. Ethiopian disabled athletics and power-lifting athletes have represented their country in the Paralympics in the 1960s and 1970s and then later, regularly since 2004. However, despite disability inclusion in the policy, the government does not provide subsidies for disability sports, as is the broad trend in Sub-Saharan Africa in general and thus preventing or slowing the development of organized disability sports (Novak 2014). Nor have policies been translated into practice to remove barriers, such as inaccessible facilities, lack of adaptive sports equipment, negative attitudes towards disability, and therefore access of persons with disabilities to sport continues to be very poor. Nevertheless, some efforts in wheelchair basketball in Ethiopia have been initiated, and in 2013 the Ethiopian Basketball Federation formed a wheelchair basketball committee with the purpose of developing and integrating wheelchair basketball into the federation's structure.

Although Ethiopia has non-disabled basketball leagues, a national basketball federation, and some organized disability sports, community-based recreational sports, ie sports where anybody can participate regardless of athletic status, is almost non-existent for persons with disabilities. That is, inclusive sport is largely not available or accessible for persons with disabilities in Ethiopia, as is often the case for countries in the Global South. Therefore, this paper focuses on access to sport rather than inclusive sport.

Wheelchair basketball is a new sport in Ethiopia. The national basketball federation lacks information on wheelchair basketball, lacks the adaptive equipment needed for the sport, and therefore has not previously provided access for persons with disabilities to this sport. The purpose of the training camps was to provide access to sport for persons with disabilities by increasing knowledge of the sport and providing basic adaptive sports equipment. The aim was to integrate wheelchair basketball into local basketball organizations and provide a foundation to support the establishment of community-based recreational wheelchair basketball teams that practise regularly and could form a wheelchair basketball league in the future.

Methodology

The fieldwork conducted in Ethiopia during 2015 is described in two parts: (1) wheelchair basketball training camps and (2) follow-up questionnaires to participants from the training camps. One of the researchers played the role of a coach for the wheelchair basketball camps. Seventy persons with physical disabilities (30 women and 40 men) participated in six wheelchair basketball training camps that were held in five regions in Ethiopia between March and May of 2015. Camps were organized with collaboration between an international humanitarian organization and government funded national and regional basketball organizations. Funding for camps and the sports equipment (e.g. wheelchairs) were provided as a donation from that international humanitarian organization.

Follow-up data from the different stakeholders of the camps were collected by the researchers through observation, informal communication, questionnaire and through emails with key informants after the camps. Questionnaires to participants were administered 7–9 months after the training camps. The questionnaire was presented to groups and translated to regional languages as needed. Participants were given as much time as they needed to answer each question. A transcriber was assigned to each illiterate participant. All completed questionnaires were translated from the local language into English. Findings through observation and informal communication were written down in a notebook. Data were compiled into an Excel data-set. Qualitative content analysis technique was used to identify key thematic areas.

Data were collected from 31 Ethiopians (44% of camp participants, 11 women, 20 men). Data were not collected from all participants due to the following reasons: they could not be reached due to lack of access for security reasons; contact information was lacking; or participants were not interested in completing the questionnaire.

Ethical issues such as informed consent, voluntary participation, privacy and right to withdraw were paid scrupulous attention to due to the politically sensitive environment in Ethiopia. In order to avoid any unintended negative consequences and to secure confidentiality, the main findings summarized in the following section deliberately hide the information of the locations where the experiences took place.

Table 1 shows the main characteristics of the participants that responded to the questionnaires. Despite the near global eradication of polio, it is still quite prevalent in Ethiopia as can be seen from the prevalence of polio among the participants. There is also a high prevalence of amputees among the participants potentially due to many of the participants being veterans of Ethiopia's civil war that lasted until 1991. The level of education among participants was quite low, and the majority gain income through self-employment. This is representative of the general population of persons with disabilities in Ethiopia, as there are many barriers for persons with disabilities to access education and gain employment.

SPORT AND DISABILITY

Table 1. Characteristics of participants.

	Ethiopia
Number of responders	
Total	31
Women	11
Men	20
Average age, years ± standard deviation	29.5 ± 8.2
Type/Cause of physical disability	
Polio	14
Amputee	10
Spina bifida	2
Spina cord injury	1
Other	4
Highest level of education	
No schooling	4
Elementary	12
Secondary	7
High school	2
Vocational training	3
University	2
Other	1
Employment status	
Employed	2
Self-employed	16
Unemployed	7
Student	2
Other	4
Number of participants that were currently doing another sport	30
Number of participants that had previously played in wheelchair basketball before camps	9
Number of participants that continued regular wheelchair basketball training after camps	19

Many of the camp participants had been affiliated to the organizers and played other sports and/or wheelchair basketball even before the camps.

Access to sports in general seemed quite high among the training camp participants. The typical sports that were reported were wheelchair racing, weight-lifting, table tennis and javelin. All sports were organized by local disability organizations, regional sports organizations and projects conducted by municipalities. It is likely that the athleticism of the participants caused recruitment bias, ie because participants were already involved in sports and interested in sports, they were more likely to register for a wheelchair basketball training camp. Also, they were more likely to be recruited or gained information about the training camps because they were already involved in organized sports and local disability organizations. Therefore, persons with disabilities not connected to disability organizations or sports organizations were to some extent excluded from the training camps because of this selection bias.

A limitation in this study is the missing qualitative information that voices the experience of the training camp participants. The community members' view is important in providing an authentic, in-depth perspective and also in avoiding colonization of research and data that 'over-reaches' (Kay 2009). Attempts were made to collect qualitative documentation on the impact of the training camps and the realization of the right to sport on persons with disabilities. However, qualitative data analysis was difficult because the data that were collected were limited. Also, continued training in the different regions was so sparse that assessing an impact on the lives of persons with disabilities could no longer be shown. Nevertheless, this study provides some insight into challenges for ensuring access of persons with disability to sport and progressing towards inclusive sport in the Global South.

Main findings and discussion

The primary outcome of the follow-up findings was that even ensuring basic provisions for disability sport was not enough to create sustainable access of persons with disabilities to sport. Regular training did not continue in the majority of the regions where wheelchair basketball training was held. Out of the total five regions from which training camp participants came, three regions had regular practices after the training camps. In one of these regions, wheelchair basketball training was already provided with the support from other donors prior to the training camps. Therefore, in actuality, wheelchair basketball was successfully introduced in only two regions out of five (40%). The reasons for why access to sport and regular training was not sustained in the majority of the regions are discussed in this section.

In order for rights of persons with disabilities to be realized, more often than not, it requires that access be provided not just in terms of sport but also in several sectors. In other words, there are several pieces that must be in place at the same time to allow participation in sport for persons with disabilities. Access includes features such as availability, accessibility and affordability. In the present case study, data collected from the participants of the camps showed that inaccessibility of the built environment was the major barrier hindering the access of persons with disabilities to opportunities in sport. Inaccessibility had several implications: most sports facilities in the regions were not accessible to wheelchair users and persons with other physical impairments; the storage facilities where the sports wheelchairs were kept were not accessible to persons with physical disabilities and required a volunteer to bring the equipment. Affordability of adaptive equipment was not an issue, because equipment was donated in each region. However, in general, the high cost of adaptive equipment is a barrier and adaptive sports equipment is not available in Ethiopia and must be purchased from international companies. Participants raised affordability as a barrier in terms of cost for transportation to reach sports facilities with a better level of accessibility but which were far from participants' homes.

Ensuring access for persons with disabilities is the responsibility of the government, whether federal or regional. Getting all key pieces for provision of access in place at the same time is complex because different governmental bodies are responsible for providing access in different sectors. Public transportation is under the transport sector, sports facilities are often under the ministry of education or sport, roads and pavements are under the infrastructure or sometimes transport sector, assistive devices are under the health and social welfare sector. Disability inclusion must be integrated in all sectors so that it is possible for persons with disabilities to participate in society in general.

Novak describes how the need for adaptive and technology-based equipment and trained coaches who have knowledge of the disability sport creates a 'disability divide' between those who have access and those who do not have access to these resources (Novak 2014). This divide in disability sports is evident between affluent countries in the Global North and the low- and middle-income countries in the Global South. This can be seen for example in comparing the number of low-income countries and athletes from these countries participating in the Paralympics to those from wealthy countries. Novak further describes how disability sports movements in the Global South have primarily been a result of funding from development agencies or other donors from the Global North. For example, with the funding from Abilis Foundation in Finland, Mozambican persons with disabilities formed the Paralympic Committee of Mozambique and entered a Paralympic team to compete in the London 2012 Paralympics.

Novak's 'disability divide' in adaptive equipment and trained coaches was not preventing access to sport in this present case study. The adaptive equipment needed for practising wheelchair basketball, namely the wheelchairs, were donated to the local organizers. Also, the training camps included coaches' clinics in order to provide trained coaches to continue with regular training. Thus, the technical support was provided to ensure sustainability, but nevertheless, in most regions, the equipment was not put to use and coaches did not continue the work. However, international aid dependence was apparent in the present case study. The camps themselves were organized with funding from international donors after which the local organizers were expected to secure local, eg governmental funding, in order to continue. One reason for the disappointingly low success rate in continuing wheelchair basketball training was the lack of funds allocated by the local sports organizations to regular training after the camps, similar to previous findings in the Global South (Wilson and Khoo 2013). So, when the funding ended, so did the training. It is quite common that disability sports do not receive government subsidies in the Global South (Novak 2014) despite many governments' sport policies including articles supporting the inclusion of athletes with disabilities. Therefore, the underlying reason appears to be lack of commitment to disability sports and allocation of funds and discriminatory attitudes towards disability rather than the lack of funds itself. Disability sports are not seen as an equal right to non-disability sports.

An integral part of the CRPD is that persons with disabilities are not simply objects for which rights are realized, but rather that persons with disabilities are a part of all steps in the process of realizing rights (UN (United Nations) 2006). In other words, duty-bearers should consult with persons with disabilities in all issues regarding them. In Ethiopia legislation and policies include articles on participation in sports of persons with disabilities, but duty-bearers, in this case sports organizations, did not consult with persons with disabilities in these matters. Not even the Ethiopian Basketball Federation's wheelchair basketball committee included a person with a disability with knowledge of disability sports. So not only is the right to sport for persons with disabilities poorly implemented, the right of persons with disabilities to be heard and participate also in the planning steps is also not realized. Appointing highly motivated persons with disabilities in positions for implementing government policies on disability sport has resulted in successfully improving provisions for disability sports in several countries in the Global South (personal interview with a program officer at the United States Department of State division devoted to sports diplomacy, February 6, 2016).

In some regions there were discriminatory processes that account for the lack of continued regular training. Sport as a human right does not mean that it uniformly includes all groups. In fact, sport can promote discrimination, and often race, class and gender exclusion are maintained in sports (Donnelly 2008). In the present case three forms of discrimination took place. Within disability communities there exist hierarchical structures differentiating disability groups, such as between different forms of impairment (Deal 2003). In many war-torn countries, veterans have a special political status because they are seen as having sacrificed for their country, and government provides additional benefits to veterans, including veterans with disabilities. In the region where regular training was provided both before and after the camps, veterans with disabilities had almost exclusive access to the sports facility, to the sports wheelchairs, and a coach attended practices regularly. In another region, similar power structures prevented persons with disabilities living in the community from accessing the sports wheelchairs, which were owned by a local educational institution. The educational institution claimed that because the sports wheelchairs were donated specifically to them, they would allow only their own students to access the sports wheelchairs and not community members.

Gender inequality is highly prevalent in disability sports but poorly described in the literature. Women with disabilities have the right to the same opportunities as men with disabilities in access to regular training and advancing in sports to internationally competitive levels, but more often than not, this is not the case in the Global North. In wheelchair basketball this is evidenced by the very small number of teams for women compared with for men in most Western countries. There is a risk when introducing disability sports in the Global South that the same gender inequalities are replicated. In addition, women with disabilities often face double discrimination because of negative societal attitudes towards gender and disability in the Global South (Katsui and Mojtahedi 2015). Women with disabilities are often kept at home by their families practically as servants, and are denied their rights to participate in society (Katsui and Mojtahedi 2015). Gender discrimination was clearly apparent in the findings of this study. At the training camps, every effort was made to ensure gender equality. However, in one of the regions where wheelchair basketball training continued to be organized after the camp by a local disability organization, training was provided only for an all-male group. Women with disabilities were not given equal access to the trainings. On the other hand, a small but significant result was achieved in other regions where more women are now attending regular wheelchair basketball training than before in other regions. In two regions where mixed gender balance was achieved in the training camps and where training has continued, women form approximately half of the players in regular practices. This is a promising start, but the goal should be that women with disabilities have the opportunity to train with their peers rather than compete against men who, generally speaking, tend to be larger and stronger.

Conclusion

This paper provides insight to some of the challenges in realizing the right of persons with disability to sport and can be used to design programmes to address the problems persons with disabilities face in accessing sport. Resources such as information on wheelchair basketball, funding for training camps and sports wheelchairs were provided from non-local donors. In other words, the foundation for improving access of persons with disabilities to wheelchair basketball was laid. In order to progress towards inclusive sports, essential provisions that are routinely provided in non-disabled sports should be provided equally in disability sports. However, the low level of continuity after the input from donors indicates that duty-bearers are not realizing this particular right for persons with disabilities in the Global South. This supports the concept presented by Novak on dependency on international development funds. Importantly, the right to sport for persons with disabilities can only be realized when duty-bearers address disability rights and gender equality in all sectors to ensure access, such as accessibility of the built environment including sports facilities and transportation, and provision of affordable assistive devices including adapted sports equipment (Novak 2014).

However, positive and inclusive attitudes towards equality, disability and the right to sport can provide powerful motivation in the development of organized disability sport. The primary reasons why continued training was successful in three regions where training camps were held was the high level of commitment among the persons with disabilities to attend practices and of coaches to provide the necessary support. As an example, one of the regions, where regular wheelchair basketball practices have been organized since the training camp, is also one of the least accessible locations compared to the other regions. Although the sports organization which is responsible for providing sports in that particular region provides no financial or other form of support for wheelchair basketball practices, a dedicated basketball coach volunteers his time and runs practices for persons with disabilities when the court is available. In addition, he brings all the sports wheelchairs from the storage facility to the court because the players are not able to access the storage. This shows that a commitment to providing equal opportunities to persons with disabilities to participate in sport can to some extent overcome even the lack of financial and structural support. This positive example, albeit encouraging, is not sustainable without a serious commitment from duty-bearers to fulfil their role in realizing the rights of persons with disabilities in all governmental sectors. Further research is needed to address the more specific roles of duty-bearers and highlight the experiences of the rights-holders, persons with disabilities in access to sport in the Global South.

Acknowledgements

The authors would like to thank the International Committee of the Red Cross, Daniel Mekonnen, Rinor Gashi and the participants for their assistance in this project.

Disclosure statement

No potential conflict of interest was reported by the authors.

References

Braye, S., K. Dixon, and T. Gibbons. 2013. "'A Mockery of Equality': An Exploratory Investigation into Disabled Activists' Views of the Paralympic Games." *Disability & Society* 28 (7): 984–996.
Carter, B., J. Grey, E. McWilliams, Z. Clair, K. Blake, and R. Byatt. 2014. "'Just Kids Playing Sport (in a Chair)': Experiences of Children, Families and Stakeholders Attending a Wheelchair Sports Club." *Disability & Society* 29 (6): 938–952.
Crawford, J. L., and M. Stodolska. 2008. "Constraints Experienced by Elite Athletes with Disabilities in Kenya, with Implications for the Development of a New Hierarchical Model of Constraints at the Societal Level." *Journal of Leisure Research* 40 (1): 128–155.
Deal, M. 2003. "Disabled People's Attitudes toward Other Impairment Groups: A Hierarchy of Impairments." *Disability & Society* 18 (7): 897–910.
Donnelly, P. 2008. "Sport and Human Rights." *Sport in Society* 11 (4): 381–394.

Federal Democratic Republic of Ethiopia. 1998. *Sport Policy of the Federal Democratic Republic of Ethiopia*. Addis Ababa: Federal Democratic Republic of Ethiopia.

IOC (International Olympic Committee). 2015. *Olympic Charter*. Lausanne: IOC.

Katsui, H., and M. C. Mojtahedi. 2015. "Intersection of Disability and Gender: Multi-layered Experiences of Ethiopian Women with Disabilities." *Development in Practice* 25 (4): 563–573.

Katsui, H., E. M. Ranta, S. A. Yeshanew, G. M. Musila, M. Mustaniemi-Laakso, and A. Sarelin. 2014. *Reducing Inequalities: A Human Rights-based Approach in Finland's Development Cooperation with Special Focus on Gender and Disability*. Turku: Institute for Human Rights.

Kay, T. 2009. "Developing through Sport: Evidencing Sport Impacts on Young People." *Sport in Society* 12 (9): 1177–1191.

Ministry of Education of Ethiopia. 2012. *Special Needs/Inclusive Education Strategy*. Addis Ababa: Ministry of Education.

Novak, A. 2014. "Disability Sport in Sub-Saharan Africa: From Economic Underdevelopment to Uneven Empowerment." *Disability and the Global South* 1 (1): 44–63.

OHCHR (Office of the UN High Commissioner for Human Rights). 2006. "Frequently Asked Questions on a Human Rights-based Approach to Development Cooperation." http://www.ohchr.org/Documents/Publications/FAQen.pdf.

SDP and IWG (Sport for Development and Peace International Working Group). 2008. "Sports and Persons with Disabilities: Fostering Inclusion and Well-being." In *Harnessing the Power of Sport for Development and Peace: Recommendations to Governments*, 167–200. Toronto: Right to Play.

UN (United Nations). 1948. *Universal Declaration of Human Rights*. Geneva: UN.

UN (United Nations). 2006. *Convention on the Rights of Persons with Disabilities, and Its Optional Protocol*. New York: UN.

Wedgwood, N. 2014. "Hahn versus Guttmann: Revisiting 'Sports and the Political Movement of Disabled Persons.'" *Disability and Society* 29 (1): 129–142.

WHO (World Health Organization) and The World Bank. 2011. *World Report on Disability*. Geneva: WHO.

Wilson, N. C., and S. Khoo. 2013. "Benefits and Barriers to Sports Participation for Athletes with Disabilities: The Case of Malaysia." *Disability and Society* 28 (8): 1132–1145.

The relationship between physical activity and self-efficacy in children with disabilities

Kim Wickman, Madelene Nordlund and Christina Holm

ABSTRACT

The main purpose of this study is to investigate whether self-efficacy in children with disabilities could be strengthened through targeted and adapted physical activities led by specially educated leaders. Children and Youth Physical Self-Perception Profile (CY-PSPP) scale were used. The study includes 45 children of 8–14 years of age with different types of impairments. The children participated in training sessions twice a week and tried out 13 different physical activities during eight months. The median in this study of total self-efficacy was 104 points, which can be compared to median points varying between 100 and 107 in previous studies based on children without disabilities. Furthermore, there was a statistically significant increase of the means in four out of six different domains of self-efficacy before and after the study was carried out. Key findings indicated that this model is successful in strengthening the children's self-efficacy and that their perceived self-efficacy was equal to that of children without disabilities.

Sport (i.e. competitive, rule-bound, structured activity) and physical activity (a broad term that encompasses many different forms of energy-expenditure, including exercise and recreation) (e.g. Day 2013; Yazicioglu et al. 2012) for children and young people with disabilities have been a quite under-researched area within the fields of disability and sport studies (Smith and Thomas 2006). Sport is an established social structure that is meaningful to individuals and society and provides an important and unique context through which broad patterns of societal relations can be investigated. For many children and youth, sport is an important part of their lives and has an impact on their identities and on how they look upon themselves and society. Consequently, sport provides an arena for development through the opportunities given to the individual to learn more about themselves and others' ability. Learning, however, is not something that only occurs in defined learning episodes, such as in being taught how to do a specific sporting exercise in the local sport club. Instead, meaningful learning is an unavoidable part of social life and participation in practice, and is transformative. It involves learning 'how to do' practices through participating in them

(Light 2010). From this perspective, children with disabilities participating in sport learn far more than just the sport-specific techniques. They also gain a range of deep, implicit, social, cultural and personal experiences that challenge their self-esteem. Through sport as a social activity, they can learn to negotiate with others, establish and keep friendships, solve conflicts and develop leadership qualities and self-esteem (Özdemir and Stattin 2012). Engaging in sports as a child or young person may thus be seen as a part of preparing for life as an adult (Karp 2010). However, studies have suggested that children and young people with disabilities tend to be excluded from sport (Kristén, Patriksson, and Fridlund 2002; Smith and Thomas 2006; Vickerman, Hayes, and Whetherly 2003). For example, Vickerman, Hayes, and Whetherly (2003) found that withdrawals are more frequent among this population (ibid.). In addition, children with disabilities have generally fewer opportunities to participate due to physical, social and emotional barriers. Their experiences are often limited due to the lack of necessary skills, overprotective adults, social isolation, time-consuming treatment and care, and difficulties in getting to and from training and matches (Taub and Greer 2000). Additionally, previous studies show that mobbing and isolation, inaccessible premises, lack of sports aids and few individually adapted activities contribute to negative experiences and exclusion (Coates and Vickerman 2010). Crushed self-esteem is quite frequently a result of discrimination (Goodwin and Watkinson 2000). So, the pathway of self-esteem linking sports participation and positive outcomes is well documented (Åström 2013). However, while the majority of researchers have focused on the importance of sport participation for individuals' self-esteem among adolescents and children without disabilities (Raustorp 2006) and adults with disabilities (Uchida, Hashimoto, and Lutz 2005) there is a dearth of research on children with disabilities.

The general purpose of the current study is to extend the knowledge-base surrounding the relationship between physical activity and self-efficacy in children with disabilities and to investigate if adapted physical activity has the potential to influence sport beliefs and, potentially, behaviours among children with disabilities. More precisely, the intention is to investigate whether self-efficacy of children with disabilities increases when they try a number of sporting activities during two school semesters, where leaders receive training in the group-adapted concepts and methodology. The study also intends to discuss whether targeted cooperation with sports federations and sports clubs is one possible approach for the Habilitation Centre (a centre that gives advice and support to families of children with disabilities) and child psychiatry when it comes to strengthening self-efficacy among children with disabilities.

Confidence and self-esteem

Confidence has been in focus in the sport social science and psychology literature for quite some time now and has been operationalized in numerous ways. For instance, the constructs of self-efficacy (Bandura 1977), sport confidence (Fox and Corbin 1989), perceived competence (Åström 2013; Dunn, Dunn, and McDonald 2012) and movement confidence (Williams and Cumming 2011) have all been proposed as measuring an individual's perception of his or her abilities. Important concepts related to the foundation of self-esteem include: self-identity, self-image, self-concept (Bailey 2003) and physical self-esteem (Fox 2000; Lindwall, Asci, and Crocker 2014). In simple terms, self-esteem is what, and how, you think and feel about yourself, or how much you value yourself. Self-esteem can also be defined as the degree to which a person is able to achieve their goals and expectations, or the relationship between an individual's performance and that individual's perceived potential (Carlock 1998; James 1980; Josephs 1992). According to Fox, 'the physical self-esteem has occupied a unique position in the self-esteem system because the body, through its appearance, attributes, and abilities, provides the substantive interface between the individual and the world' (Fox 2000).

Self-efficacy theory and sport

One of the most powerful theories for facilitating behaviour change, specifically in the domain of sport, is Bandura's self-efficacy theory (Bandura 1986). According to Bandura, self-efficacy can be described as persons' belief in their ability to handle a specific task or certain duties in a satisfactory manner (Bandura 1977). An individual who successfully executes a task will believe that she or he has the competences necessary to engage in that task in the future. Consequently, participation in sport, whether it is successful or unsuccessful, may play a role in self-efficacy and may serve as a means to promote or inhibit the child's engagement in sport. Consequently, successful experiences will lead to increased self-efficacy beliefs and may ultimately increase future participation. Further, it has also been shown to have a connection with regular exercise habits (Bandura 1997). On the other hand, there is also a connection between high self-efficacy and ability to attribute failure to something changeable, which in turn leads to continued exercise, while someone with low self-efficacy attributes failure to something she or he would not be able to change, and therefore is likely to drop out (Bandura 1997). The theory suggests that people will be more likely to engage in behaviours they believe they can successfully perform and avoid behaviours in which they feel they will be unsuccessful. In that sense, self-efficacy perceptions help to shape individuals' efforts, affective experiences and enjoyment of physical activities, particularly at higher intensities. However, you cannot generalize an individual's self-efficacy for tasks that are not similar in nature (Samson and Solmon 2011). Consequently, if a person has high self-efficacy regarding his or her performance in one specific activity it does not mean that the same person has high self-efficacy in another (Bandura 1997). Self-efficacy theory stipulates that if an individual has high self-efficacy regarding a specific activity, the likelihood increases that the individual begins or continues with the selected activity (Bandura 1997).

However, several related concepts of the self are often mislabelled as self-efficacy, when in fact they are more overarching concepts of the self and not confined within a goal-striving context (Gao et al. 2011). Some of the related concepts of the self that are commonly confused with self-efficacy include sport confidence, self-confidence, perceived competence, perceived ability, self-concept, self-esteem and outcome expectancies. Bandura also raises concern about instruments that are labelled as self-efficacy inventories when some of these instruments are actually measures of related, but more global, constructs (Bandura 2006). He developed a set of guidelines for constructing self-efficacy measures, advocating the use of domain-specification and graduations of difficulty in the development of self-efficacy inventories. Domain specification was identified as the most important of Bandura's guidelines and he states that researchers must utilize conceptual analysis and expert knowledge of what it takes to succeed in a given task (Bandura 1997).

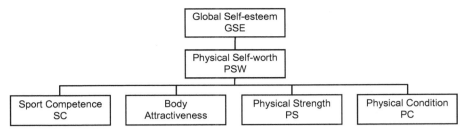

Figure 1. Sport confidence.
Note: The Hierarchical model of Physical Self Perception Profile (Fox and Corbin 1989).

When Raustorp defines physical self-efficacy, he describes it from different subgroups and how these affect/impact each other (Raustorp 2006). As a theoretical basis for this particular study, the hierarchical model of global self-esteem was applied (see Figure 1), which also was the basis for the estimation form CY-PSPP (Whitehead 1995). The hierarchical model is created to structure the concept of self-esteem and illustrate how the global self-esteem is built. The structure is composed of multiple domains, which together form the overall global self-esteem and is an important factor for mental well-being (Fortes, Ninot, and Delignières 2004, 119).

The estimation CY-PSPP (Whitehead 1995; see also Raustorp 2006) is based on the different subgroups' sports competence, bodily activity, physical strength and physical condition and within physical self-esteem and global self-esteem. Questions in the subgroups have an impact on the domain above, i.e. physical self-esteem, which in turn affects the global self-esteem. In each of these subgroups there is a specific, situation-bound self-esteem or self-efficacy, which according to Bandura implies an individual's confidence in her/his ability to manage a specific task with a certain result (Bandura 1997). Sports research on self-efficacy has previously been implemented on individuals without disabilities. It is important to emphasize here that self-efficacy beliefs are very context- and behavior-specific, and do not represent overall global traits such as self-esteem, self-concept or self-confidence (Feltz, Short, and Sullivan 2008).

Sample description

In spring 2012, 13 sports clubs in Halmstad County (Sweden) were invited to first, participate in a project with the intention to train sports coaches in adapted physical activity and then, to introduce children with disabilities to different sport activities. All 13 sport clubs accepted the invitation (total of 20 leaders) and the education included both practical and theoretical elements and occurred on three occasions (total of eight hours). All together, they represented the following sports activities: archery, golf, gymnastics, rowing, shooting, boules, bowling, karate, judo, football, climbing, dance and athletics. In August 2012, 136 children with disabilities were invited to participate in the project which intended to give them opportunities to try different sports under guidance of specially trained leaders. The target groups at the Habilitation Centre are children with physical impairments, children with neuropsychiatric diagnoses, children with severe speech and language disabilities and children with muscular diseases. In addition, the Habilitation Centre and Psychiatry for Children and Young People (BUP) in Halmstad County have a cooperation agreement concerning children with neuropsychiatric diagnoses and in consultation with BUP's department Head it was decided that 200 children from BUP's neuropsychiatric team should also be invited to take part in the sport project. Four nurses who work in the neuropsychiatric were divided into geographic areas and each of them was in charge of about a 100 children. Each of the nurses selected 50 children, who were invited to take part in the project. The nurses gave priority to the children who they thought had the greatest need to take part in the project. Forty-five (nine girls and 36 boys) of them accepted to participate in the sport activities, but due to different causes (too many already initiated activities, illness, fatigue, etc.), only 39 children (nine girls and 30 boys) finally agreed to participate in the sport activates and the survey. The children who accepted the invitation were given an accompanying information letter with an invitation to take part in the research study. The children (8–14 years) were all registered at the Habilitation Centre in Halmstad County. In the After-intervention evaluation, 36 children (eight girls and 28 boys) took part and the dropout was thereby three children. Initially, the children were offered a motivation lecture of a girl with spina bifida who had rich sporting experiences. On this occasion, the children had the opportunity to ask questions and prepare themselves for the coming activities. All in all, the children were offered 25 activity sessions with the opportunity to try the same activity twice (except from dance that only offered one occasion). Each training session lasted 60 min. All children attended the offered training sessions apart from a few children and occasions.

For the present study, a quantitative method in the form of a questionnaire was used, The Physical Self-Perception Profile (CY-PSPP) (Whitehead 1995) which gives a profile of children's and young people's physical self-esteem. The inquiry is validated and adapted for children between 10 and 14 *years of age* (Raustorp et al. 2004). The CY-PSPP consists of 36 items about children's physical self-perception. The items represent six domains: Global Self Esteem (GSE), Physical Self Worth (PSW), Sport Competence, Body Attractiveness, Physical Strength and Physical Condition (see Figure 1). Each item consists of two statements and a four-point structured alternative format. First, the child must decide which of the two statements that best describes it and then mark with (X) whether the statement is kind of true or really true for them. The assistant carefully described the procedure and read both statements for each item. Every item gives a score from one to four, where scoring four means highest self-perception on that item. Since the score key is available only for the research leader, the children do not know the points of the alternatives of the items. Maximum score of the six items of a subdomain is 24 and minimum is 6. The study was approved by the Regional Ethics in Lund (Sweden).

Intervention

The research study is a part of a cooperation project among a Swedish sports federation, local sports clubs and BUP. The study was financed by funds from the latest 'sport for all' programme, *The Lift for Sport*, launched by the Swedish Government in 2007 (see Fahlén, Eliasson, and Wickman 2015). The purpose of the project application was to initiate sports activities for children with disabilities, to create adapted activities in local sports clubs and to disseminate knowledge to sports leaders of how adaptation and implementation may concretely be carried out in the practice of sport. The sports leaders in the project were given information about different diagnoses and their consequences in everyday life, but

SPORT AND DISABILITY

also in sports contexts. They were also given instruction in pedagogy/methodology adapted to the target group. This took place in groups and through continuous advice by a sports pedagogue or by other staff members from the Habilitation Centre or BUP. The focus of the education was how the types of sport were adapted to individual preconditions and how security was created for the children and the importance of the responsible leader giving scope for variation in the exercise. The main focus of the project was to tone down the competition element and to ensure that the activity is about daring, testing and having fun instead of achieving and competing.

To measure the children's changes in perceptions related to the areas of the Physical Self-Perception Profile (CY-PSPP), we compare how they scored before and after intervention. The changes are presented in median scores as well as the range of scores (Table 1 in the result section). The significances of the repeated measurements were tested through the Wilcoxon Signed Ranks test. This non-parametric significance test was suitable due to the small sample size ($n = 45$).

Results

All in all, it seems that interventions increased the self-perceptions of the children and youth in this study (Figure 2 and Table 1). Looking at the scoring of the total self-efficacy (Total CY-PSPP), it is evident that the children/youth perceived significant increases in self-efficacy after the intervention. This change over time is statistically significant.

Looking at the scores indicating Global Self-esteem and the Physical Self-worth ranked by the children, these also increased after intervention and the observed increases of both Global Self-esteem and Physical Self-worth were statistically significant (Figures 3 and 4, and Table 1).

A closer look at the specific subgroups of self-efficacy shows that before intervention the children scored body attractiveness from 13 to 24 (median 18), and after intervention the median had increased. This increase was statistically significant (Figure 5). Further, the children also seemed to perceive that their physical strength (Figure 6 and Table 1) had increased after intervention. However, this change was only borderline significant (90% significant level). There were insignificant changes in perception before and after interventions when it came to sport competence (Figure 7 and Table 1) and physical condition (Figure 8 and Table 1).

Furthermore, the correlations between physical self-perception and each of the sub-domains before intervention were also examined in the study. One statistically significant correlation was found between self-efficacy and physical fitness ($R^2 = 0.14$, $p > 0.023$). All other correlations showed statistically insignificant relations.

Discussion

The measuring instrument CY-PSPP has never before been used on children with disabilities for the purpose of investigating the experienced self-efficacy in the target group children with disabilities. It was therefore interesting to examine how the children in the research study estimated themselves regarding self-efficacy and to compare their results with earlier similar studies. It was also of great importance to find out whether an intervention programme containing a 'trying out activity' of different sports during a period of eight

Table 1. Range, median (Md), mean (M) and standard deviation (Sd) scores for the Children and Youth Physical Self-Perception Profile (CY-PSPP) and subdomains in children with disabilities 9–14 years of age; a comparison between scores before and after intervention.

Subdomains	Before intervention (n=39)				After intervention (n=36)				Significance in changes after intervention
	Range	Md	M	Sd	Range	Md	M	Sd	
Global Self-esteem	14–24	19	18.5	3.0	15–24	21	20.9	2.5	**
Physical Self-worth	11–24	18	18.4	3.1	12–24	20.5	20.6	3.0	*
Sport Competence	7–24	17	16.9	4.0	13–24	19	18.3	3.0	
Body Attractiveness	13–24	18	17.8	2.8	14–24	20	19.5	2.4	**
Physical Strength	7–23	17	16.6	3.9	12–24	19	18.5	3.5	(*)
Physical Condition	9–24	16	16.1	3.2	9–24	17.5	17.1	3.8	
Total CY-PSPP	84–130	104	104.2	10.2	90–137	114	114.9	12.3	***

Significance tests of the results (change in scores after intervention) are based on the Wilcoxon Signed Ranks tests.
(*) = $p < 0.1$.
*$p < 0.5$; **$p < 0.01$; ***$p < 0.001$.

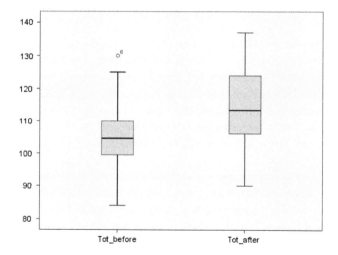

Figure 2. Total CY-PSPP.

months could affect the children's experienced self-efficacy. The most notable finding was that children with disabilities estimate themselves like children without disabilities regarding physical self-efficacy (Raustorp 2006). In the pre-measurement of the group of children with disabilities, the total median value was 104 points and in previous investigations implemented on children and young people without disabilities the median value varied between 100 and 107 points. In the subdomains Physical Self-worth, Sport Competence and Body Attractiveness, the median value was one point higher in comparison with Raustorp and colleagues (Raustorp et al. 2004). In accordance with the aim of the present study, the children's estimation results were also compared before and after the physical intervention. The mean value was calculated in the total CV-PSPP and in all its subdomains before and after the intervention. The result showed that an increase had taken place in all subdomains and in the total CV-PSPP. The difference was significant in four of the six domains regarding self-efficacy.

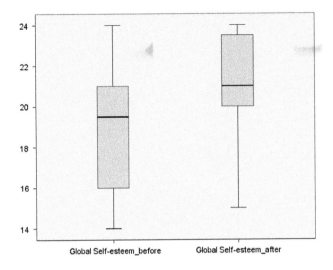

Figure 3. Physical self-worth.

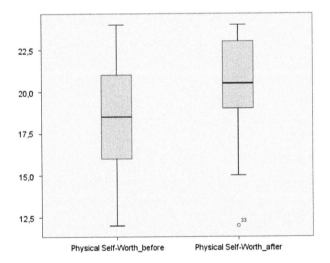

Figure 4. Global self-esteem.

In the analysis of the result and the participants' high estimation of self-efficacy, there are impact factors to be considered. One of these is the selection, which initially was a total selection, but the participation in the sports project was dependent both on the children's and their families' interest and engagement. There are therefore question marks regarding whether the selected population is entirely representative of the whole target group of children with disabilities. Probably there was already an established interest in sport among many of the participants and their families, at the same time as many also had earlier sports experiences. This may have had a positive effect on the participants' estimation of the self-efficacy and its subdomains. It is therefore difficult to draw any conclusions on whether the results can be generalized for the selected population of children with disabilities. The children who were regularly physically active in the study had a higher estimated

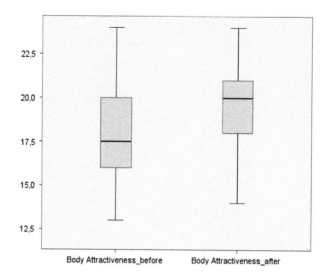

Figure 5. Body attractiveness.

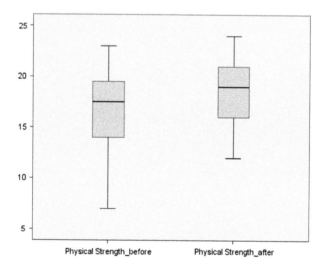

Figure 6. Physical strength.

self-efficacy than the children who were irregularly active. Another important impact factor to consider regarding a high estimation result is that most of the children in the study had an ADHD diagnosis, which often involves difficulties with executive functions. This may imply that the children have difficulties in judging dangers/risks and an overconfidence in themselves and their ability in some situations. Flaws in the two last-mentioned functions may be of importance for a higher estimation result in the study.

It is noteworthy that in the subdomain of body attractiveness, which describes how the child looks upon her/his body and what s/he thinks of it, the median value was higher in this target group in comparison with previous studies implemented on children and young people without disabilities. In the analysis of these results, attention must be paid to the fact

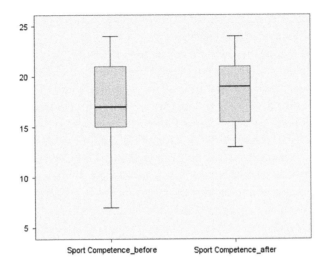

Figure 7. Sport competence.

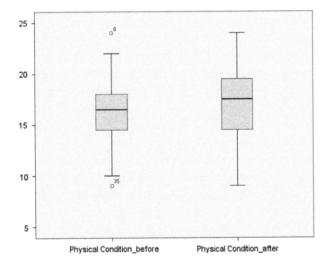

Figure 8. Physical condition.

that the majority of children in the study were children with neuropsychiatric diagnoses, which most often implies a 'well-functioning' body. The result might have been different if the majority of the participants had been children with motor disabilities. Another aspect to discuss is that the number of activity sessions varied among the children. The majority of children chose to participate in most of the activities in the project, while some of the children chose to participate only in a few activities. Maybe the result would have been different if all the children had participated on all occasions. Perhaps the increase would have been greater after the intervention with a 100% participation? A conceivable conclusion might be that the children who were selective in their choice of activities were children with great difficulties in social contexts, as a result of which the activity itself was wholly decisive for taking part or not. Therefore, a participation in only a few activities also meant a lot for these children's well-being and self-efficacy.

In the comparison among the different minimum values before and after the intervention, the result showed an increase from seven to twelve and from seven to thirteen in the subdomains of Sport Competence and Physical Strength. On the individual level this is probably of great importance for the self-efficacy and for the motivation for physical activities. Raustorp argues that an important personal factor for being physically active is the individually experienced self-efficacy (Raustorp 2006). One of the children had e.g. estimated himself almost lowest on the scale concerning sport competence and physical strength (which is six points) before the intervention and almost twice as high after the physical intervention programme. The connection among the other subdomains in CY-PSPP and self-estimated physical self-efficacy was also investigated in the study. As mentioned earlier, studies in the USA, Australia and Sweden have reported that body attractiveness and physical condition were the most important factors for boys' physical self-efficacy, while girls' self-efficacy was chiefly based on body attractiveness and sport competence (Raustorp et al. 2004). Like previous connection analyses the result showed a significant connection between self-efficacy and physical condition as regards boys. Since more than 75% of the participants in this study were boys, this was an expected result. It is worth discussing why only 12 girls chose to take part in the sports project and nine of these in the study. From experience, we know that it is generally difficult to get in touch with the girls in the Habilitation Centre's activities, where the boys dominate in both group and camp activities.

Since this target group may have difficulties in areas such as cognition, attention and concentration, the test leader chose to be available during the whole test period to be able to answer possible questions. In addition, the inquiry was implemented individually with each child in order to be able to meet possible needs for special support. This also turned out to be necessary, as some of the children had difficulties in understanding where on the questionnaire they should fill in their answer. After clarifying instructions and after the researcher had given concrete examples on the questionnaire, the children understood where they should fill in, the researcher chose to implement the investigation in a small room, without external stimuli, in order to decrease the risk of disturbing the children's concentration and attention. The researcher also chose to read the questions aloud for the children on all interview occasions. In order to further make sure that the children had understood the questions, the researcher asked the children after the inquiry had been implemented to retell what the inquiry was about. A majority of the children answered along those lines: *about myself*, *how I feel*, *if I feel strong or weak*, *if I can run far*, *who I am* or *how I am as a person*.

Through motion children develop knowledge of how the world around them functions and also how they themselves function and react in different situations – knowledge that is important for their own self-esteem. When children can feel free and secure in their own bodies together with and in the company of others, they have good chances of becoming participants in a social community. Raustorp and colleagues (2004) and Whitehead (1995) emphasize the importance of individualising physical activity, both in the physical education at school and during physical activities in the spare time. To show consideration for the individual child's needs and wishes and in that way create the best preconditions for the child to be and remain physically active. Raustorp and colleagues also argue that experienced self-efficacy is an important factor and that current research also indicates the possibility of increasing the level of the experienced self-efficacy (Raustorp et al. 2004).

Competence development of the leaders was an important part of the project. The sports leaders had been given education about the various diagnosis groups and their consequences both in everyday life and in sports contexts and education in pedagogy and methodology in Adapted Physical Activity. This took place in groups but also through continuous individual advice and feedback from the sports pedagogue, other staff from the Habilitation Centre and BUP. It was about how to adapt the different sports to individual preconditions and how to create security for the children and the importance of the responsible leader providing scope for variation in the practice. Before the implementation of the project, the sports leaders were given precise and clear guidelines and instructions for the implementation of the activities and the children's preconditions for participation. The main focus of the project was to tone down the competition element so that the activity was about daring, testing and having fun instead of measuring, achieving and competing. According to Raustorp (2006) and Fox (2000), these are important aspects to take into consideration when trying to strengthen individuals' self-efficacy. They describe the importance of giving unconditional support of task mastery minimizing ego orientation when the participant tries new things.

As mentioned earlier, several of the participants in the sports project have neuropsychiatric diagnoses, which often imply difficulties in taking initiatives and motivating oneself for actions. It is therefore important to have several leaders in each activity, who can personally guide and encourage the participants, since they have difficulties in mobilizing internal motivation. The motivation must come from outside in the forms of quick rewards – praise and encouragement can be directly decisive for how good the outcome will be. Direct feedback from the coach is important. The adapted activities also imply that the competition element is toned down and that the children are given opportunities to develop in selected sports based on individual preconditions. However, factors that can contribute to a positive experience among children in terms of socialization are awareness of the objectives of the physical activity, the experience of a long-term perspective on the activity and a more task-oriented than result-oriented nature of the physical activity.

Ethical approval

The study was approved by the Regional Ethical Review Board in Lund Sweden, Dnr. 2012/476.

Acknowledgements

This study is partly associated with an interdisciplinary project headed by Prof. Lotta Vikström, 'Experiences of disabilities in life and on line: Life course perspectives on disabled people from past society to present', which the Wallenberg Foundation *(Stiftelsen Marcus och Amalia Wallenbergs Minnesfond)* recently funded with 5 million SEK (July 2014).

Disclosure statement

No potential conflict of interest was reported by the authors.

References

Åström, P. 2013. "Included Yet Excluded? Conditions for Inclusive Teaching in Physical Education and Health." Doctoral diss., Umeå University, Umeå.

SPORT AND DISABILITY

Bailey, J. A. 2003. "The Foundation of Self-esteem." *Journal of the National Medical Association* 95 (5): 388–393.

Bandura, A. 1977. "Self-efficacy: Toward a Unifying Theory of Behavioral Change." *Psychological Review* 84: 191–215.

Bandura, A. 1986. *Social Foundations of Thought and Action: A Social Cognitive Theory*. Upper Saddle River, NJ: Prentice-Hall.

Bandura, A. 1997. *Self-efficacy: The Exercise of Control*. New York: WH Freeman and Company.

Bandura, A. 2006. "Guide for Creating Self-efficacy Scales." In *Self-efficacy Beliefs of Adolescents*, edited by F. Pajares and T. C. Urdan, 307–337. Greenwich, CT: Information Age Publishing.

Carlock, C. J. 1998. *Enhancing Self Esteem*. Philadelphia, PA: Taylor & Francis.

Coates, J., and P. Vickerman. 2010. "Empowering Children with Special Educational Needs to Speak up: Experiences of Inclusive Physical Education." *Disability and Rehabilitation* 32 (18): 1517–1526.

Day, M. C. 2013. "The Role of Initial Physical Activity Experiences in Promoting Posttraumatic Growth in Paralympic Athletes with an Acquired Disability." *Disability & Rehabilitation* 35 (24): 1–9.

Dunn, J. G. H., J. Causgrove Dunn, and K. McDonald. 2012. "Domain-specific Perfectionism in Intercollegiate Athletes: Relationships with Perceived Competence and Perceived Importance in Sport and School." *Psychology of Sport and Exercise* 13 (6): 747–755.

Fahlén, J., I. Eliasson, and K. Wickman. 2015. "Resisting Self-regulation: An Analysis of Sport Policy Programme Making and Implementation in Sweden." *International Journal of Sport Policy and Politics* 7 (3): 391–406.

Feltz, D., S. Short, and P. Sullivan. 2008. *Self-efficacy in Sport: Research and Strategies for Working with Athletes, Teams, and Coaches*. Champaign, IL: Human Kinetics.

Fortes, M., G. Ninot, and D. Delignières. 2004. "The Hierarchical Structure of the Physical Self: An Idiographic and Cross-correlational Analysis." *International Journal of Sport and Exercise Psychology* 2: 119–132.

Fox, K. R. 2000. "Self-esteem, Self-perceptions and Exercise." *International Journal of Sport Psychology* 31 (2): 228–240.

Fox, K. R., and C. B. Corbin. 1989. "The Physical Self-perception Profile: Development and Preliminary Validation." *Journal of Sport and Exercise Psychology* 11: 408–430.

Gao, Z., P. Xiang, A. M. Lee, and L. Harrison Jr. 2011. "Self-efficacy and Outcome Expectancy in Beginning Weight Training Class." *Research Quarterly for Exercise and Sport* 79 (1): 92–100.

Goodwin, D. L., and E. J. Watkinson. 2000. "Inclusive Physical Education from the Perspectives of Students with Physical Disabilities." *Adapted Physical Activity Quarterly* 17: 144–160.

James, W. 1980. *Principles of Psychology*. New York: Henry R. Holt.

Josephs, L. 1992. *Character Structure and the Organisation of the Self*. New York: Columbia University Press.

Karp, S. 2010. "Perspectives on the Meaning of Children's Sport for Adulthood." *European Journal for Sport and Society* 7 (2): 117–129.

Kristén, L., G. Patriksson, and B. Fridlund. 2002. "Conceptions of Children and Adolescents with Physical Disabilities about Their Participation in a Sports Programme." *European Physical Education Review* 8 (2): 139–156.

Light, R. L. 2010. "Children's Social and Personal Development through Sport: A Case Study of an Australian Swimming Club." *Journal of Sport and Social Issues* 34 (4): 379–395.

Lindwall, M., H. Asci, and P. Crocker. 2014. "The Physical Self in Motion: Within-Person Change and Associations of Change in Self-esteem, Physical Self-concept, and Physical Activity in Adolescent Girls." *Journal of Sport & Exercise Psychology* 36 (6): 551–563.

Özdemir, M., and H. Stattin. 2012. "Konsekvenser av att börja, fortsätta eller sluta idrotta. En longitudinell studie av ungdomars psykologiska och beteendemässiga anpassning" [Consequences of Start, Continue or Stop Playing Sports. A Longitudinal Study of Young People's Psychological and Behavioral Adaptation]. In *Är idrott nyttigt? En antologi om idrott och samhällsnytta.* [Is Sport Healthy? An Anthology of Sports and Community Benefit], edited by J. Hvenmark, 112–135. Stockholm: SISU idrottsböcker.

Raustorp, A. 2006. *Fysisk självkänsla* [Physical Self-esteem]. Uppsala: Kunskapsföretaget i Uppsala.

Raustorp, A., A. Ståhle, H. Gudasic, A. Kinnunen, and E. Mattsson. 2004. "Physical Activity and Self-perception in School Children Assessed with the Children and Youth–Physical Self-perception Profile." *Scandinavian Journal of Medicine & Science in Sports* 15 (2): 126–134.

Samson, A., and M. Solmon. 2011. "Examining the Sources of Self-efficacy for Physical Activity within the Sport and Exercise Domains." *International Review of Sport and Exercise Psychology* 4 (1): 70–89.

Smith, A., and N. Thomas. 2006. "Including Pupils with Special Education Needs and Disabilities in National Curriculum Physical Education: A Brief Review." *European Journal of Special Needs Education* 21 (1): 69–83.

Taub, D. E., and K. R. Greer. 2000. "Physical Activity as a Normalizing Experience for School-age Children with Physical Disabilities: Implications for Legitimation of Social Identity and Enhancement of Social Ties." *Journal of Sport and Social Issues* 24 (4): 395–414.

Uchida, W., K. Hashimoto, and R. Lutz. 2005. "Examination of the Hierarchical Self-esteem Model in Adults with Physical disability." *Perceptional and Motor Skills* 100 (3): 1161–1170.

Vickerman, P., S. Hayes, and A. Whetherly. 2003. "Special Educational Needs and National Curriculum Physical Education." In *Equity in Physical Education*, edited by S. Hayes and G. Stidder, 47–65. London: Routledge.

Whitehead, J. R. 1995. "A Study of Children's Physical Self-perceptions Using an Adapted Physical Self-perception Profile Questionnaire." *Pediatric Exercise Science* 7: 132–151.

Williams, S., and J. Cumming. 2011. "Measuring Athlete Imagery Ability: The Sport Imagery Ability Questionnaire." *Journal of Sport & Exercise Psychology* 3 (33): 416–440.

Yazicioglu, K., F. Yavuz, A. S. Goktepe, and A. K. Tan. 2012. "Influence of Adapted Sports on Quality of Life and Life Satisfaction in Sport Participants and Non-sport Participants with Physical Disabilities." *Disability and Health Journal* 5: 249–253.

A global perspective on disparity of gender and disability for deaf female athletes

Becky Clark and Johanna Mesch

ABSTRACT

Although the significance of gender and disability issues has gradually increased in the global society during the past three decades, there are only few studies with regard to the deaf community and sport. This article examines the level of Deaf or Hard-of-Hearing women's participation in sports and the factors for their continued underrepresentation. The *WomenSport International*'s Task Force on Deaf and Hard of Hearing Girls and Women in Sport conducted a world-wide survey to determine and assess the needs of deaf and hard of hearing girls and women in sport. A snapshot of the results and issues and future aspirations are provided.

Historically, women, members of ethnic minorities and individuals with disabilities have been basically excluded or only allowed limited access to sport (DePauw and Gavron 2005). Despite the fact that a great number of social and cultural barriers relating to equal opportunities were taken away for women in the twentieth century, women are nevertheless underrepresented and allowed limited access in mainstream sports and disability sports. Despite the length of their existence, sports for the deaf, specifically gender and deafness framed as disability, have seldom been the subject of research. Consequently, it is still difficult to measure female participation and gender progress in sports for the deaf. Even for the prestigious Deaflympics – the quadrennial Olympic equivalent event for deaf athletes governed by the International Committee of Sports for the Deaf (ICSD) – no formal studies have focused on the evolution of female participation.

To appreciate the long and rich history of the Deaflympics, it is important to understand the social and psychological dynamics that lead deaf people to desire competitions against one another (Stewart 2001; Stewart and Ammons 2011). Deaf people have no physical or mental disabilities that precludes them from competing with their hearing peers (Jordan 2001). They come together in their own competitions because social processes found in Deaf sport are designed specifically to satisfy physical, psychological and social needs of deaf individuals (Stewart 1991). Their inclusion under the rubric of sports for people with disabilities stems from a difference in communication (Ammons 1990).

Even though the existence of newspapers and magazines around the world which chiefly cater to the deaf community and mainly report on scores, championships and athletic accomplishments, limited literature is available about the past and current challenges that the deaf sport community is facing. Deaf women struggle with double discrimination and oppression on the basis of being female in a male dominated global society especially in the sports arena, and also being deaf in a world dominated by hearing people. Limited access and communication barriers to information, training and coaching is often minimal, or lacking altogether, further making it difficult for deaf girls and women to participate and develop their skills. Therefore, this article focuses on the disparity of gender and disability among deaf females in sports. Two research questions are examined: (1) how has women's participation in the Deaflympics evolved since 1924 and (2) which factors could serve as an explanation for the underrepresentation of women's participation in sports for the deaf over the years.

Gender/disability

There are nearly 1 billion (15%) people with disabilities in the world and considered as the largest, poorest and the most marginalized minority (WHO 2011). Girls and women with disabilities comprise 19.2% of the world's population in which the majority (80%) reside in developing countries (Kim 2013). Females account for 44% of the world's population with disabling hearing loss (WHO 2013; 2015). Disabling hearing loss refers to hearing loss greater than 40 decibel (dB) in the better hearing ear in adults and a hearing loss greater than 30 dB in the better hearing ear in children.

Girls and women with disabilities face double discrimination based on their gender and disability. They are at a higher risk for gender-based violence, physical and sexual abuse, and exploitation; have higher rates of illiteracy, poverty, unemployment, and poor health than women without disabilities and men with disabilities. Furthermore, research indicates that 93% of women with disabilities are not active in sport or physical activity and comprise one third of all athletes with disabilities who compete internationally (Parnes and Hashemi 2007).

The intersection of gender inequality and social and communication barriers of deafness exacerbates discrimination faced by Deaf or Hard-of-Hearing girls and women (DHHGW). Kim postulates that women with disabilities experience severe and compounded discrimination as a result of the intersection of both gender and disability rather than one or the other separately (Kim 2013).

Barriers to sport participation for girls and women with disabilities include attitudes, communication, language, culture, environmental, religious and social beliefs (Ammons 2008; Ammons and Eickman 2011; Clark and Sachs 1991; DePauw 1999; LeClair 2012; Stewart and Ammons 2011; UN Division for the Advancement of Women 2007). Girls and women with disabilities face lack of access to appropriate equipment (i.e. wheelchairs, adapted equipment, communication access such as sign language interpreters, technology, etc.) and facilities. Accommodations and funding are ongoing challenges in comparison to male athletes with disabilities.

Deafness is invisible with its own unique challenges in a world where the majority of the population can hear. Jerald M. Jordan, former president of ICSD, poignantly explained:

As a group, Deaf people do not fit into either able bodied or disabled categories. It has been the oft-repeated experience of the Deaf community that our unique needs are lost when we are lumped into either category. Our limits are not physical; rather, they are outside of us, in the social realm of communication. Among hearing people, whether able-bodied or disabled, we are almost always excluded, invisible and unserved. Among ourselves however, we have no limits. (Jordan 1996)

Just as it is in non-disabled and disabled sports (i.e. Olympics, Paralympics), Deaf sport has traditionally been dominated at all levels by men. There is also a dearth of research and statistics on DHHGW participation in sport and physical activity (Ammons 2006). Even with the passage of Article 30.5 of the United Nations Convention on the Rights of Persons with Disabilities (CRPD) (UN 2006) which defined rights in sport, physical activity and recreation, and shifted the meaning of disability globally, DHHGW continue to face double discrimination and oppression based on being female and deaf.

Deaflympics

The ICSD is the oldest sporting organization for athletes with disabilities and the second old-est multi-sport organization next to the Olympics (Deaflympics 2015). Based at the Maison du Sport International Complex in Lausanne, Switzerland, ICSD is the global governing body of the Deaflympics (formerly known as World Games for the Deaf and International Silent Games). ICSD organizes the Summer and Winter Deaflympics and oversees World Championships and other international, national and regional events. The Deaflympics are held every four years (summer and winter games alternate every two years). The Deaflympics are sanctioned by the International Olympic Committee (IOC) and recognized as the highest level of competition for elite deaf and hard of hearing athletes.

IOC recognized ICSD in 1955 as an 'International Federation with Olympic Standing' and also awarded ICSD the Olympic Cup for its meritorious services to sports for the deaf (in 1966). The IOC honored former ICSD president Jerald M. Jordan in 1995 with the Olympic Order – the highest award the IOC can give to any person – for his outstanding work of nearly a quarter century in the true spirit of the Olympic ideals.

There are no special classifications or changes in sports or rules of events for Deaf or Hard-of-Hearing (DHH) athletes in the Deaflympics (unlike the Paralympics and Special Olympics). An athlete must have a 55 dB loss or greater in the better ear to be eligible to compete in the Deaflympics. Hearing aids and cochlear implants (or any assistive hearing device) are not permitted during competition to maintain a level playing field. Visual cues such as flashing strobe lights, flags or hand signals are the only adaptations necessary.

The Summer Deaflympics consists of twenty sports including athletics, badminton, bas-ketball, beach volleyball, bowling, cycling (on the road), football (soccer), handball, judo, karate, mountain biking, orienteering, shooting, swimming, table tennis, taekwondo, tennis, volleyball, water polo, and wrestling (Freestyle and Greco-Roman). The Winter Deaflympics are much smaller with five sports: alpine and Nordic skiing, cross country skiing, curling, ice hockey and snowboarding. Some sports are male-dominant, such as cycling, handball, water polo and wrestling. Football (soccer) is the top participation sport for DHHGW in the Summer Deaflympics.

The objectives of ICSD are to develop and promote sport training and supervise com-petitions, which are organized by international, national, and regional sports federations for the deaf. It is governed by an eight member executive committee, all of whom are deaf, including the current chief executive officer. ICSD is unique from other disability sporting organizations in that membership of the national deaf federations must comprise 51% deaf individuals as mandated by the ICSD constitution. ICSD membership has grown from six to 108 national federations for the deaf representing four major world regions Africa, Americas, Asia/Pacific, and Europe (combines Asia/Pacific due to smaller DHH population in comparison to IOC's five (5) major world regions - Africa, Americas, Asia, Europe and Oceania).

DHH athletes are distinguished from all others in their special communication needs on the sports field, as well as in the social interaction that is equally part of the games. They are a diverse population with varying degrees of hearing loss, identity, educational backgrounds and communication preferences. DHH individuals who identify with 'Deaf culture' often learn sign language (there are over 141 documented sign languages in the world) (Sign Language Statistics 2015).

There is a whole variety in sign communication which varies from country to country (e.g. international signs, adaptive sign language or simply sign communication). Sign languages are thus different around the world but thanks to visually-based communication and common experiences, DHH competitors form friendships with each other (Breivik, Haualand, and Solvang 2002). Not all DHH athletes communicate in sign language, nor is it required to compete in the Deaflympics or other deaf sporting events.

The Deaflympics is one of the fastest growing sporting events in the world. It is also a major cultural event in addition to providing opportunity for elite deaf and hard of hearing athletes to compete at the highest level of competition with other DHH athletes. Deaf women and girls have participated in the Deaflympics since the beginning. To date, the Deaflympics have been hosted in 36 cities in 21 countries, with an average of 2500 athletes with deaf women comprising nearly 30% of the competitors.

Deaflympics history

Inspired by the concept of Olympism, Frenchman, Eugene Rubens-Alcais and Antoine Dresse formulated an approach to address the oppression of deafness with an 'Olympic' event for Deaf sport (Harrison 2014). It is organized and governed by and for deaf people.

The 1924 International Silent Games, now known as the Deaflympics, were held in Paris, France for first time with 148 DHH male athletes and only one female from nine European nations (Belgium, France, Great Britain, Hungary, Italy, Latvia, Netherlands, Poland and Romania). These athletes competed in six sports: athletics, cycling, football, shooting, swimming and tennis. Gymnastics was a demonstration sport in these inaugural games.

The World Records Commission (WRC) was established in 1933 for deaf world records in athletics and swimming. Shooting, speed skating, and short course swimming records were added later. The Deaflympics awards gold, silver and bronze medals to first, second and third place winners. Records of all individual, team and country categories are maintained by ICSD.

The first Winter Deaflympics were held in 1949 in Seefeld, Austria with 33 male athletes from five nations (Austria, Czechoslovakia, Finland, Sweden, and Switzerland). Competitors competed in Alpine skiing (downhill, slalom, and combined classification) and Nordic skiing (15 km and 3 × 10 relay).

Five women from three nations (Germany, Norway and Switzerland) made history as the first women to compete in the Winter Deaflympics in 1955 in Oberammergau, Germany (55 men from eight nations for combined total of 59 athletes). Eva Herland (Norway) won three gold medals in Alpine skiing (downhill, slalom and combined classification events).

Deaf and hard of hearing female athletes' participation have steadily increased in numbers across the Summer and Winter Deaflympics (personal communication, Donalda Ammons, 2015). Table 1 shows a triple increase of DHH female athletes in the Summer Deaflympics from the first games in France to 2013 Deaflympics in Bulgaria, 0.7 to 33,9% and 0% in the 1949 Winter Deaflympics to 27,4% in 2015 in Khanty-Mansiysk as shown in Table 2.

Table 1. Summer Deaflympics – Gender Statistics (International Committee of Sports for the Deaf 2011)

Year	Location	Men	Women	Total	%Women
1924	Paris	147	1	148	0.7
1928	Amsterdam	198	14	212	6.6
1931	Nurnberg	288	28	316	8.9
1935	London	178	43	221	19.5
1939	Stockholm	208	42	250	16.8
1949	Copenhagen	342	49	391	12.5
1953	Brussels	432	41	473	8.7
1957	Milan	565	70	635	11.0
1961	Helsinki	503	110	613	17.9
1965	Washington DC	575	112	687	16.3
1969	Belgrade	964	225	1189	18.9
1973	Malmö	893	223	1116	20.0
1977	Bucharest	913	237	1150	20.6
1981	Köln	893	305	1198	25.5
1985	Los Angeles	745	250	995	25.1
1989	Christchurch	726	228	954	23.9
1993	Sofia	1295	384	1679	22.9
1997	Copenhagen	1496	532	2028	26.2
2001	Rome	1562	646	2208	29.3
2005	Melbourne	1402	636	2038	31.2
2009	Taipei	1714	779	2493	31.2
2013	Sofia	1792	919	2711	33.9

Note: ICSD statistics 2010/2011 with personal communication update from ICSD re: 2013 Summer Deaflympics and 2015 Winter Deaflympics.

Table 2. Winter Deaflympics – Gender Statistics.

Year	Location	Men	Women	Total	%Women
1949	Seefeld	33	0	33	0.0
1953	Oslo	42	2	44	4.5
1955	Oberammergau	54	5	59	8.5
1959	Montana-Vermala	49	4	53	7.5
1963	Åre	47	13	60	21.7
1967	Berchtesgaden	64	13	77	16.9
1971	Adelboden	69	23	92	25.0
1975	Lake Placid	110	29	139	20.9
1979	Meribel	80	33	113	29.2
1983	Madonna di Campiglio	106	41	147	27.9
1987	Oslo	93	36	129	27.9
1991	Banff	145	36	181	19.9
1995	Ylläs	210	48	258	18.6
1999	Davos	209	56	265	21.1
2003	Sundsvall	205	42	247	17.0
2007	Salt Lake	230	68	298	22.8
2011	Vysoké Tatry	0	0	0	0.0
2015	Khanty-Mansiysk	244	92	336	27.4

Selected data from ICSD statistics (ICSD, 2011) show the highest participation rate of DHH female athletes in the Summer Deaflympics from Europe and the lowest from Africa. European DHH female athletes also had the highest average of participation in the Winter Deaflympics whereas Africa did not field a female competitor. Participation growth factors were dependent upon on venue, travel costs and funding in addition to opportunities for females to participate in their national federations.

Notable historic milestones include the selection of women to leadership positions including the selection of former Deaflympian, Maria Dolores Rojas de Bendequz of Venezuela, as the first deaf woman and Latin American to be elected to the ICSD Executive Committee in 1981. Dr. Donalda Ammons served as the first female secretary general (1997–2004) of the ICSD Executive Committee, and as its first female president (2003–2009). ICSD bestowed Dr. Ammons with an ICSD Honorary Life Member Award in 2015 for her distinguished service and contributions to ICSD and Deaf Sport. Tiffany Williams served as ICSD's first Chief Executive Officer (CEO) from 2005 to 2011.

Deaf/Hard of hearing girls and women in sport

DHHGW athletes may opt to compete with other deaf athletes in deaf sport, compete with hearing athletes, or compete with both deaf and hearing athletes. Communication mode (signing, non-signing, speech, etc.), age of onset of deafness, degree of hearing loss, type of school and social cultural environment influence the deaf athlete's preference for competing with deaf and/or hearing athletes (Kurková, Válková, and Scheetz 2011).

Although deaf people have the right to an interpreter when needed, it is not always possible to arrange for one where sports are involved (i.e. lack of funding, interpreter shortage, denial of services, etc.). Despite more opportunity for acquiring interpreting services in developed countries, DHH athletes, coaches, referees and other deaf sports staff struggle to receive communication accommodations for training in mainstream sports settings and often feel excluded. There is minimal media coverage and reporting on deaf sport in comparison to Disability Sport events (Paralympics, Special Olympics). Funding for deaf sport all over the world, especially for deaf females is a major barrier to participating, competing and leadership opportunities. These barriers relegate DHHGW to increased isolation, exclusion and invisibility in both deaf and mainstream sports.

Another factor of exclusion is a lack of communication access with their hearing counterparts. This includes: access to coaches who can communicate with them; deaf coaches who are qualified to coach at the elite levels; access/availability for funding to provide interpreters at camps or training facilities; education of the hearing world to recognize the potential of DHH athletes as contributing members of hearing teams.

Within the deaf community, DHHGW athletes feel less pressure and are able to enjoy competing/playing without communication difficulties. However, as with in any community there is discrimination based on gender, ethnicity, and different cultural, social, economic and linguistic backgrounds. Deaf sport has been strongly male-dominated for years making it difficult for DHHGW to break into sport participation and inclusion into the world of sport.

WomenSport International Task Force

WomenSport International (WSI), a non-profit organization established in 1994 as a global voice of research-based advocacy for women, officially created a new task force in 2013 to focus on issues and challenges of deaf and hard of hearing girls and women in sport globally (DHHGWIS-TF). Members of this task force include seven deaf women (including the authors) who are leaders in their field, competed in the Deaflympics, played sports at various levels and/or served in sports leadership positions representing four of the five major regions of the world (America, Asia, Europe and Oceania). The DHHGWIS-TF's purpose was to determine and assess the needs of deaf and hard of hearing girls and women in sport and advocate on their behalf. Following WSI's mission, the DHHGWIS-TF sought 'to encourage increased opportunities and positive changes' for deaf and hard of hearing girls and women at all levels of sport involvement.

Survey

A demographic survey was conducted in 2014 with the 104 member nations of ICSD to gather data on participation and leadership opportunities for girls and women in national deaf sports federations. The goal was to outline the issues and barriers related to disability in sport and physical activity in different social/cultural backdrops interconnected by gender in deaf sport community. The survey consisted of 11 questions about sport participation and leadership opportunities in 104 Deaf Sports Federation in 4 regions: Africa, Americas, Asia/Pacific and Europe. The survey was made available in both written English via email, an online survey software tool, *Survey Monkey* and in a International Sign (IS) video. Participation in the study was entirely optional. Participants in the survey were assured that the DHHGWIS-TF were the only individuals having access to the data results and data would be kept strictly confidential. The data was collected through email and *Survey Monkey*. There were not any responses via the IS video. The data was described through absolute frequencies according to the eleven survey questions (Appendix A).

Results

28 countries of 104 responded for a percentage return rate of 27%. All four regions were represented with Europe being the largest (14) followed by Asia/Pacific (8), Africa (4) and Americas (2).

Notable results

- There are about 30% Deaf and Hard of Hearing girls and women participate in either recreational or competitive sports;
- The age range majority was between 21 and 25 and 26–30 year olds at 38.5%;
- Less than 10% of the females served in leadership positions;
- Nearly 55% of the respondents indicate the level of funding for DHHGW to be between 0 and 20%, followed with 20% at 21–40%;
- National Deaf Federations reported 0% for the 15–20 age range for their female participants. Deaf and Hard of Hearing girls are not served at all!
- The percentage of annual financial support given to female athletes is at 54.2% in the 0–20% range.

Furthermore, survey participants reported the following reasons for lack of female participation in their national sports federation:

- Negative stigma towards deafness or hearing loss;
- Lack of opportunities and programs for participation, coaching, training and competition;
- Lack of financial support from local, regional and national governments for assistance in arranging training and workshops;
- Lack of research and documented facts on deaf/hard of hearing female athletes, coaches, leaders, trainers, referees, etc.;
- Lack of national policy and legislations in sport by organizers and decision makers at all levels for athletes with hearing loss.

Because of the WSI's initiative with the DHHGWIS Task Force, ICSD as the supreme body of deaf sports has become more cognizant of the greater needs of Deaf and Hard of Hearing girls and women in the sports world. As a result, ICSD with its long history of inclusion of deaf women in Deaf Sport especially at the elite level, officially endorsed the Brighton Declaration on Women and Sport at the 6th International Working Group World Conference on Women and Sport (2014) in Helsinki, Finland. The Brighton Declaration is a document which outlines concrete guiding principles on achieving women's full involvement in all areas of sport, and promotes gender equality. Additionally, to further its mission and commitment to equality in sport, ICSD established the Women in Sport Commission to gauge the needs and services of deaf girls and women in a more efficient manner.

Conclusion

This article examined the level of deaf and hard of girls and women's participation in sports and reasons for their continued underrepresentation. Although the WSI DHHGWIS TF survey study was small, it serves as a preliminary needs assessment for deaf and hard of hearing girls and women in sport. It opens the door to identifying barriers and challenging issues and provides a stepping stone to further research including interviews on local and national levels on a larger global scale.

Deaf and hard of hearing girls and women in sport compete, coach, and serve as leaders for the same reasons as other women with and without disabilities do. Ongoing advocacy, support, networking in raising awareness and promoting inclusion and equality in both mainstream and deaf/disability organizations are necessary to empower and increase participation and leadership roles for DHHGW in every aspect of sport.

Disclosure statement

No potential conflict of interest was reported by the authors.

References

Ammons, D. 1990. "Unique Identity of the World Games for the Deaf." *Palaestra* 6 (2): 40–43.
Ammons, D. 2006. "Deaflympics: Dealing with Change and Diversity." Paper presented at the 3rd IWG World Conference on Women and Sport, Kumanoto, Japan, May 11–14.

Ammons, D. 2008. "Deaf Sports & Deaflympics." Paper presented to the International Olympic Committee. https://www.jfd.or.jp/deaflympics/resources/presrep-e.pdf.

Ammons, D., and J. Eickman. 2011. "Deaflympics and the Paralympics: Eradicating Misconceptions." *Sport in Society* 14 (9): 1149–1164.

Breivik, J. K., H. Haualand, and P. Solvang. 2002. "Rome, a Temporary Deaf City!: Deaflympics 2001." *A Publication within the Anthropological Project: Transnational Connections in Deaf Worlds* (Working Paper 2-2002). http://www.ub.uib.no/elpub/rokkan/N/N02-02.pdf.

Clark, R. A., and M. L. Sachs. 1991. "Challenges and Opportunities in Psychological Skills Training in Deaf Athletes." *The Sport Psychologist* 5 (4): 392–398.

DePauw, K. P. 1999. "Girls and Women with Disabilities in Sport." *Journal of Physical Education, Recreation & Dance* 70: 50–52.

Deaflympics. 2015. Retrieved from http://www.deaflympics.com/icsd.asp, 28 December 2015.

DePauw, K. P., and S. J. Gavron, eds. 2005. *Disability Sport*. Champaign, IL: Human Kinetics.

Harrison, S. 2014. *Same Spirit - Different Team. the Politicization of the Deaflympics*. Hertfordshire: Action Deafness Books.

Jordan, J. M. 1996. "The World Games for the Deaf and the Paralympic Games." (Position Paper 1996). http://www.deaflympics.com/news.asp?the-world-games-for-the-deaf-and-the-paralympic-games.

Jordan, J. M. 2001. "CISS and the International Paralympic Committee." In *CISS 2001: A Review*, edited by J. M. Lovett, T. Giansanti and J. Eickman, 54–57. Redditch: Red Lizard.

International Committee of Sports for the Deaf (ICSD) 2011. "Statistics" (Version 1.2). Frederick: ICSD.

Kim, M. Y. 2013. "Women with Disabilities: The Convention through the Prism of Gender." In *Human Rights and Disability Advocacy*, edited by M. Sabatello and M. Schulze, 113–130. Philadelphia, PA: University of Pennsylvania.

Kurková, P., H. Válková, and N. Scheetz. 2011. "Factors Impacting Participation of European Elite Deaf Athletes in Sport." *Journal of Sports Sciences* 29 (6): 607–618.

LeClair, J. M. 2012. "Introduction: Global Organizational Change in Sport and the Shifting Meaning of Disability." In *Disability in the Global Sport Arena: A Sporting Chance*, edited by J. M. LeClair, 4–25. New York, NY: Routledge.

Parnes, P., and G. Hashemi. 2007. "Sport as a Means to Foster Inclusion, Health and Well-Being of People with Disabilities." In *Literature Reviews on Sport for Development and Peace. Commissioned by Sport for Development and Peace International Working Group (SDP IWG), Secretariat* Toronto, Canada, October 18. http://www.righttoplay.com/moreinfo/aboutus/Documents/LiteratureReviewsSDP.pdf.

Sign Language Statistics 2015. Accessed from http://www.ethnologue.com/subgroups/sign-language. 28 December.

Stewart, D. A. 1991. *A Deaf Sport: The Impact of Sports within the Deaf Community*. Washington, DC: Gallaudet University Press.

Stewart, D. A. 2001. "The Role of Deaf Sports Organizations in the Education of Deaf Children." In *CISS 2001: A Review*, edited by J. M. Lovett, T. Giansanti, and J. Eickman, 58–66. Redditch: Red Lizard.

Stewart, D. A., and D. Ammons. 2011. "Future Directions of the Deaflympics." *Palaestra* 17 (3): 45–49.

UN (United Nations) 2006. *Convention on the Rights of Persons with Disabilities, and Its Optional Protocol*. New York: UN.

UN Division for the Advancement of Women 2007. "Women 2000 and beyond: Women, Gender Equality and Sport." http://www.un.org/womenwatch/daw/public/WomenandSport.pdf.

WHO (World Health Organization) and World Bank 2011. "World Report on Disability." http://www.refworld.org/docid/50854a322.html.

WHO (World Health Organization) 2013. "Millions of People in the World Have Hearing Loss That Can Be Treated or Prevented." http://www.who.int/pbd/deafness/news/Millionslivewithhearingloss.pdf.

WHO (World Health Organization) 2015. "Deafness and Hearing Loss – Fact Sheet N°300." http://www.who.int/mediacentre/factsheets/fs300/en/.

Appendix A.

WomenSport International

WSI Task Force on Deaf and Hard of Hearing Girls and Women in Sport Survey

Name of your Organisation:
_____

Name of Contact Person:
_____

Position Title:_____

E-mail address:_____

1. How many deaf/hard of hearing **athletes** does your *Deaf Sports Federation (DSF)* have in your **country**?

    Females_____

    Males   _____

2. How many **sports** does your *DSF* offer for deaf/hard of hearing female a athletes? _____

3. Which sports are offered by your *DSF* for your deaf/hard of hearing female athletes?

SPORT	Tick √ YES	NO
Alpine Skiing	☐	☐
Athletics	☐	☐
Badminton	☐	☐
Baseball	☐	☐

Basketball	☐	☐
Beach Volleyball	☐	☐
Bowling	☐	☐
Chess	☐	☐
Cricket	☐	☐
Cross Country Skiing	☐	☐
Curling	☐	☐
Cycling Road	☐	☐
Cycling (Track)	☐	☐
Diving	☐	☐
Fencing	☐	☐
Football	☐	☐
Futsal	☐	☐
Golf	☐	☐
Gymnastics	☐	☐
Handball	☐	☐
Ice Hockey	☐	☐
Judo	☐	☐
Karate	☐	☐
Lawn Bowls	☐	☐
Mountain Biking	☐	☐
Netball	☐	☐
Orienteering	☐	☐
Rugby	☐	☐
Shooting	☐	☐
Snowboard	☐	☐
Softball	☐	☐
Squash	☐	☐
Swimming	☐	☐
Table Tennis	☐	☐
Taekwondo	☐	☐
Tennis	☐	☐
Volleyball	☐	☐
Wrestling Freestyle	☐	☐
Wrestling Greco-Roman	☐	☐
_____	☐	☐
_____	☐	☐
_____	☐	☐
_____	☐	☐

4. What is the percentage of deaf/hard of hearing female athletes participate primarily for each category?

In competition:

0-20% ☐   21-40% ☐   41-60% ☐   61-80% ☐   81-100% ☐

In fitness/recreation:

   0-20% ☐   21-40% ☐   41-60% ☐   61-80% ☐   81-100% ☐

5. What is the percentage of the total deaf/hard of hearing female athletes participate at *national/international level*?

   0-20% ☐   21-40% ☐   41-60% ☐   61-80% ☐   81-100% ☐

6. What is the **average age range** of deaf/hard of hearing female athletes in your DSF?

   15-20 ☐   21-25 ☐   26-30 ☐   31-35 ☐   over 35 ☐

7. How many deaf/hard of hearing females serve on your **DSF**:

   Executive Board?   _____
   Sub-Committees?   _____
   Staff positions?   _____
   Unpaid Volunteers   _____

8. How many deaf/hard of hearing female **referees/umpires** are there in your **DSF**? _____

9. How many deaf/hard of hearing female **coaches/trainers** are there in your **DSF**? _____

10. What is the percentage of your DSF's **annual financial support** given to female athletes?

   0-20% ☐   21-40% ☐   41-60% ☐   61-80% ☐   81-100% ☐

11. If there are no deaf/hard of hearing females in your DS, please list the possible reasons for this.

_____

_____

_____

_____

Thank You for Your Participation!

-------------------------------------END of Survey-------------------------------------

Send this form to:
WomenSport International Task Force on Deaf/Hard of Hearing Girls and Women in Sport at WSI.
DHH@gmail.com
OR
If you opt to take the IS version, please upload your answers via your YouTube account or via email and send to WSI.DHH@gmail.com.

The outcomes of running a sport camp for children and youth with visual impairments on faculty members' teaching, research, and service activities: a case study

Otávio L. P. C. Furtado, Lauren J. Lieberman and Gustavo L. Gutierrez

ABSTRACT

We explored the outcomes of running a sport camp for children and youth with visual impairment on faculty members' roles. Seven adapted physical activity faculty members were interviewed. Questionnaires and documents were also analyzed and a variety of strategies were employed to ensure the study's trustworthiness. Regarding the teaching role, disability knowledge and real life examples gave faculty more credibility in conducting their class. As for the research role, the outcomes were not shared by the majority of participants and seemed to rely on aspects such as camp maturity, directors' aptitudes, and partnerships. In turn, running the camp was a means for faculty members to perform their external service roles. These potential outcomes may become a significant part of the process by which people enact their institutional roles and may serve as a framework for future studies with a more hypothesis-driven approach.

Introduction

Technological advances and rapid globalization are particular challenges to contemporary universities. The transformation in work, leisure time, and formal schooling structures drive academic institutions often to redefine their goals if they want to keep up with the changing world. In this context, while some universities state particular educational, social, political, or spiritual aims, most of them still have fundamental goals based on the triad of teaching, research, and service (Scott 2006).

With the focus on the development of civic leaders and productive citizens (Antonio, Astin, and Cress 2000) who understand and deal intelligently with modern life (Chickering and Gamson 1987), the teaching role is of primary importance in undergraduate and graduate courses. When sharing knowledge to students and assisting students during their learning process, faculty members are enacting their teaching role. As suggested by Umbach and Wawrzynski, if educational practices, such as active and collaborative learning, engagement of students in experiences, and interaction with students are employed, certain outcomes of college are likely to occur (e.g. student learning and retention). Furthermore, the same authors found that 'faculty behaviors and attitudes affect students profoundly, which propose that faculty members may play the single-most important role in student learning' (Umbach and Wawrzynski 2005).

Alongside with teaching, research represents the core mission of universities worldwide. According to Scott, 'the research mission is valuable for the improvement of societies around the globe - creating a skilled workforce, enabling economic growth, improving health care, and encouraging knowledge production' (Scott 2006, 23). Pertaining to this matter, Reid and Stanish support that the specific body of knowledge of a given discipline is developed through research, showing a consistent link between the teaching and research roles (Reid and Stanish 2003). In large universities, the research role is more commonly part of faculty responsibilities, as these institutions have the majority of graduate courses and provide financial, human and material resources for researching. Although teaching activities are rewarded in higher education institutions, traditionally research is the most prestigious and valued among the three common faculty roles (Servage 2009).

The faculty service role, characterized by Ward as a multifaceted concept with internal and external dimensions, tends to be considered of lesser value than teaching and research because it is vaguely understood, defined, and consequently rewarded (Ward 2003). In an effort to clarify this role, Ward defines the first dimension as service to the institution and the later as a way to connect teaching and research to community and societal needs. External service is expressed through extension, consulting, service-learning, community-based action research, and community and civic service. Specifically, faculty consulting is the natural extension of scholars expertise outside the academic institution (Boyer and Lewis 1984) and service-learning is the integration of community service projects into academic course work, serving as a venue for students to acquire academic, career, social, and personal skills (Astin et al. 2000; Cutforth 2000).

According to Marston, 'a major challenge for most university faculty members is how to best channel one's interests, time, and energy in a way that most efficiently addresses each aspect of the tripartite structure' (Marston 2002, 35). In this sense, Marston explained that through directing an early childhood movement program he tried to tackle all of the three roles. Related to the teaching role he described using a variety of teaching techniques while mentoring his university students in designing and delivering movement activities. From the research perspective, he used the data collected from the program in presentations, workshops, and publications. Last, regarding the service component, Marston points that besides the provision of movement experiences to the children and the educational materials to the parents, the program was also associated to the area of public relations (i.e. a form of university outreach to the community). In a similar study, Walsh supported the idea that being able to tie teaching, research, and service activities to a university-sponsored youth sports summer camp helped to create a justifiable, longstanding project (Walsh 2011). Walsh noted it was possible to validate camp through the faculty roles by offering credits to preservice physical education teachers, by allowing graduate students to conduct research projects, and by providing local community with a sport summer camp option for their children and an employment opportunity for local students and teachers.

Although these two single case studies shed some light on how faculty roles can be integrated into a movement or sport program, it was only addressed from single case studies, including participants without disability. For instance, faculty members teaching adapted physical activity courses could also professionally benefit from running a specially designed program for participants with a given disability. According to the International Federation for Adapted Physical Activity (2016), adapted physical activity is a service delivery profession and an academic field of study, defined as 'a cross-disciplinary body of practical and theoretical knowledge directed toward impairments, activity limitations, and participation restrictions in physical activity'.

Previous studies have shown that by participating in a camp specifically designed for youths with disabilities, campers can get a reprieve from perceptions of disability isolation, increase self-reliance, and independence (Goodwin and Staples 2005). More specifically, in sport camps for children and youth with visual impairment (VI), the outcome to participants include reaching unprecedented high levels of physical activity (Lieberman et al. 2006), the acquisition of new sport skills, and the testing of individual physical limits which serve to set new self-defined standards (Goodwin et al. 2011).

One such program is Camp Abilities (CA), a developmental sport camp for children and adolescents with VI. The first CA was created in 1996 at the College at Brockport, State of New York, USA, and has been replicated at over 22 locations across the United States and in countries including Canada, Costa Rica, Finland, Ireland, Guatemala, Brazil, and Portugal (Haegele et al. 2014). Among camps, eight are run by adapted physical education faculty members and usually at their institution campus. All CA share a similar structure and mission, though specific geographical aspects may be considered in the program of each camp. Camps serve 20–55 campers who are on a one-on-one basis with coaches, from undergraduate or graduate courses, who are training to be physical education teachers, teachers of students with VI, or special education teachers. During activities, each coach-and-camper pair works together to learn, refine, and master skills, with additional support being provided by a sport specialist whenever needed (Haegele et al. 2014).

To the best of our knowledge, no studies have been published addressing the outcomes of running a sport camp for children and youth with disability in faculty members' roles. Besides that, given the increase in CA numbers and how it has been spreading worldwide in recent years, in the present study we aimed to explore, from a multiple case study perspective, the outcomes of running a sport camp for children and youth with VI on adapted physical activity faculty members' teaching, research, and service activities.

Method

Case study design

Case studies are a common type of qualitative research employed in the physical education field (Hemphill et al. 2012). This research is characterized as an exploratory case study, as there has been no empirical research conducted about the outcomes of running a sport camp for children and youth with VI on faculty members' roles. Yin states that exploratory case studies are adequate when the goal is to generate hypotheses and propositions about a specific phenomenon, the subject of this research. A multiple case study design, considered to be more robust than single case study, was used in this investigation, allowing a single set of cross-case conclusions (Yin 2009).

Table 1. Participants characteristics.

	Participant 1	Participant 2	Participant 3	Participant 4	Participant 5	Participant 6	Participant 7
Education	Master's (2012)	PhD (2002)	PhD (2007)	PhD (1996)	PhD (1993)	EdD (1992)	Master's (2012)
Faculty member since	2011	2002	2008	1995	2005	1983	2006
Faculty rank	Lecturer	Full Professor	Associate	Full Professor	Associate	Full Professor	Lecturer
Teaching level	Undergraduate	Under-graduate, Graduate (Master's)	Under-graduate, Graduate (Master's)	Under-graduate, Graduate (Master's)	Under-graduate, Graduate (Master's + PhD)	Undergraduate	Undergraduate
Camp editions	3	10	2	19	2	9	4

Legend. PhD: *Philosophiae Doctor*, EdD: *Educationis Doctor*.

Participants

Purposeful sampling was used to discover, understand, and gain insight from a specific situation (Merriam 1998). The inclusion criteria were as follows: participants had to be faculty members currently working in a higher education setting, teaching adapted physical activity / education courses, and responsible for running a CA. According to these criteria, the second author of this study (participant four), founder of the first Camp Abilities, identified eight potential participants.

Eventually, seven participants (six female and one male) took part in the study. The sample had an average of 13 years (3–31) of teaching experience in higher education, and an average of 7 years (2–19) of experience in running a camp for children and youth with VI. Additional characteristics of the participants are available in Table 1. Each case was numbered to retain anonymity.

Data collection

The first author was responsible for the data collection over a period of 14 weeks (22 October–1 February 2014). There were three data sources used in this study: (1) questionnaires, (2) document analysis, and (3) interviews. The data collection process consisted of a first contact e-mail explaining to likely participants the purpose of the study, and its procedures. Additionally, the e-mail contained copies of the informed consent and the questionnaire. After receiving the signed informed consent and the completed questionnaire the researcher proceeded with the analysis of documents related to each participant (university career progression policies and procedures; and camp website information) and subsequent scheduling of a Skype or phone interview. The project was approved by the researchers' University's Internal Review Board.

Questionnaire

The questions covered information of participant's education and professional background; characteristics of the sport camp for children and youth with VI; and Institution career evaluation.

Semi-structured interviews

Interviews were the main data collection method, considered to be a highly efficient approach to gather rich, empirical data (Eisenhardt and Graebner 2007). Interviews were used to obtain information regarding areas of the faculty members' career that could be influenced by running a camp for children and youth with VI.

The interview guide was developed in a way to ensure each participant was asked similar questions and to cover the areas of interest. The guide allowed flexibility to explore participant's responses to the questionnaire, and to investigate emerging topics likely to be important. The questionnaire and interview guide were pilot-tested with one eligible participant and provided an opportunity for checking the appropriateness of questions, the time needed for conducting the interview, and for the field researcher to practice his interviewing skills.

The interviews lasted on average 48 min and were conducted by the first author. Because of geographical distance (five in different USA states; one in Central America; one in Europe) between the respondents and the interviewer we found to be most suitable to conduct the interviews through Skype-to-telephone ($n = 4$) or non-visual Skype-to-Skype ($n = 3$) calls. All of the interviews were recorded using the MP3 Skype Recorder software 3.1. Interviews were transcribed verbatim, and each transcript was reviewed against the audio record for accuracy.

Document analysis

Electronic documents from each university related to faculty members' career progression policies and procedures, and each camp website information was also examined. This information was used to help determine the outcomes of CA on different aspects of the faculty members' career path.

Data analysis

Interviews, as the main source of evidence, questionnaires and documents, were analyzed in a three-step process of data condensation, data display and conclusion drawing/verification Data condensation occurred continuously throughout this project and consisted of decisions on choosing the conceptual framework, the cases, the research questions and the data collection approaches. As the research proceeded, this phase also included: writing summaries, coding, discovering potentially new themes, and developing sub-themes (Miles, Huberman, and Saldaña 2014). Three a priori themes were developed (teaching, research, and service) based on the literature presented in the introduction of this paper and the research questions. Derived from inductive and deductive approaches an initial coding list was created, and served as the foundation to the data analysis (Miles, Huberman, and Saldaña 2014; Ryan and Bernard 2003; Yin 2009). In order to reduce bias and ambiguity two researchers independently analyzed the data, and subsequently through discussion achieved consensus of findings.

In the next phase a strategy called stacking comparable cases was employed, consisting of a mixed technique of case and variable oriented approaches. First each case was displayed in a matrix and analyzed in depth. Then, we stacked the case-level displays in a meta-matrix (lines and columns) with all the cases, and explored similarities and differences across cases and variables, allowing the development of assertions and propositions (Miles, Huberman, and Saldaña 2014).

Trustworthiness

We employed a variety of strategies to ensure the study's trustworthiness. To establish content validity of the data collection instruments, two experts in qualitative research and three adapted physical activity faculty members reviewed and provided feedback on the elements of the questionnaire and interview guide (Haynes, Richard, and Kubany 1995). Before field work commenced, both instruments were pilot-tested allowing further adjustments. To increase construct validity, the development of a sufficiently operational set of measures was accomplished by using multiple data sources (documents, questionnaires, and interviews). In addition, member checks were performed when participants had the opportunity to check and confirm the accuracy of interview transcriptions (Yin 2009).

A comprehensive approach was used to analyze the data. The first and second authors independently performed the coding of the data and, through discussion, reached consensus on disagreements. Analytic triangulation occurred with the aid of a peer debriefer, a colleague with experience in camps for children with disabilities, who reviewed and provided critical feedback on the methods employed (Brantlinger et al. 2005). To address reliability, or the ability of different researchers to reach the same conclusions about the same case studies, we created a formal computerized database including all documents, questionnaires, and interviews (Yin 2009).

Results

The three themes developed were first, teaching; second, research; and third, service. Based on careful analysis of the results, this section will describe each theme and how directing a camp can be related to faculty members' roles. The themes are described using the participant's own words.

Teaching

Participants mentioned teaching to be their main institutional role and added that by running a camp for children and youth with VI has been a rich opportunity for their professional development and to physical education students (Figure 1).

From the faculty professional development perspective two common outcomes were reported to be potentially beneficial from running a camp. First, it was *a way of acquiring more knowledge* about individuals with VI participating in physical activities. Participant five illustrates this by saying that 'I didn't really get involved in sports for the visually impaired (before), so it has increased my knowledge and my awareness'. Another common thread was the *advantage of teaching based in real life situations*, which was richly expressed by participant six:

> I get a chance to role model the teaching methods that I'm teaching them in class. So I use all of those things to help me identify that what I am teaching them is real. It reiterates that the things that I'm teaching are real. So that's professional development for me. And there's no doubt in my mind that with every camp something happens where I have to learn a lot more.

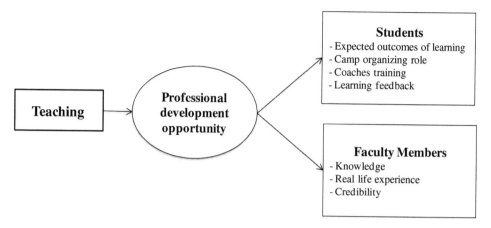

Figure 1. Visual representation of the theme teaching.

> It's one of the highest forms of professional development, to actually do it actively where you actually do the things that you believe are best practice. And then it gives you more information on how to teach better. And that's professional development to me.

In another perspective, participants expressed some form of enthusiasm when talking about the potential learning to their students who participated in camp. In broad terms, they expected student to learn how to work with this specific group of individuals with sensory impairment as a result of the training provided to coaches prior to camp, and from the one-to-one relationship with campers. In particular, they made clear their desire of students to reach an understanding of issues around VI; specific instructional strategies (e.g. guiding techniques, auditory signals, tactile teaching techniques); equipment and, as mentioned by participant five 'I want them to walk away feeling comfortable with working with individuals with visual impairments'.

For a majority of the participants, camp volunteers had an opportunity to perform and receive feedback for improvement on existing knowledge. Except for participant four, who reasoned to have a mixed group of undergraduate and graduate volunteers from different universities, all participants mentioned giving feedback to students about their coaching role. In two situations when students received course credits for their participation in camp, they were formally evaluated at the end of camp. In the remaining camps, feedback was given during or after activities as exemplified by the words of participant six:

> It's the perfect time for me to meet with the students to express my opinion about how they're doing. So they have a formative, not a summative, assessment. I can get to each one of them and say, 'You're right on. You're doing exactly what you're supposed to be doing. You're picking up things well, and I like your leadership'.

Evening chats or after camp gatherings were said to be moments to analyze situations, to discuss experiences, and to share memories. Overall, these moments were associated with personal and professional development. Nonetheless, in circumstances when a coach did not work as expected, extreme measures could be taken, such as the exclusion from camp, as reported participant two.

It is also important to note the opportunity for coaches to increase their disability awareness, to meet specialists in the field, and, for some students who took part in the organization

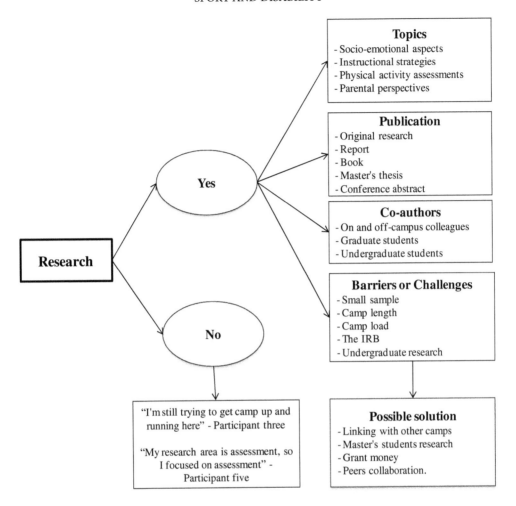

Figure 2. Visual representation of the theme research.

of camp, the chance 'to understand what goes into running a program like this, costs to run the camp, how do you raise the money', from participant six words. To stress the value of this experience for coaches, participant one says: 'The physical education students learn much more than they would learn in one semester in the classroom'.

Research

The second theme related to research. Based on our findings, the majority of participants develop some kind of camp-related research, except for faculty three and five who explained, respectively, that: 'I'm still trying to get camp up and running here' and 'My research area is assessment, so I focused on assessment'. From those who answered yes, four sub-themes emerged within the broad theme of research: *publication, topics, co-authors, and barriers* (Figure 2).

Overall, participant four was responsible for most of the camp-related peer reviewed publications – 22 articles. *Publication* from this and other participants also included case

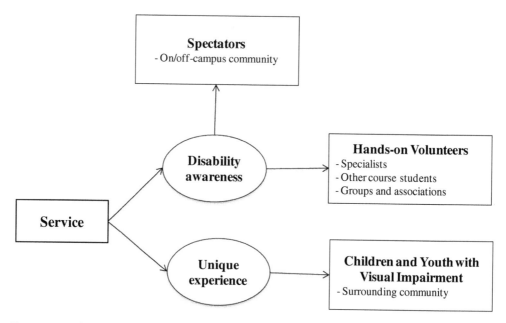

Figure 3. Visual representation of the theme service.

reports, conference abstracts, and books (pertaining to VI pedagogical aspects and a book on how to start a camp). *Topics* commonly addressed in the research comprised socio-emotional outcomes of camp attendees; sport or physical activity instructional strategies for youth with VI; physical activity and motor development status; and parental perspectives. *Co-authors* were on and off-campus colleagues, graduate and undergraduate students.

Although camp can be a fruitful opportunity to do research, a number of *barriers* have been identified from the data. One issue refers to the small number of camp participants (i.e. campers: average of 25, ranging from 12 to 53; coaches: average of 32, ranging from 17 to 70), which becomes more pronounced when the campers heterogeneous characteristics are considered (i.e. gender, age, and VI classification). Another matter relates to the limited available time (ranging from three to seven days), since camp is already fully scheduled with the program activities. Furthermore, it was acknowledge the challenge to get the research project approved by the IRB and to have only undergraduate students involved in research projects.

Service

A third theme is service. For cases six and seven, camp is linked to an undergraduate or graduate class in a physical education course (or related courses such as kinesiology, sport studies), thus being here categorized on a service-learning perspective (Figure 3). In this situation, coaches of children or youth with VI have to be regular students, unless there are more kids than coaches, when on or off-campus volunteers are allowed to participate. On the other hand, when camp is not associated with a course class (cases one to five) or when students can opt to apply for practicum credits (cases two, four and five) we fit it into the faculty consulting category, another aspect of external service. It is important to note that even when off-campus volunteers collaborate as coaches the majority of them were graduated or were physical education or adapted physical education students.

Within the theme service, two reoccurring sub themes were found: *disability awareness* and *unique experience*. The first sub theme included two main groups of people who were captivated by curiosity or seeking for a civic engagement opportunity. Some faculties expressed that camp activities were positive to raise attention of spectators on-campus to children with VI. Participant two said 'we go to the cafeteria, we move around, we do activities, and everybody who comes around will see us, and they will say, what's happening here? ... Everybody's really impressed'. In regard to the off-campus community, participant five explained that by having kids with VI riding a conference bike in the surroundings of the university, it 'provides people in the community with a bigger awareness of visual impairment'.

The disability awareness sub theme also embraced a civic engagement opportunity for groups of hands-on volunteers. These groups included visual impairment and adapted physical education specialists, on-campus students (other than physical education students), parents of campers and members of local organized groups and associations. A second sub theme that emerged was the unique experience of children and youth with VI who participated in a sport camp specifically designed for them. For example, participant 7 says a meaningful aspect of running Camp was,

> ... seeing the campers having such a good time and developing and growing during the week. They've even set up Facebook pages where they keep in touch with each other, and just to see the friendships that have blossomed and the different things that they go on and do. You can really see that you've had an impact, a positive impact on somebody's life.

Discussion

The purpose of this study was to investigate the outcomes of running a sport camp for children and youth with VI on adapted physical activity faculty roles'. Regardless of participants' characteristics our results indicate a clear benefit on their teaching and service activities, whereas the outcomes on the research area is not so evident, and seems to rely on factors such as camp characteristics (i.e. partnerships, starting year, number of participants) and personal motivation.

Teaching a specific subject should require a good wealth of knowledge, often derived from theory (e.g. text books, evidence-based practice guidelines), and enhanced from practical, real-world experiences (Fry, Ketteridge, and Marshall 2008). In this way, directing a sport camp for children with VI was reckoned to empower participants, not only to increase disability understanding, but also to teach using examples anchored in real life situations, which was mentioned to give them more credibility in class. Although not assessed in this study, most likely these benefits would occur in the first years of running the camp, following the characteristic learning-curve pattern. Therefore, long term professional development goals could help to keep directors engaged in this demanding task, and could include teaching others how to run camps, working with other agencies or organizations to produce accessible equipment and encouraging students to go into the field of visual impairment among other long term projects.

In this study the participants reported high learning expectation to students participating as coaches. The one-on-one instruction, a rule for CA, provides a unique opportunity to train and prepare future professionals such as teachers for those with VI, adapted physical education teachers, physical education teachers, and sport coaches (Lieberman et al. 2013), and may be more efficient in promoting learning outcomes when compared to disability simulation laboratory experiences, commonly used in undergraduate courses (Leo and Goodwin 2013). For instance, Roper and Santiago reported that the hands-on aspect of a service-learning project was beneficial to promote positive attitude changes and to develop undergraduate kinesiology students' interpersonal and problem solving skills for working with students with disabilities in a physical activity setting (Roper and Santiago 2014). In another study, physical education students enrolled in an adapted physical education class participated in a physical activity-based service-learning programming, and enhanced their academic and civic learning (Richards et al. 2015). More specifically, a previous study done at CA has also showed that immersion in a sports camp practicum improved attitudes of pre-service teachers toward children with VI and deafblindness (Lieberman and Wilson 2005).

Plausibly, there is a continuum of activities influencing students' attitudes towards disability, in which camp engagement can assume one of the higher ranks. This continuum would begin with in-class disability concepts and simulations (Leo and Goodwin 2014), then would evolve to hands-on experiences within university adapted physical activity classes, and would proceed to immersion in experiences more closely related to their profession, such as summer camps (Ellis, Lepore, and Lieberman 2012) or Special Olympics (Diacin and VanSickle 2014). Overall, positive outcomes are likely to occur to all groups of coaches. However, those performing activities as part of a course (service-learning) are expected to benefit more when compared to those working as volunteers or to earn practicum credits (Astin et al. 2000), and it could be explained by the deliberate emphasis on reflection, which is distinctive in service-learning approaches (Diacin and VanSickle 2014).

Based on our analysis, we further identified several teaching outcomes which could be matched to most of the principles for good practice in undergraduate education proposed by Chickering and Gamson (1987). These outcomes included: (a) frequent out-of-class contact between students and faculty throughout the length of camp; (b) situations of reciprocity and cooperation among students working in small groups and in diverse activities; (c) active learning, when coaches had the chance to instruct, reflect, and write about it; (d) prompt feedback on coaches performance; and (e) emphasis for time on task in a very tight camp's schedule. Nonetheless, these outcomes were more frequently observed in camps using a service-learning approach than in those having coaches working for practicum credits or as volunteers. While the high load of activities, very common in these camps, served to provide leadership opportunities for some students performing a camp organization role, it also seemed to be a source of concern and anxiety to new directors, who wanted to get camp up and running before becoming more committed to teaching or research outcomes.

Coincidently or not, the older and bigger camp (case four) was responsible for most of the research developed among camps. Whilst many factors may play a role in the determination of the quantity of research developed in such a particular setting, based on our results we postulate that camp maturity, directors' aptitudes (internally driven to conduct research), partnership with other faculties, and collaboration with graduate students are key elements in designing and conducting a research project in such a short and tight schedule. For example, participant four along with other three faculty from the same department and one director from another camp (case one) received a specific grant to developed a multi-site investigation. With the collaboration of graduate and undergraduate students, the researchers were able to assess the health related fitness status of 152 children with VI aged 10–17, in five different camps throughout the United States of America (Lieberman et al. 2010). This collaborative strategy was positive to enhance study validity by increasing its statistical power, a common issue in quantitative disability research, due to the small samples typically available, and may be a desirable approach for future studies.

Our study detected that while some studies done at camps were published in congress and symposiums, providing little knowledge to the international audience, they are an outstanding opportunity for undergraduate and graduate students to develop intellectual and scientific skills. On the other hand, other research published in specialized peer reviewed journals are among the most cited literature regarding the field of physical activity for children and youth with VI, collaborating to the creation of a specialized body of knowledge useful to researchers and practitioners (Hand, Lieberman, and Stuart 2006; Lieberman and McHugh 2001; Robinson and Lieberman 2014; Shapiro et al. 2005). Nonetheless, the level of evidence derived from those investigations is still to be determined.

Reid, Bouffard, and MacDonald have recognized the challenge to determine what works in adapted physical activity as research may be constrained by the multifactor complexity with numerous variables and interactions at several levels (Reid, Bouffard, and MacDonald 2012). We recognize that low sample size, heterogeneity of participants (e.g. gender, age, visual impairment classification), and program's short duration are common issues of this one-on-one instruction sport and recreation situation. Thus, the transferability of research outcomes to other physical activity settings are not fully understood.

The development of a CA, here characterized as a service delivery model (Haegele et al. 2014) represented a means for faculty to perform their external service roles. According to Ward, by 'making teaching and research relevant and connected to community and societal needs' (Ward 2003, 69), faculty are supporting their institutional missions of public service. The participants of this study reported the institution's administrators recognized their entrepreneurship efforts. Administrators usually mentioned the beneficial gain to the image of the institution and, conceivably as a result, kept supporting camps either by providing access to facilities, to financial, or to human and material resources. From a career promotion perspective, since running camps had a direct relationship to faculty disciplinary expertise, it was viewed as a service role, either way through faculty consulting or service-learning.

Examining the mission statements of the CA explored in this study, we found their main goal is to empower children and youth with VI to be physically active and dynamic members of their schools, communities, and society in general. While the outcomes for campers seem to go beyond the mere development of sports knowledge and skills, and may include experiences of group membership and shared emotional connection to peers (Goodwin et al. 2011), additional outcomes can affect the broader societal context. Although the camps are segregated in nature, we believe it can favor social inclusion due its effect on disability awareness and positive intergroup contact between hands-on volunteers and spectators with children and youth with VI playing sports or during ordinary activities, such as walking with or without a guide, having meals, or even washing hands (Pettigrew and Tropp 2006). In addition, every sport totally includes each participant which is more inclusive than most 'inclusive' camps. However, to what extent participants are affected in regard to their attitudes towards people with disabilities is a topic for future studies.

Although we believe it would be interesting to establish the impact of running a camp for children and youth with VI on the participants' career progression, we also understand it would be a very complex task to be accomplished, because of the variety of faculty tenure status (i.e. two lecturers, two associate and three full professors), along with the need to scrutinize each institution's tenure criteria. That was beyond the purpose of this study. This task requires a much deeper involvement with extra data and can be the aim of a future investigation. Lastly, the present case study generated hypotheses and propositions about the outcomes of running a sport camp for children and youth with VI on adapted physical education faculty members' roles, providing a framework for studies with a more hypothesis-driven approach.

Conclusions

In this exploratory multiple case study we highlighted several outcomes from running a sport camp for children and youth with VI. Regarding the teaching role, the directing experience empowered faculty members by improving their disability knowledge and by allowing them to teach using real life examples, which would give them more credibility in class. The expected outcomes for coaches-students included the application of theory to practice, attitudinal changes, and frequent out-of-class contact between students and faculty throughout the length of camp. As for the research role, although the published studies helped to created a specialized body of knowledge about physical activity for children and youth with VI, the outcomes were not shared by the majority of participants and seemed to rely on aspects such as camp maturity, directors' aptitudes, partnership with other researchers, and collaboration with graduate students. In turn, running the camp was a means for faculty members to perform their external service roles, either by consulting or on a service-learning approach. Finally, the exact impact of directing a summer camp for children and youth with a given disability on adapted physical activity faculty members' progression career is still to be determined. Nevertheless, the present study provided valuable information to faculty members willing to consider a service program as a part of their long-term professional development plan.

Disclosure statement

No potential conflict of interest was reported by the authors.

Funding

This work was supported by the CAPES Foundation – Ministry of Education of Brazil [grant number 18852-12-2].

References

Antonio, A. L., H. S. Astin, and C. M. Cress. 2000. "Community Service in Higher Education: A Look at the Nation's Faculty." *The Review of Higher Education* 23 (4): 373–397.

Astin, A. W., L. J. Vogelgesang, E. K. Ikeda, and J. A. Yee. 2000. *How Service Learning Affects Students*, edited by Higher Education Research Institute. Los Angeles, CA: University of California.

Boyer, C. M., and D. R. Lewis. 1984. "Faculty Consulting: Responsibility or Promiscuity?" *The Journal of Higher Education* 55 (5): 637–659.

Brantlinger, E., R. Jimenez, J. Klingner, M. Pugach, and V. Richardson. 2005. "Qualitative Studies in Special Education." *Exceptional Children* 71 (2): 195–207.

Chickering, A. W., and Z. F. Gamson. 1987. "Seven Principles for Good Practice in Undergraduate Education." *AAHE Bulletin* 3: 1–7.

Cutforth, N. J. 2000. "Connecting School Physical Education to the Community through Service-learning." *Journal of Physical Education, Recreation & Dance* 71 (2): 39–45.

Diacin, M. J., and J. L. VanSickle. 2014. "Service Learning with Special Olympics: Student Volunteers' Reflections of Their Experiences at the World Summer Games." *Palaestra* 28 (1): 14–23.

Eisenhardt, K. M., and M. E. Graebner. 2007. "Theory Building from Cases: Opportunities and Challenges." *Academy of Management Journal* 50 (1): 25–32.

Ellis, M. K., M. Lepore, and L. Lieberman. 2012. "Effect of Practicum Experiences on Pre-professional Physical Education Teachers' Intentions toward Teaching Students with Disabilities in General Physical Education Classes." *Revista Brasileira De Educação Especial* 18 (3): 361–374.

Fry, H., S. Ketteridge, and S. Marshall. 2008. *A Handbook for Teaching and Learning in Higher Education: Enhancing Academic Practice*. New York: Routledge.

Goodwin, D. L., and K. Staples. 2005. "The Meaning of Summer Camp Experiences to Youths with Disabilities." *Adapted Physical Activity Quarterly* 22 (2): 160–178.

Goodwin, D. L., L. J. Lieberman, K. Johnston, and J. Leo. 2011. "Connecting through Summer Camp: Youth with Visual Impairments Find a Sense of Community." *Adapted Physical Activity Quarterly* 28 (1): 40–55.

Haegele, J. A., L. J. Lieberman, M. Lepore, and M. Lepore-Stevens. 2014. "A Service Delivery Model for Physical Activity in Students with Visual Impairments: Camp Abilities." *Journal of Visual Impairment and Blindness* 108 (6): 473–483.

Hand, K., L. Lieberman, and M. Stuart. 2006. "Beliefs about Physical Activity among Children Who Are Visually Impaired and Their Parents." *Journal of Visual Impairment & Blindness* 100 (4): 223–234.

Haynes, S. N., D. Richard, and E. S. Kubany. 1995. "Content Validity in Psychological Assessment: A Functional Approach to Concepts and Methods." *Psychological Assessment* 7 (3): 238–247.

Hemphill, M. A., K. A. R. Richards, T. J. Templin, and B. Blankenship. 2012. "A Content Analysis of Qualitative Research in the Journal of Teaching in Physical Education from 1998 to 2008." *Journal of Teaching in Physical Education* 31 (3): 279–287.

Leo, J., and D. Goodwin. 2013. "Pedagogical Reflections on the Use of Disability Simulations in Higher Education." *Journal of Teaching in Physical Education* 32 (4): 460–472.

Leo, J., and D. Goodwin. 2014. "Negotiated Meanings of Disability Simulations in an Adapted Physical Activity Course: Learning from Student Reflections." *Adapted Physical Activity Quarterly* 31 (2): 144–161.

Lieberman, L. J., and E. McHugh. 2001. "Health-related Fitness of Children Who Are Visually Impaired." *Journal of Visual Impairment and Blindness* 95 (5): 272–287.

Lieberman, L. J., M. E. Stuart, K. Hand, and B. Robinson. 2006. "An Investigation of the Motivational Effects of Talking Pedometers among Children with Visual Impairments and Deaf-blindness." *Journal of Visual Impairment & Blindness* 100 (12): 726–736.

Lieberman, L. J., H. Byrne, C. O. Mattern, C. A. Watt, and M. Fernández-Vivó. 2010. "Health-related Fitness of Youths with Visual Impairments." *Journal of Visual Impairment and Blindness* 104 (6): 349–359.

Lieberman, L., M. Lucas, J. Jones, D. Humphreys, A. Cody, B. Vaughn, and T. Storms. 2013. "Part IV – Sport Groups." *Journal of Physical Education, Recreation & Dance* 84 (8): 36–40.

Marston, R. 2002. "Addressing the University's Tripartite Mission through an Early Childhood Movement Program." *Journal of Physical Education, Recreation & Dance* 73 (5): 35–41.

Merriam, S. B. 1998. *Qualitative Research and Case Study Applications in Education: Revised and Expanded from Case Study Research in Education*. San Francisco, CA: Jossey-Bass Publishers.

Miles, M. B., A. M. Huberman, and J. Saldaña. 2014. *Qualitative Data Analysis: A Methods Sourcebook*. Thousand Oaks, CA: SAGE.

Pettigrew, T. F., and L. R. Tropp. 2006. "A Meta-analytic Test of Intergroup Contact Theory." *Journal of Personality and Social Psychology* 90 (5): 751–783.

Reid, G., and H. Stanish. 2003. "Professional and Disciplinary Status of Adapted Physical Activity." *Adapted Physical Activity Quarterly* 20 (3): 213–229.

Reid, G., M. Bouffard, and C. MacDonald. 2012. "Creating Evidence-Based Research in Adapted Physical Activity." *Adapted Physical Activity Quarterly* 29 (2): 115–131.

Richards, K. A. R., A. D. Eberline, S. Padaruth, and T. J. Templin. 2015. "Experiential Learning through a Physical Activity Program for Children with Disabilities." *Journal of Teaching in Physical Education* 34 (2): 165–188.

Robinson, B. L., and L. J. Lieberman. 2014. "Effects of Visual Impairment, Gender, and Age on Self-determination." *Journal of Visual Impairment and Blindness* 98 (6): 351–366.

Roper, E. A., and J. A. Santiago. 2014. "Influence of Service-learning on Kinesiology Students' Attitudes toward P–12 Students with Disabilities." *Adapted Physical Activity Quarterly* 31 (2): 162–180.

Ryan, G. W., and H. R. Bernard. 2003. "Techniques to Identify Themes." *Field Methods* 15 (1): 85–109.

Scott, J. C. 2006. "The Mission of the University: Medieval to Postmodern Transformations." *The Journal of Higher Education* 77 (1): 1–39.

Servage, L. 2009. "The Scholarship of Teaching and Learning and the Neo-liberalization of Higher Education: Constructing the "Entrepreneurial Learner." *The Canadian Journal of Higher Education* 39 (2): 25–44.

Shapiro, D. R., A. Moffett, L. Lieberman, and G. M. Dummer. 2005. "Perceived Competence of Children with Visual Impairments." *Journal of Visual Impairment and Blindness* 99 (1): 15–25.

Umbach, P. D., and M. R. Wawrzynski. 2005. "Faculty Do Matter: The Role of College Faculty in Student Learning and Engagement." *Research in Higher Education* 46 (2): 153–184.

Walsh, D. 2011. "Strategies for Developing a University-Sponsored Youth Sports Summer Camp." *Journal of Physical Education, Recreation and Dance* 82 (9): 24–50.

Ward, K. 2003. *Faculty Service Roles and the Scholarship of Engagement. Higher and Adult Education Series*. San Francisco, CA: Jossey-Bass ERIC.

International Federation for Adapted Physical Activity. 2016. "Definition of Adapted Physical Activity." http://ifapa-international.net/definition/

Lieberman, L. J. S. Wilson. 2005. "Effects of a Sports Camp Practicum on Attitudes toward Children with Visual Impairments and Deafblindness." *RE:View: Rehabilitation Education for Blindness and Visual Impairment* 36 (4), 141–153.

Yin, R. K. 2009. *Case Study Research: Design and Methods*. 4th ed. Thousand Oaks, CA: Sage.

Sense of belonging: is inclusion the answer?

Melissa H. D'Eloia and Pollie Price

ABSTRACT
The Americans with Disabilities Act mandated the inclusion of people with disabilities in all aspects of social and civil life in the United States including sports. As a result, sport and recreation programmes designed for typically developing youth began to include children with disabilities. One popular recreation context providing sport activities for youth with disabilities is summer camp. Research on inclusive camps has shown mixed results, with some studies suggesting that children with disabilities continue to experience exclusion from physical activity and leadership opportunities, social isolation, and stigma. This conceptual and argumentative essay will review current research on inclusive camps and will argue that, until the mechanisms of inclusive camps are better understood and applied in practice, camps for children with disabilities may be the best delivery system to promote inclusion and a sense of belonging, arguably one of the most important outcomes of camp.

Sense of belonging: are inclusive environments the answer for youth with disabilities?

In the 1970s, people with disabilities in the United States reacted to social oppression and exclusion, activating the disability rights movement that eventually led to passage of the Rehabilitation Act of 1973, Section 504, the Individuals with Disabilities Education Act (IDEA) (U.S. Department of Justice 1975), and the Americans with Disabilities Act (ADA) (U.S. Department of Justice 1990). This new legislation impacted programmes for youth with disabilities and promoted their inclusion in all areas of social life, beginning with schools and moving into sport and recreation services. The National Recreation and Park Association echoed this legislation by adopting in 1999 a position statement that encouraged all agencies that provide park, recreation and sport services to incorporate inclusion practices (NRPA 1999). As a result, sport and recreation programmes (particularly those offered during school) designed for typically developing youth were mandated to include youth with disabilities, while programmes specifically designed for youth with disabilities became socially stigmatized and accused of creating participation barriers (Carter and LeConey 2004) as well as perpetuating the inequality and segregation of persons with disabilities (DePauw and Doll-Tepper 2000).

Summer camp is a popular sport and recreation context in the United States, serving over 10 million people, including youth with disabilities (American Camp Association 2010). Under the summer camp umbrella lie specialty sport camps, where youth with and without disabilities engage in variety of sport-specific activities to increase skill development as well as build more physically active and healthy lifestyles. Sport camps for youth with disabilities offers a unique context where the stigmas associated with disability, physical performance, and appearance are challenged and transformed increasing positive perceptions of ability and self (Goodwin et al. 2011).

Summer camp programmes that serve youth with disabilities fall into three structural types: (1) Segregated programmes designed specifically for campers with disabilities in a barrier-free environment; (2) Therapeutic and medical summer camp programmes designed to meet specific health-related outcomes; and (3) Inclusive summer camp programmes where youth with and without disabilities participate together in a least-restrictive environment aimed at promoting maximum participation regardless of ability (Disability World 2015). Prior to the ADA, majority of the summer camp programmes for youth with disabilities were segregated, providing optimum accessibility across activities and facilities, and utilizing highly trained staff who understood how to promote maximum participation among campers with disabilities. Despite the substantial body of literature tying these programmes to an array of positive social and health-related outcomes for youth with disabilities (e.g. Bluebond-Langner et al. 1990; Rynders, Schleien, and Mustonen 1990; Bluebond-Langner, Perkel, and Goertzel 1991; Brannan, Arick, and Fullerton 1996; Candler 2003; Goodwin and Staples 2005; Hill and Sibthorp 2006; Gillard, Witt, and Watts 2011; D'Eloia and Sibthorp 2014), segregated programmes have fallen out of favour. Many summer camp programmes have adopted models of inclusion, which in the eyes of disability activists and recreation scholars, is the most socially just.

Research with respect to inclusive camp experiences has shown mixed results. Some research points to the success of inclusion and suggests these practices promote acceptance and a sense of belonging among youth with and without disabilities (Boyd et al. 2008; Cho 2005; Divine and O'Brien 2007; Goodwin and Watkinson 2000; Kristen, Patriksson, and Fridlund 2003). Despite these successes, other research has demonstrated that inclusive camp programmes may have caused more harm than good for children with disabilities. For example, research on inclusive camp programmes has shown that children with disabilities continue to experience rejection and ridicule from their nondisabled peers, which results in feelings of isolation, loneliness, marginalization, disempowerment, exclusion, and physical, emotional, and social stigma (Germ and Schleien 1997; Blinde and McCallister 1998; Taub and Geer 2000; Bedini 2002; Devine 2004). Although social acceptance of youth and a sense of belonging are widely considered fundamental outcomes of the summer camp experience, these same outcomes appear the most challenging to intentionally programme in inclusive camp settings.

While models of best practices for inclusive camp programmes exist, there is a gap between theory and practice. Many camp programmes that were developed for typical children have been retrofitted to include children with disabilities and lack the intentional programming needed to promote awareness, a sense of community and belonging, and equal participation. The idea that inclusive settings still struggle to provide youth with disabilities opportunities to be socially included and to feel a sense of belonging seems to support Georg Simmel's notion that the social inclusion of people with disabilities in our society is 'spatially proximal yet socially distant' (as cited in Milner and Kelly 2009, 48). Scholars continue to make significant strides towards developing best practice of inclusion (e.g. Schleien et al. 2009), however, much more research is needed in order to know how to create intentional programming to promote a sense of belonging, reciprocity in social relationships between children with and without disabilities, and equal opportunity for participation and skill development.

A sense of belonging: the most significant outcome of camp participation?

A sense of belonging is defined by the American Heritage Dictionary as 'acceptance as a natural member or part' (American Heritage Dictionary 2009). Belonging, also commonly referred to as connectedness, attachment, membership and relatedness, is broadly concerned with individual perceptions of feeling connected to and cared for by others (Ryan 1995; La Guardia et al. 2000). A positive sense of belonging encompasses perceptions of warmth, closeness, caring, and support (Eccles and Gootman 2002) and may lead to a variety of positive emotions including happiness and joy when properly satisfied (Fajans 2006). As a result, people who feel a strong sense of belonging may experience a variety of physical and psychological benefits (Milner and Kelly 2009; Pitonyak 2010). On the contrary, persons lacking a sense of belonging within a setting can feel left out, ignored, and may be disinclined to participate (Hall 2009). Numerous authors argue that belonging is a fundamental human need, and that individual perceptions of belonging can result in both negative and positive effects (Ainsworth 1979; Baumeister and Leary 1995; Deci and Ryan 2000; Maslow 1954). Baumeister and Leary conducted an extensive review of the literature and concluded that the human need for belonging is universal (1995). They defined belonging as 'a pervasive drive to form and maintain a minimum quantity of lasting, positive, and significant inter-personal relationships' (Baumeister and Leary 1995, 497). Experiencing sense of belonging can occur over a variety of contexts provided the right mechanisms are in place. Research shows the elements that produce a sense of belonging include participation, no fear of being judged, sharing in tradition, and not feeling like a burden to others (Hall 2009). The drive to satisfy the human need to belong is quite profound, and as a result acts as a primary motivator to engaging in goal-directed activity intended to gratify this need (Deci and Ryan 2000). Beth Mount stated, '[l]oneliness is the only real disability' (as quoted by Pitonyak 2010, 5) suggesting that for many people with disabilities, the suffering they experience is more likely from their feelings of loneliness rather than the impairment itself. Thus, the goal of any service programme should then be to help people with disabilities maintain and develop positive and lasting relationships (O'Brien 1987). This research supports the argument that a sense of belonging should be a primary outcome of camp participation for youth with disabilities.

IDEA, ADA, social model of disability and inclusion

People with disabilities have commonly been stigmatized as socially undesirable, isolated from community resources, and often lack a sense of belonging. The reaction of people with disabilities to these alienating experiences gave rise to the disability rights movement in the 1970s. The Social Model of Disability emerged as a result of the disability rights movement, which asserted that people with disabilities have a right to participate in and contribute to society (Zola 1982; Shapiro 1994; Longmore 2003; Shakespeare 2006). The term 'inclusion' represents the disability community's idea that all people feel welcomed, valued, and incorporated into the fabric of society without restrictions or limitations of any kind. Disability rights advocates argued for inclusion and this social movement led to both the creation of the Social Model of Disability and important legislation addressing disability rights (IDEA; ADA). Inclusion efforts aimed to decrease the segregation of persons with disabilities and to foster an authentic sense of belonging to the community at-large (Bullock and Mahon 2000; Watson and Keith 2002). The IDEA and the ADA fully support the inclusion of youth with disabilities in all areas of life, including school, work, recreation and sport.

Sections 202 and 302 of the ADA mandated that sport service providers make services available and accessible to people with disabilities. According to this legislation, organizations that provide separate-but-equal services are discriminatory. Some scholars within the field of sport and recreation claim that specialized services add to the discrimination of people with disabilities by perpetuating the 'us' vs 'them' dichotomy (Miller, Schleien, and Bowens 2010). There are numerous textbooks (e.g. Dattilo 2002; Brannan et al. 2003; Smith et al. 2005) and research articles (e.g. Bendini 1990; Sable 1995; Arick et al. 2001; Devine and Lausha 2002; Devine and O'Brien 2007; Milner and Kelly 2009) advocating for inclusive practices. One unifying theme within this literature is the idea that sport programmes must move beyond best practice models of inclusion, and instead view inclusion as the standard practice within the recreation profession at large.

Research indicates that the intention of the legislation, the intent of inclusion as a social policy, and the Social Model of Disability as the reification of the disability rights movement may not be operationalized in building inclusive sport programmes. Further, some inclusive sport programmes could be causing more harm to children with disabilities by promulgating negative and stigmatizing attitudes and behaviours that promote alienation and social exclusion. While research has described a variety of beneficial outcomes that result from inclusion programmes, we still do not know how social inclusion is achieved. When we do know the mechanisms of inclusion, they are not always apparent in the programmes themselves. Irrespective of what makes programmes successful in implementing inclusion, youth with disabilities may still need exclusive experiences.

Successes and weaknesses of inclusion

The majority of the research on inclusion has stemmed from the educational literature including physical education. One theme ensuing from this body of literature is that students' perceptions of belonging are highly dependent on their social environment. More specifically, studies suggest that youth do not perceive the school context as a place to seek meaningful peer and adult relationships (Furrer and Skinner 2003). Schools often employ organizational practices and policies that thwart students' sense of community (Osterman 2000) and have been described by some students and researchers as 'alienating institutions' (Anderman and Maehr 1994). Youth with disabilities are no strangers to feeling alienated within the school context. For example, the common inclusion practice of hiring assistants for children with disabilities to help increase their academic performance raises the question of whether or not this service further promotes inclusion or if, in fact, it creates learned helplessness and stigma (Egilson and Traustadottir 2009).

The inclusion of youth with disabilities in regular classrooms has been a controversial topic among educators, parents, and scholars, and has been subject to research about the effectiveness of inclusion practices. Inclusive schools enable students with and without disabilities to participate in the classroom together and are based on the premise that least restrictive and integrated environments benefit these students equally. Inclusion advocates assert that youth with disabilities have the right to receive an education alongside youth without disabilities, and believe that inclusion, compared to segregation, will lead to stronger social and academic achievement and a stronger sense of belonging (Bunch and Valeo 1997, 2004). Schools that adopt inclusion practices purport to embrace diversity and see it as a valued and expected attribute (Bunker 1994). Inclusive settings that are optimally functioning provide youth with disabilities a context where everyone belongs (Stainback and Stainback 1990), learns new skills, feels more efficacious and gains physical strength (Goodwin and Watkinson 2000; Kristen, Patriksson, and Fridlund 2003). One such model school is Patrick O'Hearn Elementary School in Dorchester, Massachusetts (Patriot Ledger 2012). The school was organized around the concept of full inclusion and is built on three intentions: (1) inclusion is the cultural attitude and norm; (2) staff and families are skilful and committed to adapt the curriculum to make it accessible for children of all abilities, while still meeting standards and (3) a collaborative model manifests the commitment of everyone to help each other do their best and to figure out how to meet each child's learning needs. In 2007, the school had some of the highest test scores in the state.

While many teachers recognize these benefits and support the ideology of inclusion, they also report feeling inadequately prepared, unsupported, and express difficulty in effectively facilitating inclusion practices (Hodge et al. 2004). The lack of teacher knowledge, support, and experience in including youth with disabilities in programming has led to a variety of negative outcomes for these youth. For example, one of the largest obstacles many children with disabilities who try to adapt and integrate into an inclusive school setting face is the negative bias and discriminatory behaviour of children without disabilities (Cho 2005). Many youth with disabilities have reported feeling excluded, ridiculed, and isolated by their nondisabled peers (Blinde and McCallister 1998; Goodwin and Watkinson 2000; Place and Hodge 2001). Research has also shown that youth with disabilities who attend an integrated school setting report having less autonomy, fewer social interactions with peers (Eriksson and Granlund 2004), a lower quality of life (Silvana, Watson, and Keith 2002), and experience more restricted participation in school activities than students without disabilities (Ericksson et al. 2007; Simeonsson et al. 2001). Furthermore, there is a high turnover rate of assistants for those with disabilities in inclusive school settings and the adjustment period to a new aid provides a new set of stressors and barriers to full inclusion (Egilson and Traustadottir 2009).

In addition, inclusion practices have been criticized for implementing a one-size-fits all standard for students with disabilities (Gordon 2006). These practices promote homogeneity, where youth with disabilities experience an increased pressure to fit the social perceptions of what is 'normal' (Stainback et al. 1994; Bunch and Valeo 2004). The conditions for what is considered normal are often established by the dominant nondisabled class and do not echo the voices of youth with disabilities. Because of these pressures, youth with invisible disabilities, for example, have been shown to deny having a disability and engage in the practice of 'passing' where they try to pass as nondisabled (Watson et al. 2000), often by attempting to conceal their disability and not socializing with others who have disabilities.

The dominant social view of what people believe to be 'normal' is further promoted by teachers and scholars who identify and use peer role models in an inclusive classroom. The inclusion literature points to youth without disabilities as the ideal peer role model in this context. Youth with disabilities, according to some inclusion advocates, are seen as inappropriate role models because they may teach other youth with disabilities inappropriate and unacceptable behaviours (Bunch and Valeo 2004). This further perpetuates the perception that youth with disabilities are less capable than their nondisabled peers. There is evidence that contradicts the above assertion and reveals that peer mentors who have similar disabilities help promote social acceptance and improve self-esteem (Devine and Dawson 2010).

While education scholars believe teachers and administrators ought to foster a sense of belonging within the school structure, many students perceive more opportunities for student interaction during out-of-school time than when they are at school (Goodlad 1984). After-school programmes, on the other hand, tend to be more interpersonal in nature as they encourage youth to engage in social activities that help build close bonds with their peers and programme staff (Grossman and Bulle 2006). Research within the after-school setting points to process-level variables, including programme activities and staff practices, as critical and intentionally planned ingredients that foster interpersonal relationships and a sense of relatedness (Rhodes 2004).

There is dearth of research investigating the relationship between program-level processes and participant outcomes. Understanding both the how and why programmes achieve their outcomes is essential for staff to implement evidence-based practices and to replicate participant outcomes. One prevalent out-of-school sport and recreation context is summer camp. As previously mentioned, some research suggests that inclusive settings like summer camp may provide a 'mixed bag' of experiences where the interactions between persons with and without disabilities are not experienced equally (Devine and O'Brien 2007).

According to the above research, two fundamental ingredients are missing from the relationship between persons with and without disabilities: reciprocity and intimate sharing. Both reciprocity and intimate sharing are essential to the development of lasting friendships and feelings of belonging (Hagerty et al. 1993; Duck 1994; Milner and Kelly 2009). The lack of reciprocity may be attributed to the hierarchical nature of these relationships, where youth with disabilities traditionally have a lower position of status than their nondisabled peers (Bunch and Valeo 2004). The social inequality between participants in an inclusive context appears to be most prominent when an activity is competitive (Wilhite, Devine, and Goldenberg 1999), when the friendships between youth with and without disabilities are initiated through a buddy system (Matheson, Olsen, and Weisner 2007) or emphasize a helping and caretaker role (Staub 1998), and when participation is limited due to social, behavioural or physical skills (Bedini 2002).

Further complicating friendship development between youth with and without disabilities is stigma. Youth with disabilities are one of the most stigmatized groups in the world. (UNICEF 2005). Stigma surrounding the concept of disability acts as a barrier to friendship. Youth with disabilities report having fewer friendships and the research describes these friendships as being lower in quality (Wiener and Schneider 2002). Salmon examined how teenagers with disabilities negotiate stigma to create lasting friendships and found that all of the participants in the study chose self-exclusion, where they sought friendships with peers have disabilities (Salmon 2013). For the participants in this study, they achieved a more profound sense of belonging through friendships where the experience of stigma and disability was shared. Regardless of these challenges, friendships between youth with and without disabilities are mutually beneficial and achievable when the roles are balanced (Matheson, Olsen, and Weisner 2007) the social and environmental context is accessible providing optimum participation in physical activity for all youth is premised on the idea that it promotes full participation and social acceptance, yet some camp research suggests that an inclusive setting may highlight rather than minimize the differences between programme participants (Glover 2004). Some research questions whether the term 'inclusion' acts more like a cloak that camouflages the social inequalities that are present within inclusive camp settings (Devine and Parr 2008). Often, relationships between youth with and without disabilities require the child with a disability to conform to the culturally prescribed roles defined primarily by persons without disabilities (Cote and Levine 2002). Children with disabilities try to appear, act, and behave as nondisabled in order to gain the social acceptance of youth without disabilities (Gilson, Tusler, and Gill 1997). Because of this, many youth with disabilities begin to feel uncomfortable interacting with peers who have disabilities, internalize stigmas associated with disability (Gill 1997) and develop negative self-perceptions (Groff and Kleiber 2001).

Research within the camp setting mimics these negative outcomes suggesting that inclusion settings can both mask and emphasize participant differences (Devine and Parr 2008). These negative outcomes are attributed to two programme factors within the camp setting: programme type and staff. Programmes that were competitive in nature and skill focused, which are inherent to sports in particular, produced more negative attitudes and paternalistic perceptions about individuals with disabilities (Devine and Wilhite 1999). In addition to programme type, staff also played a role in reinforcing negative perceptions about inclusion, stereotypes, and the need to overprotect people with disabilities (Conatser, Block, and Lepore 2000; Grenier 2006; Tripp and Rizzo 2007). These underlying processes can be obstacles to relatedness in inclusive camp settings. This research suggests that relatedness may not be an outcome of inclusive camps for youth with disabilities, and that camps may not be built to promote attitudes and behaviours of inclusion, and may provide more harm than good. Due to the restorative qualities of the summer camp environment, camps exclusively for youth with disabilities have been described as offering its participants a 'therapeutic landscape' in which they can achieve an increased sense of independence, improved understanding of their physical potential and foster social belonging (Gesler, 1992 p. 737; Goodwin and Staples 2005). In spite of the intentions of the ADA and the Social Model of disability, might we consider exclusive camps as important experiences for youth to have? In the next section, we will review current research on camps for youth with disabilities.

Camps for youth with disabilities

Summer camp provides a prominent out-of-school sport and recreation context for youth with disabilities to interact and develop meaningful relationships. At camp, youth with disabilities engage in a multitude of physical activities ranging from outdoor sports such as horseback riding, skiing and rock climbing to more traditional sport activities like swimming, basketball and volleyball. Organized residential camp programmes for specific groups (e.g. children with disabilities) have been an established part of the American culture since the early 1900s and are generally believed to provide positive experiences for youth with disabilities. Research has linked camp participation to positive outcomes, such as acquiring new outdoor skills (Rynders, Schleien, and Mustonen 1990; Candler 2003), increased self-esteem (Tiemens, Beveridge, and Nicholas 2007; Dawson, Knapp, and Farmer 2012), improved social skills, greater independence (Brannan, Arick, and Fullerton 1996), diabetes management (Hill and Sibthorp 2006), developing empathy for others (Henley 1999), an overall sense of not being alone, and feelings of normalcy (Gillard, Witt, and Watts 2011). In addition to these outcomes, camp also seems to provide youth with disabilities a place where they can freely explore their identity, discover the different meanings associated with disability (Goodwin and Staples 2005) feel less socially isolated (Michalski et al. 2003) and develop group membership and community (Goodwin et al. 2011). The research indicates that a sense of belonging is one important outcome of camp participation for children with disabilities, if not for all children of all abilities. Despite these positive outcomes, research suggests that camps designed specifically for youth with disabilities may be experiencing the sting of stigmatizing attitudes and perceptions that these experiences are promoting the segregation and alienation of youth with disabilities (Goodwin and Staples 2005).

Summer camp programmes that are specifically designed for youth with disabilities possess unique programme processes that are not present in inclusive settings and can act as a therapeutic landscape (Michalski et al. 2003). Gesler coined the term 'therapeutic landscape' (1992) suggesting that different geographic settings may have restorative qualities that foster a variety of healing and treatment-related outcomes. In addition to various health-related benefits, summer camps for youth with disabilities are well-suited to provide opportunities to meet and interact with similar others, identify with peer role models who have disabilities (Tiemens, Beveridge, and Nicholas 2007; Devine and Dawson 2010) and experience mutual self-help processes (Bluebond-Langner et al. 1990; Bluebond-Langner, Perkel, and Goertzel 1991). Research suggests that these opportunities primarily occur during two distinct times: structured time and unstructured time (Hough and Browne 2009). While structured time presents campers with opportunities to learn new communication and cooperation skills, unstructured time seems to foster elements such as closeness, shared understanding, and a sense of belonging among campers with disabilities (Tiemens, Beveridge, and Nicholas 2007). These results depart from research within the inclusive camp setting, which describes unstructured time as problematic (Devine and Lashua 2002). During unstructured time in an inclusive context, youth with disabilities perceived a lack of social acceptance among peers without disabilities (Devine and Parr 2008).

Furthermore, summer camp can provide a context where youth with disabilities begin to identify and integrate with other youth who have disabilities, a process Gill refers to as 'coming home' (Gill 1997). For youth with disabilities, being around similar others has been linked to identity exploration (Goodwin and Staples 2005) and feeling 'normal' (Gillard and Watts 2008; Gillard, Witt, and Watts 2011). For example, Groff and Kleiber (2001) found that children who had opportunities to interact with other youth who have disabilities lead to a deeper understanding of themselves. Identity exploration results at camp when participants engage in activities that allow youth with disabilities to share their personal stories, freely express their feelings, and offer support and guidance to their fellow peers (Goodwin and Staples 2005). Summer camp programmes that are specially designed for youth with disabilities provide a supportive environment for these youth to engage in challenging experiences, take on meaningful roles, learn new skills, identify with peer role models who share similar characteristics, and socially connect with similar others, all of which contributes to a sense of belonging.

One of the major tenets of positive youth development is that youth need opportunities for challenging experiences in order to grow into productive and thriving adults (Roth and Brooks-Gunn 2003). These opportunities are often depicted in youth development models as one of the necessary programme mechanisms that are directly linked to the outcome of sense of belonging (Connell, Gambone, and Smith 2000). Due to societal barriers, as well as some over-protective parents, many youth with disabilities have fewer opportunities to engage in challenging activities with similar peers that are fun and social in nature (Barton 1998; Clough and Corbett 2000; Groff and Kleiber 2001). Summer camp programmes that are designed specifically for youth with disabilities could be reframed as a least-restrictive environment where these youth are given numerous opportunities to work collectively and support each other as they navigate a variety of challenging situations. There is an increasing body of literature stating that summer camps for those with disabilities can elicit positive outcomes, however, this research runs into the same problem that was seen in the inclusive evidence – participant outcomes could not be traced back to specific factors within the camps which make replication of results variable (Candler 2003; Devine and Dawson 2010). More research needs to be done concerning the specific camp mechanisms that are yielding the desired outcomes.

Important programme mechanisms

Camp programmes that are specifically designed for children with disabilities encourage these youth to take on a variety of roles, including leadership and mentoring peers. Through structured camp activities, youth with disabilities are asked to solve problems, make difficult decisions, and encourage their group members. These experiences can foster feelings of trust, mutual respect, and solidarity (Battistich et al. 1991), all of which are associated with a general sense of relatedness. The camp context provides youth with disabilities with opportunities to try on the adult roles (e.g. leadership and mentorship) for which they are preparing. Youth with disabilities need opportunities to actively participate in a variety of roles (leader, team participant, decision-maker, etc.) and camp for youth with disabilities may provide one setting for these youth to engage in these experiences.

Exclusive camp settings provide youth with disabilities opportunities to engage in different challenging learning experiences. Through participation in camp activities, youth with disabilities can acquire new social and physical skills, experience a sense of independence, and develop increased self-confidence (Goodwin and Staples 2005). The types of learning experiences that occur during camp are of a different nature than the types of learning that occur during school time. At camp, learning occurs through social interaction where youth with disabilities are asked to work together and to engage in problem-solving processes rather than at school where they participate in more rudimentary tasks (Grossman and Bulle 2006). In addition, camp can also provide educational sessions that help youth with disabilities learn about themselves and how to move beyond their disability (Gillard, Witt, and Watts 2011). Camp staff can provide a learning environment that celebrates disability by implementing strategies and activities that integrate disability knowledge and encourage youth with disabilities to become active learners.

Youth with disabilities who attend a specialized summer camp may begin to identify friends and role models who share their unique identities and experiences. Peers can act as excellent role models for each other. According to social cognitive theory (Bandura 1986), people can quickly learn new behaviours through observation and imitation of others. Through peer role modelling, youth with disabilities can learn new skills, develop stronger emotional competencies, learn how to effectively navigate their disability (Bluebond-Langer et al. 1991), and experience feelings of normalcy (Goodwin and Staples 2005), all of which may promote a sense of belonging.

Unstructured and informal social opportunities are a unique process that camps for youth with disabilities can provide. The youth development literature asserts that informal social opportunities are essential to the development of authentic peer and adult relationships (Grossman and Bulle 2006). Unstructured time provides youth with disabilities opportunities to share stories, discover common interests, and develop mutual understandings, all of which can lead to feelings of relatedness (Gillard 2009). During unstructured time children with disabilities engage in intimate discussions where they talk about their physical symptoms, fears and challenges (Bluebond-Langner et al. 1990; Kiernan, Gromley, and MacLachlan 2004). This type of informal sharing is an essential element of the unique opportunities that exclusive camps present youth with disabilities to make connections and experience a sense of belonging.

Conclusion

We end this discussion with big questions. Which type of camp is better? Inclusive camps, when intentionally programmed to promote inclusion, full participation, positive skill development, and social reciprocity, may be very important experiences for children with and without disabilities to have. Clearly, shaping attitudes in youth will impact attitudes, behaviours and practices in adulthood and could help to move society at large into a more inclusive culture for all people of all abilities. Much more research is needed on what mechanisms need to be put into place and how to implement them so that inclusive camps promote positive youth development, manifest societal attitudinal change, execute legislation, and above all, do no harm.

The authors make the case that camps specifically for youth with disabilities offer experiences that are not available in many inclusion-oriented contexts. Camp provides youth with disabilities a fun, challenging, and least-restrictive environment where they can join together, learn from one another, and experience an authentic sense of belonging. Camp programmes should engage youth with disabilities in learning experiences, peer role modelling, challenging experiences, meaningful roles, and valuable social experiences.

What should camp programmes offer youth with disabilities to facilitate the above processes? The camp experience should engage participants with disabilities in recreational and learning opportunities, and provide an environment where they can learn about disabilities, develop social skills, and become more independent. Camp staff should encourage youth with disabilities to engage in meaningful roles where the campers develop as leaders and mentors to other youth with disabilities. Finally, camp staff should provide campers with disabilities unstructured time where they can share personal stories, discuss their feelings and develop meaningful interpersonal connections. Perhaps camps for children with disabilities could open up with intentional programming that would include children without disabilities.

Parents and their children with disabilities need both options from which to choose based on the types of outcomes that are offered: learning to socially negotiate in a circle of difference and diversity, and recognizing oneself in familiar others and feeling 'at home'. The need for friendship, affiliation, reciprocity and a sense of belonging is such a powerful yet basic human need. Surely, a sense of belonging in the world is an important outcome of summer camp participation in either model.

Disclosure statement

No potential conflict of interest was reported by the authors.

References

Ainsworth, M. D. 1979. "Infant-mother Attachment." *American Psychologist* 34 (10): 932–937.

American Heritage® Dictionary of the English Language. 2009. (4th ed.). New York: Houghton Mifflin.

Anderman, E. M., and M. L. Maehr. 1994. "Motivation and Schooling in the Middle Grades." *Review of Educational Research* 64 (2): 287–309.

Arick, J. R., S. Brannan, A. Fullerton, and J. Harris. 2001. "The National Inclusive Camp Practices (NICP) Study: Research on Practices and Effects of Inclusive Programs 1997–2001." In *Including Youth with Disabilities in Outdoor Programs: Best Practices, Outcomes, and Resources*, edited by S. Brannan, 205–235. Champaign, IL: Sagamore.

Bandura, A. 1986. *Social Foundations of Thought and Actions: A Social Cognitive Theory*. Englewood Cliffs, NJ: Prentice Hall.

Barton, L. 1998. "Markets, Managerialism and Inclusive Education." In *Managing Inclusive Education: From Policy to Experience*, edited by P. L. Clough Barton, 331–344, London: Paul Chapman.

Battistich, V., M. Watson, D. Solomon, E. Schaps, and J. Solomon. 1991. "The Child Development Project: A Comprehensive Program for the Development of Prosocial Character." In *Handbook of Moral Behavior and Development: Application*, edited by W. M. Kurtines and J. L. Gerwirtz, 1–34. Hillsdale, NJ: Lawrence Erlbaum Associates.

Baumeister, R. F., and M. R. Leary. 1995. "The Need to Belong: Desire for Interpersonal Attachments as a Fundamental Human Motivation." *Psychological Bulletin* 117 (3): 497–529.

Bedini, Leandra A. 1990. "Separate but Equal?" *Journal of Physical Education, Recreation, and Dance* 61 (8): 40–44.

Bedini, L. A. 2002. "'Just Sit Down So We Can Talk:' Perceived Stigma and Community Recreation Pursuits of People with Disabilities." *Therapeutic Recreation Journal* 34: 55–68.

Blinde, M. E., and S. G. McAllister. 1998. "Listening to the Voices of Students with Physical Disabilities: Experiences in the Physical Education Classroom." *Journal of Physical Education, Recreation, and Dance* 69 (6): 64–68.

Bluebond-Langner, M., D. Perkel, and T. Goertzel. 1991. "Pediatric Cancer Patients' Peer Relationships." *Journal of Psychosocial Oncology* 9 (2): 67–80.

Bluebond-Langner, M., D. Perkel, T. Goertzel, K. Nelson, and J. McGeary. 1990. "Children's Knowledge of Cancer and Its Treatment: Impact of an Oncology Camp Experience." *The Journal of Pediatrics* 116 (2): 207–213.

Boyd, C. M., J. L. Fraiman, K. A. Hawkins, J. M. Labin, M. B. Sutter, and M. R. Wahl. 2008. "Effects of the Star Intervention Interactions Between Campers with and without Disabilities during Inclusive Summer Day Camp Activities." *Education and Tr apirnoinggra imn on Developmental Disabilities* 43 (1): 92–101.

Brannan, S. A., J. R. Arick, and A. Fullerton. 1996. *A National Evaluation of Residential Camp Programs Serving Persons with Disabilities*. Reston, VA: The Council for Exceptional Children.

Brannan, S. A., A. Fullerton, J. R. Arick, G. M. Robb, and M. Bender. 2003. *Including Youth with Disabilities in Outdoor Programs: Best Practices, Outcomes, and Resources*. Champaign, IL: Sagamore.

Bullock, C. C., and M. J. Mahon. 2000. *Introduction to Recreation Services for People with Disabilities: A Person-centered Approach*. 2nd ed. Champaign, IL: Sagamore.

Bunch, G., and A. Valeo. 1997. *Inclusion: Recent Research*. Toronto: Inclusion Press.

Bunch, G., and A. Valeo. 2004. "Student Attitudes Toward Peers with Disabilities in Inclusive and Special Education Schools." *Disability & Society* 19 (1): 61–76.

Bunker, L. K. 1994. "Virtual Reality: Movement's Centrality." *Quest* 46 (4): 456–474.

Candler, C. 2003. "Sensory Integration and Therapeutic Riding at Summer Camp: Occupational Performance Outcomes." *Physical and Occupational Therapy in Pediatrics* 23 (3): 51–64.

Carter, M. J., and S. P. LeConey. 2004. *Therapeutic Recreation in the Community: An Inclusive Approach.* 2nd ed. Champaign, IL: Sagamore Publishing.

Cho, H. 2005. "'Nikang Nekang' Therapeutic Camp: Beyond the Barrier Between the Challenged and the Unchallenged." *WFOT Bulletin* 52 (1): 5229–5234.

Clough, P., and J. Corbett. 2000. *Theories of Inclusive Education: A Student's Guide.* London: Paul Chapman.

Conatser, P., and M. Lepore. 2000. "Aquatic Instructors' Attitudes Toward Teaching Students with Disabilities." *Adapted Physical Activity Quarterly* 17: 197–207.

Connell, J., M. Gambone, and T. Smith. 2000. *Youth Development: Issues, Challenges and Directions.* Philadelphia, PA: Public/Private Ventures.

Cote, J. E., and C. G. Levine. 2002. *Identity Formation, Agency, and Culture.* London: Lawrence Erlbaum.

Dattilo, J. 2002. *Inclusive Leisure Services Responding to the Rights of People with Disabilities.* 2nd ed. State College, PA: Venture Publishing .

Dawson, S., D. Knapp, and J. Farmer. 2012. "Camp War Buddies: Exploring the Therapeutic Benefits of Social Comparison in a Pediatric Oncology Camp." *Therapeutic Recreation Journal* 46 (4): 313–325.

Deci, E. L., and R. M. Ryan. 2000. "The 'What' and 'Why' of Goal Pursuits: Human Needs and the Self-determination of Behavior." *Psychological Inquiry* 11 (4): 227–268.

D'Eloia, M. H., and J. Sibthorp. 2014. "Relatedmess for Youth with Disabilities: Testing a Recreation Program Model." *Journal of Leisure Research* 46 (4): 462–482.

DePauw, K. P., and G. Doll-Tepper. 2000. "Toward Progressive Inclusion and Acceptance: Myth or Reality? The Inclusion Debate and Bandwagon Discourse." *Adapted Physical Activity Quarterly* 17 (2): 135–143.

Devine, M. A. 2004. "Being a 'Doer' instead of a 'Viewer:' The Role of Inclusive Leisure Contexts in Determining Social Acceptance for People with Disabilities." *Journal of Leisure Research* 90 (2): 137–159.

Devine, M. A., and S. Dawson. 2010. "The Effect of a Residential Camp Experience on Self Esteem and Social Acceptance of Youth with Craniofacial Differences." *Therapeutic Recreational Journal* 54 (2): 105–120.

Devine, M. A., and B. Lashua. 2002. "Constructing Social Acceptance in Inclusive Leisure Contexts: The Role of Individuals with Disabilities." *Therapeutic Recreation Journal* 36 (1): 65–83.

Devine, M. A., and M. B. O'Brien. 2007. "The Mixed Bag on Inclusion: An Examination of an Inclusive Camp Using Contact Theory." *Therapeutic Recreation Journal* 41 (3): 201–222.

Devine, M. A., and M. Parr. 2008. "Come on in, but Not Too Far: Social Capital in an Inclusive Leisure Setting." *Leisure Sciences* 30 (5): 391–408.

Devine, M. A., and B. Wilhite. 1999. "Theory Application in Therapeutic Recreation Practice and Research." *Therapeutic Recreation Journal* 33 (1): 9–45.

Disabled World. 2015. "Disability Camps: Children, Teens & Adults with Disabilities." http://www.disabled-world.com/entertainment/camps/.

Duck, S. 1994. *Meaningful Relationships: Talking, Sense, and Relating.* Thousand Oaks, CA: Sage.

Eccles, J., and J. Gootman. 2002. *Community Programs to Promote Youth Development.* Washington, DC: National Academy Press.

Egilson, S. T., and R. Traustadottir. 2009. "Assistance to Pupils with Physical Disabilities in Regular Schools: Promoting Inclusion or Creating Dependency?" *European Journal of Special Needs Education* 24 (1): 21–36.

Eriksson, L., and M. Granlund. 2004. "Perceived Participation: A Comparison of Students with Disabilities and Without Disabilities." *Scandinavian Journal of Disability Research* 6 (3): 206–224.

Eriksson, L., J. Welander, and M. Granlund. 2007. "Participation in Everyday School Activities for Children with and Without Disabilities." *Journal of Developmental and Physical Disabilities* 19 (5): 485–502.

Fajans, J. 2006. "Autonomy and Relatedness: Emotions and the Tension between Individuality and Sociality." *Critique of Anthropology* 26 (1): 103–119.

Furrer, C. J., and E. Skinner. 2003. "Sense of Relatedness as a Factor in Children's Academic Engagement and Performance." *Journal of Educational Psychology* 95 (1): 148–162.

Germ, P. A., and S. Schleien. 1997. "Inclusion Community Leisure Services: Responsibilities for Key Players." *Therapeutic Recreation Journal* 31 (1), 22–37.

Gesler, W. M. 1992. "Therapeutic Landscapes: Medical Issues in Light of the New Cultural Geography." *Social Science & Medicine* 34 (7), 735–746.

Gill, C. J. 1997. "Four Types of Integration in Disability Identity Development." *Journal of Vocational Rehabilitation* 9 (1): 39–46.

Gillard, A. 2009. "At Home, I'm Clark Kent. at Camp, I'm Superman: Outcomes and Processes of a Camp for Youth with HIV/AIDS". Unpublished Doctoral diss. College Station: Texas A&M.

Gillard, A., and C. E.Watts. 2008. "Initial Findings from a Programs Evaluation of a Camp for Youth with Disabilities". Presented at the ACA Conference, Austin, TX, February.

Gillard, A., P. A. Witt, and C. E. Watts. 2011. "Outcomes and Processes at a Camp for Youth with HIV/AIDS." *Qualitative Health Research* 21 (11): 1508–1526.

Gilson, S. F., A. Tusler, and C. Gill. 1997. "Ethnographic Research in Disability Identity: Self-determination and Community." *Journal of Vocational Rehabilitation* 9 (1): 7–17.

Glover, T. 2004. "Social Capital in the Lived Experiences of Community Gardeners." *Leisure Sciences* 26: 143–162.

Goodlad, J. I. 1984. *A Place Called School*. New York: McGraw-Hill.

Goodwin, D. L., and K. Staples. 2005. "The Meaning of Summer Camp Experiences to Youths with Disabilities." *Adapted Physical Activity Quarterly* 22 (2): 160–178.

Goodwin, D. L., and E. J. Watkinson. 2000. "Inclusive Physical Education from the Perspective of Students with Physical Disabilities." *Adapted Physical Activity Quarterly* 17 (2): 144–160.

Goodwin, D. L., L. J. Lieberman, K. Johnston, and J. Leo. 2011. "Connecting Through Summer Camp: Youth with Visual Impairments Find a Sense of Community." *Adapted Physical Activity Quarterly* 28 (1): 40–55.

Gordon, S. 2006. "Making Sense of the Inclusion Debate Under IDEA." *Bringham Young University Education and Law Journal* 1 (1): 189–226.

Grenier, M. 2006. "A Social Constructionist Perspective of Teaching and Learning in Inclusive Physical Education." *Adapted Physical Activity Quarterly* 23 (3): 245–260.

Groff, D. G., and D. A. Kleiber. 2001. "Exploring the Identity Formation of Youth Involved in an Adapted Sports Program." *Therapeutic Recreation Journal* 35 (4): 318–332.

Grossman, J. B., and M. J. Bulle. 2006. "Review of What Youth Programs Do to Increase the Connectedness of Youth with Adults." *Journal of Adolescent Health* 39 (6): 788–799.

Hagerty, B. M. K., J. Lynch-Sauer, K. L. Patusky, and M. Bouwsema. 1993. "An Emerging Theory of Human Relatedness." *Image: The Journal of Nursing Scholarship* 25 (4): 291–296.

Hall, S. A. 2009. "The Social Inclusion of Young Adults with Intellectual Disabilities: A Phenomenology of Their Experiences." *Journal of Ethnographic and Qualitative Research* 4: 24–40.

Henley, D. 1999. "Facilitating Socialization Within a Therapeutic Camp Setting for Children with Attention Deficits Utilizing the Expressive Therapies." *American Journal of Art Therapy* 38: 40–50.

Hill, E., and J. Sibthorp. 2006. "Autonomy Support at Diabetes Camps: A Self-determination Theory Approach to Therapeutic Recreation." *Therapeutic Recreation Journal* 40 (2): 107–125.

Hodge, S. R., J. Ammah, K. Casebolt, K. Lamaster, and M. O'Sullivan. 2004. "High School General Physical Education Teachers Behaviors and Beliefs Associated with Inclusion." *Sport, Education and Society* 9 (3): 395–419.

Hough, M. S., and L. Browne. 2009. "Connecting Camp Mechanisms to Camper Outcomes: A Case for Program Theory." Symposium conducted at the Nation American Camp Association Conference, Orlando, FL, February 17–20, 2009.

Kiernan, G., M. Gormley, and M. MacLachlan. 2004. "Outcomes Associated with Participation in a Therapeutic Recreation Camping Programme for Children from 15 European Countries: Data from the 'Barretstown Studies.'" *Social Science & Medicine* 59 (5): 903–913.

Kristen, L., G. Patriksson, and B. Fridlund. 2003. "Parentsi Conceptions of the Influences of Participation in a Sports Programme on Their Children and Adolescents with Physical Disabilities." *European Physical Education Review* 9 (1): 23–41.

La Guardia, J. G., R. M. Ryan, C. E. Couchman, and E. L. Deci. 2000. "Within-person Variation in Security of Attachment: A Self-determination Theory Perspective on Attachment, Need Fulfillment, and Well-being." *Journal of Personality and Social Psychology* 79 (3): 367–384.

Longmore, P. 2003. *Why I Burned My Book and Other Essays on Disability*. Philadelphia, PA: Temple University Press.

Maslow, A. 1954. *Motivation and Personality*. New York: Harper.

Matheson, C., R. J. Olsen, and T. Weisner. 2007. "A Good Friend is Hard to Find: Friendship Among Adolescents with Disabilities." *American Journal on Mental Retardation* 112 (5): 319–329.

Michalski, J. M., F. Mishna, C. Worthington, and R. Cummings. 2003. "A Multi-method Impact Evaluation of a Therapeutic Summer Camp Program." *Child and Adolescent Social Work Journal* 20 (1): 53–76.

Miller, K. D., S. J. Schleien, and F. Bowens. 2010. "Support Staff as an Essential Component of Inclusive Recreation Services." *Therapeutic Recreation Journal* 44 (1): 35–49.

Milner, P., and B. Kelly. 2009. "Community Participation and Inclusion: People with Disabilitites Defining Their Place." *Disability and Society* 24 (1): 47–62.

National Recreation and Park Association. 1999. "Position Statement on Inclusion." *Parks & Recreation* 34 (12): 94.

O'Brien, J. 1987. *Frameworks for Accomplishment*. Litonia, GA: Responsive Associates.

Osterman, K. F. 2000. "Students' Need for Belonging in the School Community." *Review of Educational Research* 70 (3): 323–367.

Patriot Ledger. 2012. "Pass or Fail: Special Education in Massachusetts." http://www.youtube.com/watch?v=Mnj7ZURXj20&feature=related.

Pitonyak, D. 2010. "The Importance of Belonging." http://www.dimagine.com/Belonging.pdf.

Place, K., and S. R. Hodge. 2001. "Social Inclusion of Students with Physical Disabilities in General Physical Education: A Behavioral Analysis." *Adapted Physical Activity Quarterly* 18 (4): 389–404.

Rhodes, J. E. 2004. "The Critical Ingredient: Caring Youth–Staff Relationships in After-school Settings." *New Directions for Youth Development* 2004: 145–161.

Roth, J., and J. Brooks-Gunn. 2003. "What Exactly is a Youth Development Program? Answers from Research and Practice." *Applied Developmental Science* 7 (2): 94–111.

Ryan, R. M. 1995. "Psychological Needs and the Facilitation of Integrative Processes." *Journal of Personality* 63 (3): 397–427.

Rynders, J., S. Schleien, and T. Mustonen. 1990. "Integrating Children with Severe Disabilities for Intensified Outdoor Education: Focus on Feasibility." *Mental Retardation* 28 (1): 7–14.

Sable, J. 1995. "Efficacy of Physical Integration, Disability Awareness, and Adventure Programming on Adolescent's Acceptance of Individuals with Disabilities." *Therapeutic Recreation Journal* 21 (3): 206–217.

Salmon, N. 2013. "'We Just Stick Together': How Disabled Teen Negotiate Stigma to Create Lasting Friendship." *Journal of Intellectual Disability Research* 57 (4): 347–358.

Schleien, S., K. Miller, and J. Lausier. 2009. "Search for Best Practices in Inclusive Recreation: Programmatic Findings." *Therapeutic Recreation Journal* 43 (1): 27–41.

Shakespeare, T. 2006. *Disability Rights and Wrongs*. New York: Routledge.

Shapiro, J. P. 1994. *No Pity: People with Disabilities Forging a New Civil Rights Movement*. New York: Three Rivers Press.

Silvana, M. R., K. Watson, and D. Keith. 2002. "Comparing the Quality of Life of School-age Children with and without Disabilities." *Mental Retardation* 40 (4): 304–312.

Simeonsson, R. J., D. Carlson, G. S. Huntington, J. S. McMillen, and J. L. Brent. 2001. "Students with Disabilities: A National Survey of Participation in School Activities." *Disability and Rehabilitation* 23 (1): 49–63.

Smith, R. W., D. R. Austin, D. W. Kennedy, Y. Lee, and P. Hutchison. 2005. *Inclusive and Special Recreation: Opportunities for Persons with Disabilities*. 3rd ed. Dubuque, IA: Brown & Benchmark.

Stainback, S., and W. Stainback. 1990. "Inclusive Schooling." In *Support Networks for Inclusive Schooling: Interdependent Integrated Education*, edited by W. Stainback and S. Stainback, 2–23. Baltimore, MA: Brookes.

Stainback, S., W. Stainback, K. East, and M. Sapon-Chevin. 1994. "A Commentary of Inclusion and the Development of a Positive Self-identity by People with Disabilities." *Exceptional Children* 60 (6): 486–490.

Staub, D. 1998. *Delicate Threads. Friendships Between Children With and Without Special Needs in Inclusive Settings*. Bethesda, MD: Woodbind House.

Taub, D. E., and K. R. Greer. 2000. "Physical Activity as a Normalizing Experience for School-age Children with Physical Disabilities: Implications for Legitimation of Social Identity and Enhancement of Social Ties." *Journal of Sport and Social Issues* 24 (4): 395–414.

Tiemens, K., H. L. Beveridge, and D. B. Nicholas. 2007. "Evaluation of a Therapeutic Camp Program for Adolescents with a Facial Difference." *Social Work with Groups* 30 (2): 57–71.

Tripp, A., T. L. Rizzo, and L. Webbert. 2007. "Inclusion in Physical Education: Changing the Culture." *Journal of Physical Education, Recreation, and Dance* 78 (2): 32–48.

UNICEF. 2005. Summary Report. Violence Against Disabled Children, UN Secretary General's Report on Violence Against Children; Thematic Group on Violence Against Disabled Children. Findings and Recommendations. Accessed June 10 2016. http://www.unicef.org/videoaudio/PDFs/UNICEF_Violence_Against_Disabled_Children_Report_Distributed_Version.pdf

U.S. Department of Justice. 1975. *The Individuals with Disabilities Education Act*. http://nichy.org/wp-content/uploads/docs/PL108-446.pdf.

U.S. Department of Justice. 1990. *The Americans with Disabilities Act*. http://www.ada.gov/cguide.htm#anchor62335.

Watson, S., and K. Keith. 2002. "Comparing the Quality of Life of School-age Children with and Without Disabilities." *Mental Retardation* 40 (4): 304–312.

Watson, N., T. Shakespeare, S. Cunningham-Burley, C. Barnes, M. Corker, J. Davis, and M. Priestley. 2000. *Life as a Disabled Child: A Qualitative Study of Young People's Experiences and Perspectives: Final Report to the ESRC*. Edinburgh: University of Edinburgh Department of Nursing Studies.

Wiener, J., and B. H. Schneider. 2002. "A Multisource Explo-Ration of the Friendship Patterns of Children with and Without Learning Disabilities." *Journal of Abnormal Child Psychology* 30 (2): 127–141.

Wilhite, B., M. A. Devine, and L. Goldenberg. 1999. "Self-perceptions of Youth with and Without Disabilities: Implications for Leisure Programs and Services." *Therapeutic Recreation Journal* 33 (2): 15–28.

Zola, I. 1982. *Missing Pieces: A Chronicle of Living with a Disability*. Philadelphia, PA: Temple University Press.

Between a rock and a hard place: the impact of the professionalization of the role of the teaching assistant in mainstream school physical education in the United Kingdom

Jackie Farr

ABSTRACT

National surveys of the role of the teaching assistant (TA) in the United Kingdom and the para-educator in the USA have explored and revealed trends in the recruitment, training, deployment and perception of their roles. Recent subject-specific research in the UK has further considered how TAs construct their role when supporting disabled pupils in a specific curriculum subject in a mainstream setting. In light of the implementation of a new code of practice in England from 2014 which changes the way in which a child with special educational needs and disabilities is supported in schools and beyond, this paper explores the roles of TAs working in secondary mainstream schools in the UK who are employed to support disabled children in Physical Education. It considers the way in which the role of the TA has evolved and developed in England following 'Workforce Reform' in 2003 and draws on research and literature from a number of sources to explain and update the nomenclature and responsibilities of the para-professional who seems to work '*subdoceo*' (from the Latin meaning 'to teach as an assistant'). It is an attempt to consolidate what we know about these roles in a specific subject and to reaffirm the trends identified from the existing small body of work in the UK. In doing so, this paper aims to provide a platform for further research but will also remind teachers of their role in ensuring that their collaboration with and deployment of these 'paraprofessionals' is paramount to the best interests of the child.

Introduction and context

Following a large-scale study which reported on the broader issues around Physical Education (PE), inclusion and special educational needs and disabilities (SEND), Vickerman and Blundell proposed a 'Seven Cs' model (Vickerman and Blundell 2012) as a means to consolidate the existing knowledge-base and research activity in the area of the role of the teaching assistant (TA) in fostering inclusive practice. In particular, the model calls for a collective view of the role of the learning support assistant (LSA) or TA in supporting pupils with SEND in mainstream school PE. This article is an attempt to contribute to that collective view.

The role of these professionals in creating access and entitlement to the curriculum is clear: that there are tensions in what this role is perceived to be is also apparent from the literature in the UK and internationally. The tension inherent in the TA's role where they find themselves caught between a rock and a hard place[1] (Farr 2010) is not necessarily helped by the ever-increasing standards and targets dominating professional practice in education in the UK.

It appears that the TA has always been and remains a fully (if poorly) paid-up member of Estelle Morris' 'mum's army' (Morris 2001) and that whilst this army recruits a passionate workforce, they are increasingly and in light of severe teacher shortages and teacher workload in the UK, being used to fulfil a role for which they are both underprepared and underqualified. Routine covering of teaching by TAs is noted by the teaching unions (ATL 2013). In the main, that they are not qualified to do so is uncontested in research to date although there will surely be instances where well-qualified graduates, teachers even, make career or lifestyle decisions to work with young people in education in a less-challenging role than that of the teacher. Indeed, further research into whether teachers take the 'road less travelled' at some point in their career and step back from teaching but remain in education would be illuminating. Indeed, this may yet be an unintended consequence of the perceived teacher burnout and workload currently being experienced across the sector. Of concern however is that 'the least qualified staff members are teaching students with the most complex learning characteristics' (Giangreco and Broer 2005, 31).

Research to date has revealed some obvious similarities: where studies were conducted which considered the perceptions of the TAs themselves about their role, it was clear that training and time for collaboration (with the teacher) were the most commonly cited as issues and recommendations. By training, this not only referred to Continuing Professional Development (CPD) for TAs but extended to how teachers were trained to deploy TAs. These are handled well in a number of studies or reports which seek to explore the depth and diversity that is 'being' a TA (Farr 2010), for example Blatchford et al. (2007), Farr (2010), Vickerman and Blundell (2012), Malian (2011), and Maher (2014). However, research also alludes to a situation where TAs are somewhat trapped between understanding their role in a generic, inclusive process in a mainstream school and being able to articulate how they achieve this, yet continuing to lack the pedagogical understanding required to adapt to an increasingly instructional role. Farr (2010) and Malian (2011) have identified this as being in part due to the acceleration of professional expectations of the role.

According to teachers' unions in the UK, there continues to be an unprecedented and higher than ever use of TAs or support staff being used to support teaching. Their role however, has also shifted into one in which they are frequently used as substitute teachers. The seminal longitudinal DISS study (Blatchford et al. 2009) in the UK revealed this tendency, as did a similar study in the USA (Malian 2011). Recent journalistic forays into the topic have reported the way in which schools deploy these support staff with varying degrees of success or efficiency (e.g. Sobel 2013; Webster 2014; Hodge 2015).

> As the political commitment towards the inclusion of pupils with SEN and disabilities in mainstream PE has increased, there has emerged a correlative increase in the emphasis placed upon the role of LSAs in assisting teachers. (Green and Hardman 2005, 231)

Depending on others: the origins of an assistance model

Historically, definitions of what it means to be disabled have focused on the language of loss and tragedy and were symbolic of suffering and bravery. Media representation tells of triumph over adversity and courage in the face of extreme hardship or 'handicap' (*sic*). Stories in the media which perpetuate the hegemony of the 'super-crip' are noted for example by Hockenbury (1995), Harnett (2000), McCarthy and Hurst (2001), Magasi (2008), and Silva and Howe (2012). Central to the tragedy view, or heroic narrative, is the notion that impairment renders an individual powerless, with a focus on inability and deficiency. Images of passivity and helplessness reinforced an inferior status and charitable campaigns would use perceived human tragedy to great effect.

Legislation relating to disabled people in the early part of the twentieth century in England served to categorize on the basis of the medical condition or impairment. The eugenics model of the 'management' of disability was about surveillance, the application of therapies, doing 'to' rather than 'for' (Finkelstein 1981). This normalising culture created opportunities for segregation and, as Snyder and Mitchell (2005) observed, led to a form of social obedience or, in education, towards a deficit model of disability (Ainscow 1999). In the early 1990s, a theoretical perspective which emerged and was adopted by disabled academics and researchers, known as the social model, underpinned the work of various structures and organizations, propelled by an emancipatory agenda, which found it useful to adopt 'terms of reference' for disability. Indeed, these definitions themselves may have played their part in shaping both policy and practice related to disabled people. This agenda, driven through a new disability studies model or paradigm (Oliver and Barton 2000) could also be said to have influenced policy and practice in the development of roles for people who act on behalf of or alongside disabled people.

The evolution of role of the TA in supporting a disabled child in mainstream schools seems to be shaped by such a discourse: indeed, a discourse of power relations may cause the TA to be both a respondent to a contractual obligation on the one hand whilst retaining some intrinsic, personal qualities (Sikes, Lawson, and Parker 2007) and motivation on the other. In discussions about teaching, this is referred to as a humanistic approach or as 'emotional practice' (Hargreaves 1998, 825; Reiter 2000; Sutton and Wheatley 2004). Thus, the role of the TA is not only one with, increasingly, a set of prescribed skills, attributes and competencies, but one whose existence is at odds with a contemporary construction of disability, placing them between a rock and a hard place. Indeed, public sector reform, along a competency-based model of performance (Coffield et al. 2007) may not be helpful in retaining or reinforcing the qualities of a role which is based on relationships. In this regard, are there tensions in the dichotomous role of the TA as both instructor/teacher and care-giver? Does a focus on professionalising the role move the TA towards an instructional model and away from a humanistic one? There are indeed 'contradictory demands' for the TA (Hem and Heggen 2003, 101).

In the last 10–15 years, the role of the TA has been packaged and professionalized, brought into the structure and fabric of the school without always the most appropriate support. The definition of the role of the TA may be increasingly shaped by a discourse which, perhaps in response to societal agenda for disability rights, has moved so far away from a humanistic construction as to have rendered itself sterile and functional. Research indicates that this is likely to be at odds with the personal or vocational motivation of the

TA themselves. The very nature of the role of the TA is thus grounded in a notion that, in order to be included in mainstream education, a physically disabled pupil needs some sort of additional assistance. Role definitions for a TA, such as they are, or indeed of anyone working with disabled people may well be structured in line with a dominant orthodoxy, having less and less to do with the personal, the social, the moral or the humanistic.

Dependency culture

Whilst Oliver noted that disabled people should continue to seek the most appropriate and professional 'intervention' (Oliver 1999, 6) from the construction of mutually dependant relationships, the transformation of disabled people's lives, in his opinion, has been facilitated through social and political activism and not through any equivalent transformation of professional practice. It may be that the construction and perception of the TA's role is, indeed, bounded by a model of disability which, it is contended elsewhere, is somewhat outdated. In turn, this may reinforce a dependant or passive acceptance on the part of the disabled pupil who receives support shaped by adult discourse. Indeed, Allan (1996) and, to an extent, Sebba and Sachdev (1997) noted the clarity with which we might understand these pupils' experiences as resulting from studying how such discourses are constructed to medicalize or marginalize (Allan 1996; Sebba and Sachdev 1997). Indeed, there is an argument here that this perpetuates a simplistic view of a medical model whereby disabled pupils are fitted into an existing structure through a process of adaptation and modifying activities (Smith, as quoted in Fitzgerald 2009, 32).

The idea that disabled young people may be conditioned into dependency and passivity within an educational context is reproduced by several authors in the field of disability studies. Davis and Watson, for instance, describe this as a 'normalising discourse' (Davis and Watson 2001, 675) in the context of their investigation into inclusive versus special schooling. Indeed, a reinforcement of medical model values appears to be implicit in policy from Warnock (1978) to the Special Educational Needs and Disabilities Act (DfES 2001). The discourse of inclusion is still rooted in the language of dependency and may create an environment which does not necessarily advance inclusive education with integrity. Ainscow (2007) contends that this deficit model detracts from the real issue: that disabled children are not adequately served in apparently inclusive schools (Ainscow 2007).

How is inclusion created in mainstream secondary schools?

There is a plethora of scholarship into how inclusion works in theory and how the 'professions' work to provide meaningful experiences. Previous research ranges from the logistics of inclusion (physical access, staff training and awareness, see Avramadis and Norwich 2002; Smith 2004) to the benefits of special schools over mainstream provision (Davis and Watson 2001). Subject-specific teachers' views are sought (Smith and Green 2004; Brent 2005; Morley et al. 2005; Vickerman and Coates 2009) as are those of the parents (Sloper, Rabiee, and Beresford 2007; Yssel et al. 2007) some consider the views of disabled young people (Davis and Watson 2001; Fitzgerald, Jobling, and Kirk 2003; Morris 2003; Kelly, MacArthur, and Gaffney 2008); a few studies consider the views of TAs (Farr 2010; Maher 2014) or 'para-educators' (a term found in North American literature, see Malian 2011), while fewer still look at peer relationships (Allan 1997; Shevlin and O'Moore 2000;

Blackmore 2008). That there remains a dearth of studies which focus specifically on the personal narrative of the TA is noted by several authors internationally including Bourke and Carrington (2007) and Lawson et al. (2006) and has been addressed in part through recent research by Farr (2010), Vickerman and Blundell (2012) and Maher (2014).

Ferguson notes that through strategies in school, such as personalized learning, the curriculum could be said to be becoming 'more engaging' for individual pupils (Ferguson 2008, 114). Curriculum design and the application of principles of differentiation should ensure that learning is both the focus and the result. Lloyd, however, argues that the current system of education still constructs difference 'as a negative condition' in which a child with SEND can only achieve success with assistance (Lloyd 2008, 234). However, whilst the notable differences may be regarded negatively, I resist the perception that all forms of support or assistance are somehow disempowering.

In addition, the rather mechanistic way in which standards and targets in all schools are measured suggests that a concept of a truly inclusive school is still clearly both a philosophical and pedagogical leap for education. Lloyd talks about 'compensatory normalisation' which derives because the education system of the twenty-first century is set-up to be target-driven and 'standards-saturated' (Lloyd 2008, 234, 228). A focus on additional teacher training, resources (both physical and human) or access, for example, has ensured a culture which never really looks beyond these targets and standards (Rose 2001).

What's in a name?

The language of disability can be hazardous, but so too is the language surrounding the titling and naming of the educational support staff who work in this emerging profession as well as the naming of the profession itself. Studies in Europe, the USA and Australia often use the term 'paraeducator' or 'paraprofessional'. There may be obvious reasons for this in that in these countries, a 'teaching assistant' is more likely to be a graduate, working alongside a professor in a college or university (e.g. Park 2004; Muzaka 2009). Giangreco et al. (1997, 7) used the term 'instructional assistants', whilst further studies consider the way in which therapists (physios, occupational therapists and so on) contribute to collaborative and inclusive classroom learning (e.g. Hemmingsson, Gustavsson and Townsend 2007). The latter is, however, largely concerned with medical or physiotherapy support rather than support for learning per se.

Bedford et al. note the negative impact of terms such as 'support staff', 'adults other than teachers' and 'non-teaching staff' (Bedford, Jackson, and Wilson 2008, 8). Indeed, in their reporting of a study into teachers' relationships with TAs, one sample school had noted a *positive* impact on relationships between TA and teacher when the TA was renamed 'assistant teacher' (Bedford, Jackson, and Wilson, 2008, 21). In the UK, the DfES encourages the use of 'TA' as a 'preferred generic term' (DfES 2000, 3). Despite this, however, it is still common to see the term LSA in recent research and policy documents in the UK (Smith, as quoted in Fitzgerald 2009, 33; Veck 2009; Vickerman and Blundell 2012; Maher 2014). One wonders at the inconsistency of terminology, particularly with the shift from 'learning' support to support for 'teaching'. Kerry argues that the label 'TA' reinforces the idea that *teaching* is the central component in education as opposed to *learning* (Kerry 2005, 375).

Clarifying the role: hierarchies

Naming the profession is one thing, interpreting the nature of the role is quite another and authors have agreed on the importance of role clarity:

> The key to effective support appears to depend on a clarification of the assistant's role. (Jerwood 1999, 128)

The literature calls for a clarification of TA roles as one of the most regularly cited issues or recommended outcomes from research (for instance, Clayton 1993; Minondo, Meyer, and Xin 2001; Moran and Abbott 2002; Kerry 2005). In Jerwood's small-scale study of seven TAs, it was noted that they themselves were unclear about their role and had specific concerns about their interaction with the teacher (Jerwood 1999). Egilson and Trausdottir's respondents relied on their 'own knowledge, skills or initiatives' in the absence of role definition (Egilson and Trausdottir 2009, 23). Of interest were Jerwood's findings which noted the strength of a 'faculty-based' TA, one attached to a subject rather than a pupil (Jerwood, supported by Lacey 2001). When the case study school moved to adopt this model, TAs found their roles easier, clearer and were generally more positive about their positions. Other partners in the process (teachers, parents and pupils) were also clearer about the nature of the TA's duties. In particular, pupils' perceptions shifted to a position where they viewed the TA as a resource rather than a 'minder' for particular children (Jerwood 1999, 128).

Studies by Kerry (2005) and Kessler, Bach, and Heron (2007), for instance, attempt to create a typology of assistant roles, the former for TAs specifically, the latter for assistants across education and social welfare. These typologies appear hierarchical in construction: in the case of Kerry, from 'dogsbody' (Kerry 2005, 376) incorporating the infamous phrase 'pig-ignorant-peasant',[2] to mobile paraprofessional and teacher-support staff. Kessler, Bach, and Heron (2007) identify an 'apprentice' who, as an assistant, is preparing for a move into the 'profession'. Malion considers this to be challenging to the ease with which collaboration can take place between teachers and TAs (Malian 2011). The assumption here of course is that this is an upward move, with higher status. This hierarchical system applied to evolving professions is likely to ensure that the subject of the assisting (in this case, the disabled pupil) is at the bottom of the pile rather than being a central focus.

A similar perspective is gleaned from Bedford, Jackson and Wilson's research into relationships between teachers and TAs. According to the authors, the perception of terms such as 'support staff' is that they have negative connotations. This reinforces a 'them' and 'us' relationship where the qualities inherent in one profession seem to be of higher value (professionally) than those of someone in a supporting or assisting role (Bedford, Jackson, and Wilson 2008).

With inconsistency in nomenclature, there is little room for role clarity and thus also for representing the role to stake-holders such as parents, not least pupils and teachers. If a school attaches a name to a role (and there are discrepancies from school to school as well as within establishments, see Farr 2010) then that may subsequently impact on preferred models of CPD. Indeed, assumptions may be made about a role which may render some training out of reach to the TA and thus hinder a positive pupil–teacher–TA relationship, both pedagogical and personal.

The growth of a profession

Michael Giangreco with others (see the various references) used both qualitative and quantitative data over a period of time to assess the growth and impact of the role of this person who supports disabled pupils in mainstream (or 'general')[3] as opposed to special education. In particular, Giangreco, Edelman, Broer and Doyle's extensive review of the US literature and Pivik, McComas and Laflamme's in Canada, both conducted in 2002, revealed that it was case law and parental choice which had originally determined the need for paraprofessional support in North America as far back as 1975 (Giangreco et al. 2002; Pivik, McComas, and Laflamme 2002). Kliewer and Biklen trace the work of the parents' movement in this regard as far back as the 1940s in the US; the latter's efforts to secure improved educational opportunities and conditions in care were unmatched by equivalent moves in science and medicine with their focus remaining on eugenics and their perception that a disabled child was 'not capable of being educated' (Kenned, as quoted in Kliewer and Biklen 2000, 193).

In the UK, however, central government policy has determined the rise in TA deployment. Since 1997, figures show the rapid growth of support staff in schools in a variety of roles, mostly to support or release teachers from administrative tasks (Morris 2001). In a four-year period, by 2003, the number of TAs had risen by over 50% (Kessler, Bach, and Heron 2007, 1648). Writing in 2007, for instance, Callaghan bases his assertion (that the number of TAs had tripled in 10 years) on Parliamentary figures (Callaghan 2007) and indeed, Moran and Abbott trace the beginning of this rise to the 1981 Education Act with its focus on integration (Moran and Abbott 2002). Indeed, in the early years of the developing role, Clayton noted that, traditionally, these assistants undertook housekeeping or caring roles, they were in fact seen as 'domestic helpers' (Clayton 1993).

Defining the role

According to the literature, TAs in the UK appear to play an increasingly instructional role in the classroom and there is some evidence to suggest that the training and job descriptions for example do, in fact, reinforce that an instructional role is the appropriate one, particularly with regard to PE. Palladino, Cornoldi, Vianello, Scruggs and Mastropieri reported that in Italian schools, where inclusion has prevailed for over 30 years (a similar length of time to both the US and the UK), instruction is exclusively the remit of the teacher, whereas matters of personal care or mobility, for example, are the domain of the TA (Palladino et al. 1999): a clearer delineation of roles, which appears not to be so straightforward in the UK. Indeed, increasingly, there is a notion that the TA is re-imaged as a teacher in all but name (Quicke 2003).

Early papers in the study of the TA's generic role noted lack of training and preparation of the TA themselves (Farrell, Balshaw, and Polat 1999; Lacey 2001), others point to the lack of training of teachers to manage the engagement of the TA in a mainstream class (Dew-Hughes, Brayton, and Blandford 1998). Callaghan identifies class size as a significant factor in increasing the need for adult classroom support and notes particularly the use of TAs in increasing numbers with disabled pupils (Callaghan 2007). The growth in the deployment of TAs to support individuals, particularly in secondary schools, is further supported by the research of Neill who found that the existence of more 'specialist' TAs in the secondary sector matched the higher level of academic functioning as opposed to similar roles in primary schools (Neill 2002). Dunne and Goddard's research into the perceptions by TAs of their role also noted the 'specific' nature of this role in secondary schools, whereas primary TAs retained one which was more holistic (Dunne and Goddard 2004, 7). Their study into the perception of 90 TAs on what constituted good practice elicited feedback which, when analysed, revealed that secondary TAs appeared better able to exercise initiative than their colleagues in the primary sector. TAs in this study also placed importance on being able to plan lessons or undertake evaluation, monitoring and assessment, tasks which do not feature in either the DfES Good Practice Guide (2000) or the Standards for Higher Level Teaching Assistants (HLTAs) (DfES 2000, 2003b).

Moran and Abbott researched the specific roles of the TA in Northern Ireland but used a sample which represented both special and mainstream provision which was cross-phase and spanned a wide range of impairments. More importantly, the semi-structured interviews conducted by the researchers were with the Heads of each of the sample schools or units and related to the management view of the TA's role and not to any view expressed by the TA themselves. However, they did conclude by noting the importance of teacher and TA working collaboratively (Moran and Abbott 2002, 164), a view supported by Andrew Smith and Ken Green and identified by Michael Giangreco as an important factor in successful inclusion (Giangreco 1997; Smith and Green 2004). In particular, the need for the teacher to be trained to manage the TA effectively has been highlighted (Farrell, Balshaw, and Polat 1999) and this is reinforced when, from 2005 onwards, the DfES identified the TA's professional role as being commensurate with a need for dedicated CPD (Groom 2006).

Subdoceo: the TA as teacher

The National Agreement (DfES 2003a), published shortly after Time for Standards (DfES 2002) highlighted the contribution, deemed as 'significant' (DfES 2004) and 'subtle' (Howes 2003, 148) made by support staff to the efficient running of schools and to raising standards but makes it clear that the roles of teachers and TAs are not interchangeable. Furthermore, Howes notes that the National Agreement may fail to do justice to the complexities of this role (Howes 2003, 148, 142).

Brown et al. stress the importance of recognizing the challenges to learning presented by students with complex disabilities and acknowledged that they

> ... are in dire need of continuous exposure to the most ingenious, creative, powerful, competent, interpersonally effective and informed professionals ... (Brown et al. 1999, 252)

> ... a tall order indeed.

Generally, the literature suggests that the TA is increasingly taking on an instructional or semi-teaching role and that they often take sole responsibility for the education of more challenging pupils (Moyles and Suschitzky 1997; Veck 2009). Indeed, Warnock had noted that disabled students in mainstream schools are almost entirely taught by TAs (Warnock 2005), whilst MacBeath et al. (2006) observed 'a tendency for TAs to isolate "their" child from group learning activities' (in Shah 2007, 430). Giangreco (1997) and Block (1999) talk about TAs 'hovering' around disabled children, thereby socially isolating them from the peer group whilst occasionally authors describe the assistant as being 'velcroed at the hip' (Meyer 2001, 17; and Sikes, Lawson, and Parker 2007). Farrell, Balshaw, and Polat (1999) definition of good practice for the role of the TA noted that they should be neither 'glued' to the child nor present a barrier between the child and the teacher, something which could lead to 'learned helplessness' (Seligman 1975).

That these roles may also be gender-biased is a feature of literature and previous research:

> The majority of assistants in schools are mums ... it is not a good idea to have your mum with you always, even if she is not really your mum. (O'Connell 2005, 17)

It is acknowledged that, in the primary sector of education, there is a dearth of male role models (Skelton 2003; Cushman 2005; Carrington and McPhee 2008) and recent research indicates the predominant gender-bias in the employment of TAs in both primary and secondary provision (Blatchford et al. 2009). In a large-scale study by Dew-Hughes, Brayton and Blandford, the authors noted that 96% of respondents to their survey across 62 local authorities were women (Dew-Hughes, Brayton, and Blandford 1998) and this was similar to subject-specific data revealed by others (e.g. Farr 2010; Vickerman and Blundell 2012; and Maher 2014).

Ida Malion suggested that their role was evolving from an 'independent tutor' to a 'collaborative partner' (Malian 2011). In Herold and Dandolo's study, when a visually impaired pupil was asked to say who his PE teacher was, he in fact named the LSA (Herold and Dandolo 2009). The DISS study reported that where TAs were increasingly deployed with one child for the duration of the school day, the time spent by that child in being taught by the teacher lessened. That teachers and TAs were rarely provided with opportunities for collaborative planning and feedback was also revealed through the DISS study (Blatchford et al. 2009).

Including disabled pupils in PE: curricular concerns

The value of physical activity, and by default, PE, for *all* young people is unchallenged at a fairly simplistic level in the literature in this field (Bailey et al. 2006) and includes social and affective aspects of learning leading to the production of social capital (Bailey et al. 2006; Capel 2007). Consequently, the perceived value to young *disabled* people of engaging in PE is also a consideration in the literature (Coates and Vickerman 2008). For instance, it can be a significant normalizing experience (Taub and Greer 2000) and might facilitate students to 'background their disability' (Brittain 2004, 86). Equally, and despite schools in general and perhaps PE specifically, becoming more accessible to disabled young people, their experiences in a supposedly inclusive setting may not have value (Penney and Evans 1995). Barrie Houlihan reported on a survey which found that whilst 79% of PE department Heads in 38 mainstream schools claimed an 'inclusive' or suitable curriculum, physically disabled pupils in particular 'did not have access to the full range of activities' (Houlihan 2003, 11).

The evolution of the National Curriculum for Physical Education (NCPE) between 1991 and 2000 also corresponded to the rise in the number of disabled pupils attending mainstream schools; by 1999, the then Department for Education and Employment (DfEE) was beginning to recognize the subsequent need for flexibility within the programmes of study. However, by the time the first NCPE texts were written and published, Len Barton observed that the new curriculum's emphasis on games and performance 'would not easily accommodate pupils with physical disabilities' (Barton 1993, 51). This was supported by research undertaken by Fitzgerald (2003), further corroborated by Vickerman (2007), who found that pupils' perception of difference or lack of ability centred on an ideology focused on either the teacher or the existing curriculum promoting competitive or team games. This 'privileging' of games over other activities was noted as a feature of the 1999 NCPE (Penney and Evans 1999) and Penney would later note that the so-called 'marginalised' activities such as dance and swimming were, in fact potentially more inclusive (Penney 2002). By 2014, Anthony Maher was suggesting that the latest iterations of the NCPE, with opportunities to deliver activities more flexibly, might actually cause pupils with SEND to be disenfranchised once more (Maher 2014): further research on the impact of the latest curricular models in PE on pupils with SEND would be important.

The dominant physicality of the PE curriculum, at face value, and certainly in the eyes of some teachers, seems to dictate the perceived lack of ability with which a child with SEND might engage with content. Barton noted that '... physical education is the creation of and for able-bodied people' and that it gives priority to certain types of human movement (Barton 1993, 49). Armour (1999) and ten years later, Jerlinder, Danermark and Gill have also articulated that an embodiment discourse for PE appears not to be compatible with the inclusion of a physically disabled young person (Armour 1999; Jerlinder, Danermark, and Gill 2009). This is aligned to an emerging post-modern disability perspective in which impairment is seen as part of the disabling process (Corker and Shakespeare 2002). A sociology of impairment would indeed consider the body as central to this disabling process (Hughes and Paterson 1997).

Teachers in Morley et al.'s study observed the limiting effect and therefore greater degree of challenge apparent in a programme of physical activity for the physically disabled child. They perceived this as one of the factors which created a barrier to successful inclusion (Morley et al. 2005). The view from disability studies, however, might be that this represented a fairly clear example of the 'problem' occurring as a result of the impairment and not, as a social model perspective might suggest, that the curriculum is the barrier. Penney and Evans noted the NCPE's efforts to distance itself from labelling children as having (and therefore being) a problem (Penney and Evans 1995).

Communities of practice: professionalizing the role

Houlihan and Green note that, during the 1960s and 1970s, educational debate centred on secondary school structure rather than curriculum concerns or subject-specific discourse. They also attest to the lack of belief by the PE profession in their subject at this time following earlier remarks of Peters who discussed the value of any subject for inclusion in the curriculum and concluded that games was not a 'serious pursuit' and that it 'throws very little light on much else' (Peters 1966, 159, in Houlihan and Green 2006). Through a critical review of journal articles from that point onwards, Houlihan and Green present clear evidence for an insecurity within the profession.

Furthermore, Game Plan (DfES 2002) followed closely by the PE, School Sport and Club Links (DfES 2003b) and the Physical Education and Sport Strategy for Young People, ostensibly threatened the nature and delivery of PE as a curriculum subject and provided the potential for other professionals from the wider field of sport and sports coaching to provide physical activity in schools (Houlihan and Green 2006; Keay 2006). This expansion of a community of practice (Wenger 2000) is not restricted to visiting coaches from national governing bodies of sport however, but stretches to the use of TAs, technicians etc. Beck discusses what are deemed to be the competencies of the teaching profession (as set out by the Training and Development Agency for Schools) and includes the observation that the 2007 document 'Professional Standards for *Teachers*' (emphasis added) has recently:

> ... enlarged at both ends ... to include ... developing national occupational standards for teaching/classroom assistants and professional ... standards for higher level teaching assistants. (Beck 2009, 7)

Thus, tensions between a range of professional bodies responsible for both the development and delivery of school sport and PE resulted in a general perceived lack of clarity and focus according to Houlihan and Green or of 'pedagogical authority' (Harjunen 2009, 109). More significantly, it is the impact of policy in terms of the growing and changing role of the Physical Educationist[4] in schools which appears to give rise to the concept that the teacher's role may have been de-professionalized.

There appear to be similar arguments put forward in respect of changes in the roles of health workers. In identifying the potential challenge, or indeed threat, to the deprofessionalization of teachers' roles 'in the guise of re-professionalisation' (Beck 2008, 119) a comparison could be made with the shift in roles in the medical profession where nurses increasingly take on tasks previously undertaken by doctors (Morris 2001; Neill 2002). That is not to say, however, that there are negative aspects to widening the scope of the role (or the subject). It may well be that teachers are both protective of their subject knowledge and threatened by change. However, an activist teacher (Sachs 2003) or Thorburn's 'new professional' (Thorburn 2005), embraces change, responds positively to engaging with other professionals: many hands make light work, perhaps. If the 'new' professionalism embraces these concepts such as more professional dialogue, creating environments of trust (Frowe 2005) and restructuring time and space, how does this relate to an 'old' model which, Thorburn alleges, has been slow to change or reactive and has had exclusive membership? Indeed as Hellison and Templin suggest:

> If you are non-reflective, you may allow others to make your curriculum decisions. (Hellisson and Templin 1991, 3)

Judyth Sachs notes the requirement for the activist (or reflective) teacher to work collectively and collaboratively with others. Risk-taking is considered worthwhile in order to improve learning opportunities for all involved in the education process (Sachs 2003). Using Wenger's concept of mutual engagement (Wenger 2000), Sachs notes that the contribution and knowledge of others is deemed significant in promoting an activist profession which is both effective and which builds on social capital (Sachs 2003). In supporting this transformation and moving towards communities of practice, she challenges the whole notion of teacher identity and thus provides us in PE with a tangible model on which to build successful partnerships with every professional body or individual with an interest in physically educating young people. Clearly, the relationship between the teacher and the TA is one such partnership.

Additionally, the TA's relationship may be with the subject as much as with the pupil and the teacher and therefore the TA's understanding of the nature of that subject might also be important. Furthermore, it may be that the pupil's learning is directly affected by the ability of the TA to engage fully with the subject knowledge in situations where the teacher devolves responsibility for delivery to the TA. This was explored by research conducted into the role perception of TAs supporting physically disabled pupils in PE in one large local authority (Farr 2010).

The teaching assistant in physical education

In the context of PE, a higher duty of care (British Association of Advisers and Lecturers in PE [BAALPE]) in practical lessons exists for this subject and substantial case law should alert employers or Headteachers to proceed cautiously when deploying staff (BAALPE 2005). In particular, this applies when allowing inexperienced or unqualified staff to supervise activities where a higher degree of risk is involved. Since August 2003, regulations have been in place in England in which the circumstances under which support staff can undertake 'specified work' are clarified.

BAALPE's recommendation is for staff other than teachers in the context of PE to be HLTAs as a benchmark for ensuring appropriate supervision. Bedford, Jackson, and Wilson (2008) reported on the 'controversial' content of the standards introduced for HLTA status which, they note, were similar to those for classroom teachers. The use of the word 'controversial' in their discussion would further serve to reinforce the unease and concern prevalent amongst teachers at this time regarding the perceived status of their respective roles. It is clear from BAALPE's guidelines that the overall responsibility for *learning* lies with the qualified teacher, however, the document identifies those who may also assist and support the work of a qualified teacher, including TAs and HLTAs.

Research into the employment of TAs by Blatchford et al. similarly noted that the role of the teacher and the TA were not interchangeable (Blatchford et al. 2007). Delegation of duties to support staff is also deemed to be at the discretion of the teacher (or subject to a risk assessment) but the fact that BAALPE note the need for these people to be 'well informed, well qualified and well trained' (BAALPE 2005) confers or implies an implicit acceptance of their growing professional status. Furthermore, not all the evidence supports the notion that TAs are 'teachers in waiting' (from Kessler, Bach, and Heron 2007; Farrell, Balshaw, and Polat 1999). Conversely, Howes' review of the National Agreement highlighted a relationship between teacher and TA as being one in which the teacher leads and manages, and not one of collaboration and partnership (Howes 2003).

Reaffirming the trends

So, there remain certain clear trends and themes from existing research:

(1) The need to collaborate: what Vickerman and Blundell note as a 'critical factor' (Vickerman and Blundell 2012, 150) and what Malion refers to as 'teaming' (Malian 2011): the American term of paraprofessional which places clarity on the different but parallel role.
(2) The need for training – both of TAs 'on the job' and of teachers to be helped to deploy TAs. Sobel (2013) and Hodge (2015) note that children could flourish when supported appropriately but that TAs needed support, training and development to ensure this.

To these I offer:

(1) Recognizing the value of the vocational context of the role which may have been lost in a drive to standardize and professionalize (this would perhaps also be true of the health professions).

(2) Recognizing that this is a unique and bifurcated role as long as it remains less about supporting the teacher and more about supporting the pupil.

(3) A need for clear delineation of roles.

Conclusion

A competency-driven and skill-based role is one half of a dichotomous construction. Tickle's qualities of empathy and compassion (Tickle, as referred to in Korthagen 2004), for instance, are not included in any assessment of TA competence although, of course, any assessment of a value-laden perception of a role is fraught with difficulty. These qualities are not particularly easy to align with a contemporary disability discourse which has occasionally made it difficult to view the impairment as central to a process. This stance was critiqued by Geoff Lindsay and others including Tom Shakespeare for example who argued that there was room for both an impairment-focused view and one which accounts for barriers caused by society, systems or structures, both of which were to be considered in constructing the 'needs' of the disabled pupil (Lindsay 2003; Shakespeare 2006). The definition of the role of the TA may be increasingly shaped by a discourse which, in response to a politically driven societal agenda for disability, has moved so far away from a humanistic construction as to have rendered itself sterile and functional – and this may even be at odds with the personal or vocational motivation of the TAs themselves. Thus, I contend, the TA struggles to please all masters and appears to have a role which requires an:

> … interface between aspects of one's personal virtues and one's professional life, between personhood and teacherhood. (Tickle, as quoted in Korthagen 2004, 123)

In an earlier study (Farr 2010), the TA largely constructed their role as an advocate whose relationship with the pupil is accepting and supportive and whose motivation for being in the role is to facilitate an inclusive process (even though they were undecided about what such a process looks like). In other words, this role is intuitive, reflective and responsive: it is shaped as much by personal as professional experience although, increasingly, the 'personal' is removed from training and accreditation. The feeling is that the TA is an individual with a particular 'sense' of their role, who constructs it somewhat haphazardly dependant on the strength of their relationships with pupils and teachers and their own level of confidence in the subject matter. Indeed, public sector reform, along a competency-based model of performance (Coffield et al. 2007), may not be helpful in retaining or reinforcing the qualities of a role which is based on relationships. In becoming more 'professional', has the TA's role become less organic, less humanistic (Reiter 2000) and perhaps less connected to the child? In this regard, are there tensions in the dichotomous role of the TA as instructor and caregiver, for instance? Does the existing training per se move the TA towards an instructional model and away from a humanistic one? This tension or polarity between the professional and vocational places the TA between a rock and a hard place.

Notes

1. An English adage meaning to be caught between two different but equally challenging and difficult situations.

2. This was allegedly said by Nigel de Gruchy of the UK Teachers' Union, the NASUWT during a so-called 'paranoic period' in which the teaching professions felt somewhat threatened by the emerging role of the TA (in Kerry 2005, 376).
3. In the US, a 'general' education setting is the equivalent term to the UK's 'mainstream' school.
4. This is a widely adopted term, (see e.g. Armour 1999; Penney and Evans 1995; Whitehead 2006).

Disclosure statement

No potential conflict of interest was reported by the author.

References

Ainscow, M. 1999. *Understanding the Development of Inclusive Schools.* London: Falmer Press.
Ainscow, M. 2007. "Taking an Inclusive Turn." *Journal of Research in Special Educational Needs* 7 (1): 3–7.
Allan, J. 1996. "Foucault and Special Educational Needs: A 'Box of Tools' for Analysing Children's Experiences of Mainstreaming." *Disability & Society* 11 (2): 219–234.
Allan, J. 1997. "With a Little Help from My Friends? Integration and the Role of Mainstream Pupils." *Children & Society* 11: 183–193.
Armour, K. R. 1999. "The Case for a Body-focus in Education and Physical Education." *Sport, Education and Society* 4 (1): 5–15.
ATL (Association for Teachers and Lecturers). 2013. *Teaching on the Cheap is Selling Children Short: Schools Use Teaching Assistants and Cover Supervisors to Teach Children.* http://www.atl.org.uk/.
Avramadis, E., and B. Norwich. 2002. "Teachers' Attitudes Towards Integration/inclusion: A Review of the Literature." *European Journal of Special Needs Education* 17 (2): 129–147.
BAALPE (British Association for Advisers and Lecturers in Physical Education). 2005. *Workforce Reform: Essential Safe Practice in Physical Education and School Sport.* Leeds: Coachwise.
Bailey, R., K. Armour, D. Kirk, M. Jess, I. Pickup, and R. Sandford. 2006. *The Educational Benefits Claimed for Physical Education and School Sport: An Academic Review.* BERA Physical Education and Sport Pedagogy Special Interest Group.
Barton, L. 1993. "Disability, Empowerment and Physical Education." In *Equality, Education and Physical Education*, edited by J. Evans. London: Falmer.
Beck, J. 2008. "Governmental Professionalism: Re-professionalising or De-professionalising Teachers in England?" *British Journal of Educational Studies* 56 (2): 119–143.
Beck, J. 2009. "Appropriating Professionalism: Restructuring the Official Knowledge Base of England's 'Modernised' Teaching Profession." *British Journal of Sociology of Education* 30 (1): 3–14.
Bedford, D., C. K. Jackson, and E. Wilson. 2008. "New Partnerships for Learning; Teachers' Perspectives on their Developing Professional Relationships with Teaching Assistants in England." *Journal of In-Service Education* 34 (1): 7–25.
Blackmore, T. 2008. "'Half of My Friends Don't Even See Me as Disabled:' What Can Field, Capital and Habitus Reveal About Disability Inclusion and Exclusion?" Presentation to the 4th Biennial Disability Studies Conference. Lancaster: Lancaster University.
Blatchford, P., A. Russell, P. Bassett, P. Brown, and C. Martin. 2007. "The Role and Effects of Teaching Assistants in English Primary Schools (Years 4 to 6) 2000–2003. Results From the Class Size and Pupil–Adult Ratios (CSPAR) KS2 Project." *British Educational Research Journal* 33 (1): 5–26.
Blatchford, P., P. Basset, P. Brown, C. Martin, A. Russell, and R. Webster. 2009. *Deployment and Impact of Support Staff Project.* DCSF-RB148. Institute of Education. London: University of London.
Block, M. E. 1999. "Did We Jump on the Wrong Bandwagon? Problems With Inclusion in Physical Education." *Palaestra* 15 (3): 1–7.
Bourke, P., and S. Carrington. 2007. "Inclusive Education Reform: Implications for Teacher Aides." *Australasian Journal of Special Education* 31 (1): 15–24.

Brent, H. 2005. "Physical Education Teachers' Reflections on Preparation for Inclusion." *Physical Educator* 62 (1): 44–56.

Brown, L., K. Farrington, T. Knight, C. Ross, and M. Ziegler. 1999. "Fewer Paraprofessionals and More Teachers and Therapists in Educational Programs for Students with Significant Disabilities." *The Association for Persons with Severe Handicaps* 24 (4): 250–253.

Brittain, I. 2004. "The Role of Schools in Constructing Self-perceptions of Sport and Physical Education in Relation to People With Disabilities." *Sport, Education & Society* 9 (1): 75–94.

Callaghan, T. 2007. "Assistants Won't Help the Profession." *Times Educational Supplement*, February 9, 24.

Capel, S. 2007. "Moving Beyond Physical Education Subject Knowledge to Develop Knowledgeable Teachers of the Subject." *Curriculum Journal* 18 (4): 493–507.

Carrington, B., and A. McPhee. 2008. "Boys 'Underachievement' and the Feminization of Teaching." *Journal of Education for Teaching* 34 (2): 109–120.

Clayton, T. 1993. "From Domestic Helper to 'Assistant Teacher' – The Changing Role of the British Classroom Assistant." *European Journal of Special Needs Education* 8 (1): 32–44.

Coates, J., and P. Vickerman. 2008. "Let the Children Have Their Say: Children with Special Educational Needs and Their Experiences of Physical Education – A review." *Support for Learning* 23 (4): 168–175.

Coffield, F., S. Edward, I. Finlay, A. Hodgson, K. Spours, R. Steer, and M. Gregson. 2007. "How Policy Impacts on Practice and How Practice Does Not Impact on Policy." *British Educational Research Journal* 33 (5): 723–741.

Corker, M., and T. Shakespeare, eds. 2002. *Disability/postmodernity: Embodying Disability Theory*. London: Continuum.

Cushman, P. 2005. "Let's Hear it from the Males: Issues Facing Male Primary School Teachers." *Teaching and Teacher Education* 21 (3): 227–240.

Davis, J. M., and N. Watson. 2001. "Where are the Children's Experiences? Analysing Social and Cultural Exclusion in 'Special' and 'Mainstream' Schools." *Disability & Society* 16 (5): 671–687.

Dew-Hughes, D., H. Brayton, and S. Blandford. 1998. "A Survey of Training and Professional Development for Learning Support Assistants." *Support for Learning* 13 (4): 179–183.

DfES. 2000. *Working With Teaching Assistants: A Good Practice Guide*. London: DfES.

DfES. 2001. *The Special Education Needs and Disability Act (SENDA)*. London: HMSO.

DfES. 2002. *Time for Standards: Reforming the School Workforce*. London: DfES.

DfES. 2003a. *Raising standards and tackling workloads: a national agreement. Time for Standards*. London: DfES.

DfES. 2003b. *Standards for HLTAs*. London: DfES.

DfES. 2004. *Pedagogy and Practice: Teaching and Learning in Secondary Schools. Unit 4: Lesson Design for Inclusion*. London: DfES.

Dunne, L., and G. Goddard. 2004. "Good Practice for TAs: A Matter of Perception." *Cutting Edge* 4 (4): 7–8.

Egilson, S. T., and R. Trausdottir. 2009. "Assistance to Pupils with Physical Disabilities in Regular Schools: Promoting Inclusion or Creating Dependency?" *European Journal of Special Needs Education* 24 (1): 21–36.

Farr, J. 2010. "Between a Rock and a Hard Place? Teaching Assistants Supporting Physically Disabled Pupils in Mainstream Secondary School Physical Education: The Tensions of Professionalising the Role." Doctoral thesis published online in the Greenwich Academic Literature Archive (GALA), University of Greenwich. http://gala.gre.ac.uk/6609/.

Farrell, P., M. Balshaw, and F. Polat. 1999. *The Management, Role and Training of Teaching Assistants*. DfES No 161. London: DfEE.

Ferguson, Dianne L. 2008. "International Trends in Inclusive Education: The Continuing Challenge to Teach Each One and Everyone." *European Journal of Special Needs Education* 23 (2): 109–120.

Finkelstein, V. 1981. "Disability and the Helper/helped Relationship: An Historical View." In *Handicap in a Social World*, edited by A. Brechin, P. Liddiard, and J. Swain. London: Open University Press.

Fitzgerald, H. 2003. "Still Feeling like a Spare Piece of Luggage? Embodied Experiences of (Dis)ability in Physical Education and School Sport." *Physical Education and Sport Pedagogy* 10 (1): 41–59.

Fitzgerald, H., ed. 2009. *Disability and Youth Sport*. London: Routledge.

Fitzgerald, H., A. Jobling, and D. Kirk. 2003. "Valuing the Voices of Young Disabled People: Exploring Experiences of Physical Education and Sport." *European Journal of Physical Education* 8 (2): 175–201.

Frowe, I. 2005. "Professional Trust." *British Journal of Educational Studies* 53 (1): 34–53.

Giangreco, M. F. 1997. "Key Lessons Learned about Inclusive Education. Summary of the 1996 Schonell Memorial Lecture." *International Journal of Disability* 44 (3): 193–206.

Giangreco, M. F., and S. M. Broer. 2005. "Questionable Utilization of Paraprofessionals in Inclusive Schools: Are We Addressing Symptoms or Causes?" *Focus on Autism and Other Developmental Disabilities* 20 (1): 10–26.

Giangreco, M. F., S. Edelman, S. M. Broer, and M. B. Doyle. 2002. "Paraprofessional Support of Students with Disabilities: Literature from the past decade." *Exceptional Children* 68 (1): 45–63.

Giangreco, M. F., S. Edelman, T. E. Luiselli, and S. Z. C. Macfarland. 1997. "Helping or Hovering? Effects of Instructional Assistant Proximity on Students with Disabilities." *Exceptional Children* 64: 7–18.

Green, K., and K. Hardman. 2005. *Physical Education: Essential Issues*. London: Sage.

Groom, B. 2006. "Building Relationships for Learning: The Developing Role of the Teaching Assistant." *Support for Learning* 21 (4): 199–203.

Hargreaves, A. 1998. "The Emotional Practice of Teaching." *Teaching and Teacher Education* 14 (8): 835–854.

Harjunen, E. 2009. "How Do Teachers View Their Own Pedagogical Authority?" *Teachers and Teaching* 15 (1): 109–129.

Harnett, A. 2000. "Escaping the 'Evil Avenger' and the 'Supercrip': Images of Disability in Popular Television." *Irish Communications Review* 8: 21–29.

Hellisson, D. R., and T. J. Templin. 1991. *A Reflective Approach to Teaching Physical Education*. Leeds: Human Kinetics.

Hem, M. H., and K. Heggen. 2003. "Being Professional and Being Human: One Nurse's Relationship with a Psychiatric Patient." *Journal of Advanced Nursing* 43 (1): 101–108.

Hemingsson, H., A. Gustavsson, and E. Townsend. 2007. "Students with Disabilities Participating in Mainstream Schools: Policies That Promote and Limit Teacher and Therapist Cooperation." *Disability & Society* 22 (4): 383–398.

Herold, F., and J. Dandolo. 2009. "Including Visually Impaired Students in Physical Education Lessons: A Case Study of Teacher and Pupil Experiences." *British Journal of Visual Impairment* 27 (1): 75–84.

Hockenbury, J. 1995. *Moving Violations*. New York: Hyperion.

Hodge, K. 2015. "How Teaching Assistants Can Make a Real Difference in the Classroom." *The Guardian*, April 1.

Houlihan, B. 2003. *Sport and Society: A Student Introduction*. London: Sage.

Houlihan, B., and K. Green. 2006. "The Changing Status of School Sport and Physical Education: Explaining Policy Change." *Sport, Education and Society* 11 (1): 73–92.

Howes, A. 2003. "Teaching Reforms and the Impact of Paid Adult Support on Participation and Learning in Mainstream Schools." *Support for Learning* 18 (4): 147–153.

Hughes, B., and K. Paterson. 1997. "The Social Model of Disability and the Disappearing Body: Towards a sociology of impairment." *Disability & Society* 12 (3): 325–340.

Jerlinder, K., B. Danermark, and P. Gill. 2009. "Normative Approaches to Justice in Physical Education for Pupils with Physical Disabilities – Dilemmas of Recognition and Redistribution." *Disability & Society* 24 (3): 331–342.

Jerwood, L. 1999. "Using Special Needs Assistants Effectively." *British Journal of Special Education* 26 (3): 127–129.

Keay, J. 2006. "What is a PE Teacher's Role? The Influence of Learning Opportunities on Role Definition." *Sport, Education and Society* 11 (4): 369–383.

Kelly, B., J. MacArthur, and M. Gaffney. 2008. "'Some People Think I Am Different, but I See Myself as an Equal Person to Everyone Else.' Exploring Identities of Young Disabled People at School." Presentation to the Fourth Biennial Disability Studies Conference, Lancaster: Lancaster University.

Kerry, T. 2005. "Towards a Typology for Conceptualising the Roles of Teaching Assistants." *Educational Review* 57 (3): 373–384.

Kessler, I., S. Bach, and P. Heron. 2007. "Comparing Assistant Roles in Education and Social Care: Backgrounds, Behaviours and Boundaries." *The International Journal of Human Resource Management* 18 (19): 1648–1665.

Kliewer, C., and D. Biklen. 2000. "Democratizing Disability Inquiry." *Journal of Disability Policy Studies* 10 (2): 186–206.

Korthagen, F. A. J. 2004. "In Search of the Essence of a Good Teacher: Towards a More Holistic Approach in Teacher Education." *Teaching and Teacher Education* 20: 77–97.

Lacey, P. 2001. "The Role of Learning Support Assistants in the Inclusive Learning of Pupils with Severe and Profound Learning Difficulties." *Educational Review* 53 (2): 157–167.

Lawson, H., M. Parker, and P. Sikes. 2006. "Seeking Stories: Reflections on a Narrative Approach to Researching Understandings of Inclusion." *European Journal of Special Needs Education* 21 (1): 55–68.

Lindsay, G. 2003. "Inclusive Education: A Critical Perspective. The Gulliford Lecture." *British Journal of Special Education* 30 (1): 3–12.

Lloyd, C. 2008. "Removing Barriers to Achievement: A Strategy for Inclusion or Exclusion?" *International Journal of Inclusive Education* 12 (2): 221–236.

MacBeath, J., M. Galton, S. Steward, A. MacBeath, and C. Page. 2006. *The Costs of Inclusion: A study of Inclusion Policy and Practice in English Primary, Secondary and Special Schools*. Cambridge: University of Cambridge Faculty of Education.

Magasi, S. 2008. "Infusing Disability Studies into the Rehabilitation Sciences." *Topics in Stroke Rehabilitation* 15 (3): 283.

Maher, A. J. 2014. "Special Educational Needs in Mainstream Secondary School Physical Education: Learning Support Assistants Have Their Say." *Sport, Education and Society* 21 (2): 262–278.

Malian, I. 2011. "Paraeducators Perceptions of Their Roles in Inclusive Classrooms: A National Study of Paraeducators." *Electronic Journal for Inclusive Education* 2 (8): 1–26.

McCarthy, D., and A. Hurst. 2001. "A Briefing on Assessing Disabled Students." Learning and Teaching Support Network, Assessment Series No. 8.

Meyer, L. H. 2001. "The Impact of Inclusion on Children's Lives: Multiple Outcomes, and Friendship in Particular." *International Journal of Disability, Development and Education* 48 (1): 9–31.

Minondo, S., L. H. Meyer, and J. L. Xin. 2001. "The Role and Responsibilities of Teaching Assistants in Inclusive Education: What's Appropriate?" *Research and Practice for Persons with Severe Disabilities* 26 (2): 114–119.

Moran, A., and L. Abbott. 2002. "Developing Inclusive Schools: The Pivotal Role of Teaching Assistants in Promoting Inclusion in Special and Mainstream Schools in Northern Ireland." *European Journal of Special Needs Education* 17 (2): 161–173.

Morley, D., R. Bailey, J. Tan, and B. Cooke. 2005. "Inclusive Physical Education: Teachers' Views of Including Pupils with Special Educational Needs and/or disabilities in Physical Education." *European Physical Education Review* 11 (1): 84–107.

Morris, E. 2001. *Professionalism and Trust – The Future of Teachers and Teaching*. DfES Speech to the Social Market Foundation, November 12.

Morris, J. 2003. Including All Children: Finding Out About the Experiences of Disabled Children. *Children & Society* 17 (5): 337–348.

Moyles, J., and W. Suschitzky. 1997. "The Employment and Deployment of Classroom Support Staff: Head Teachers' Perspectives." *Research in Education* 58: 21–34.

Muzaka, V. 2009. "The Niche of Graduate Teaching Assistants: Perceptions and Reflections." *Teaching in Higher Education* 14 (1): 1–12.

Neill, S. R. S. J. 2002. *Teaching Assistants: A Survey Analysed for the National Union of Teachers*. Coventry: The University of Warwick Teacher Research and Development Unit.

O'Connell, P. 2005. "'A Better Future'? Young adults with complex physical and communication needs in mainstream education." The Dare Foundation, presented by Dawns Seals, BERA, The University of Glamorgan. http://disability-studies.leeds.ac.uk/library/.

Oliver, M. 1999. *The Disability Movement and the Professions*. www.disability-archive@leeds.ac.uk.

Oliver, M., and L. Barton. 2000. "The Emerging Field of Disability Studies: A View From Britain." Paper presented at the conference 'Disability Studies: A Global Perspective', Washington, DC.

Palladino, P., C. Cornoldi, R. Vianello, T. E. Scruggs, and M. A. Mastropieri. 1999. "Paraprofessionals in Italy: Perspectives from an Inclusive Country." *Research and Practice for Persons with Severe Disabilities* 24 (4): 254–258.

Park, C. 2004. "The Graduate Teaching Assistant (GTA); Lessons from North American exoerience." *Teaching in Higher Education* 9 (3): 349–361.

Penney, D. 2002. "Equality, Equity and Inclusion in Physical Education and School Sport." In *The Sociology of Sport and Physical Education: An Introductory Reader*, edited by A. Laker. London: RoutledgeFalmer.

Penney, D., and J. Evans. 1995. "The NCPE: Entitlement for All?" *British Journal of Physical Education* 26 (2): 6–13.

Penney, D., and J. Evans. 1999. *Politics, Power and Practice in Physical Education*. London: Spon Press.

Pivik, J., J. McComas, and M. Laflamme. 2002. "Barriers and Facilitators to Inclusive Education." *Exceptional Children* 69 (1): 97–107.

Quicke, J. 2003. "Teaching Assistants: Students or Servants?" *FORUM* 45 (2): 71–74.

Reiter, S. 2000. "Society and Disability: A Model of Support in Special Education and Rehabilitation." *Focus on Exceptional Children* 32 (8): 1–14.

Rose, R. 2001. "Primary School Teacher Perceptions of the Conditions Required to Include Pupils with Special Educational Needs." *Educational Review* 53 (2): 148–156.

Sachs, J. 2003. "Teacher Activism: Mobilising the Profession." Plenary address presented to the British Educational Research Association Conference, Heriot Watt University, Edinburgh.

Sebba, J., and D. Sachdev. 1997. *What Works in Inclusive Education?*. Ilford: Barnardo's.

Seligman, M. E. 1975. *Helplessness: On Depression, Development, and Death*. London: WH Freeman/Times Books/Henry Holt.

Shah, S. 2007. "Special or Mainstream? The Views of Disabled Students." *Research Papers in Education* 22 (4): 425–442.

Shakespeare, T. 2006. *Disability Rights and Wrongs*. London: Routledge.

Shevlin, M., and A. O'Moore. 2000. "Fostering Positive Attitudes; Reactions of Mainstream Pupils to Contact with Their Counterparts Who Have Severe/Profound Intellectual Disabilities." *European Journal of Special Needs Education* 15: 200–217.

Silva, C. F., and P. D. Howe. 2012. "The (In)validity of Supercrip Representation of Paralympian Athletes." *Sport & Social Issues* 36 (2): 174–194.

Sikes, P., H. Lawson, and M. Parker. 2007. "Voices On: Teachers and Teaching Assistants Talk about Inclusion." *International Journal of Inclusive Education* 11 (3): 355–370.

Skelton, C. 2003. "Male Primary Teachers and Perceptions of Masculinity." *Educational Review* 55 (2): 195–209.

Sloper, P., P. Rabiee, and B. Beresford. 2007. *Oucomes for Disabled Children*. Research Works. York: SPRU, University of York.

Smith, A. 2004. "The Inclusion of Pupils with Special Educational Needs in Secondary School Physical Education." *Physical Education and Sport Pedagogy* 9 (1): 37–54.

Smith, A., and K. Green. 2004. "Including Pupils with Special Educationl Needs in Secondary School Physical Education: A Sociological Analysis of Teachers' Views." *British Journal of Sociology of Education* 25 (5): 593–607.

Snyder, S. L., and D. T. Mitchell. 2005. *Cultural Locations of Disability*. Chicago, IL: The University of Chicago Press.

Sobel, D. 2013. "Teaching Assistants are the Unsung Heroes of Education." *The Guardian*, October 2.

Sutton, R. E., and K. F. Wheatley. 2004. "Teachers' Emotions and Teaching: A Review of the Literature and Directions for Future Research." *Educational Psychology Review* 15 (4): 327–358.

Taub, D. E., and K. R. Greer. 2000. "Physical Activity as a Normalizing Experience for School-age Children with Physical Disabilities: Implications for Legitimation of Social Identity and Enhancement of Social Ties." *Journal of Sport and Social Issues* 24 (4): 395–414.

Thorburn, M. 2005. "Emerging Models of Professionalism: The Changing Expectations of Physical Education Teachers." *Education in the North* 13: 47–53.

Veck, W. 2009. "From an Exclusionary to an Inclusive Understanding of Educational Difficulties and Educational Space: Implications for the Learning Support Assistant's role." *Oxford Review of Education* 35 (1): 41–56.

Vickerman, P. 2007. "Training Physical Education Teachers to Include Children with Special Educational Needs: Perspectives from Physical Education Initial Teacher Training Providers." *European Physical Education Review* 13 (3): 385–402.

Vickerman, P., and M. Blundell. 2012. "English Learning Support Assistants' Experiences of Including Children with Special Educational Needs in Physical Education." *European Journal of Special Needs Education* 27 (2): 143–156.

Vickerman, P., and J. K. Coates. 2009. "Trainee and Recently Qualified Physical Education Teachers' Perspectives on Including Children with Special Educational Needs." *Physical Education & Sport Pedagogy* 14 (2): 137–153.

Warnock, M. 1978. *Report of the Committee of Enquiry into the Education of Handicapped Children and Young People*. London: HMSO.

Warnock, M. 2005. *Special Educational Needs and Disability: A New Look*. London: Philosophy of Education Society of Great Britain.

Webster, R. 2014. "Relying on Teaching Assistant Support for SEN Students is a False Economy." *Teacher Network, The Guardian*. Accessed April 17. www.theguardian.com

Wenger, E. 2000. "Communities of Practice and Social Learning Systems." *Organisation* 7 (2): 225–246.

Whitehead, M. 2006. "Meaningful Existence, Embodiment and Physical education." *Journal of Philosophy of Education* 24 (1): 3–14.

Yssel, N., P. Engelbrecht, M. Oswald, I. Eloff, and E. Swart. 2007. "Views of Inclusion: A Comparative Study of Parents' Perceptions in South Africa and the United States." *Remedial and Special Education* 28 (6): 356–365.

The fiddle of using the Paralympic Games as a vehicle for expanding [dis]ability sport participation

P. David Howe and Carla Filomena Silva

ABSTRACT
In this paper, we highlight the need to explore the excessive significance given to the Paralympic Games as a vehicle for the encouragement of participation of people with a disability within sport. The media spectacle around the games that the International Paralympic Committee (IPC) has worked tirelessly to develop has become, for policy-makers and the public alike, a sufficient outlet for disability sport provision. The honourable goals of the IPC articulated through the ethos of Paralympism have been assumed to be valid for all people with a disability, yet in terms of widening participation, their utility is limited. This paper first illuminates the relationship between the International Olympic Committee and the IPC before we turn our attention to the ethos of Paralympism. Highlighting the necessity for 'sport for all', we use a human rights lens, aided by a capabilities approach to facilitate better ways to educate the public about the need for equality of access to sporting participation opportunities.

Introduction

Today the Paralympic Games are presented as part of the Olympic Festival, and are formally part of the Olympic Movement. Internationally the International Paralympic Committee (IPC) and the International Olympic Committee (IOC) signed an agreement in 2001, which benefited the IPC by providing it with long-term financial support, access to high quality facilities in which to hold the Paralympics, and countless other commercial opportunities. For the IOC, the positive publicity garnered praise for the charitable support of the IPC at a time when the organization's core values were being publicly scrutinized in light of scandals associated with the 2002 Salt Lake City Winter Olympic Games. In 2003, this agreement was amended to transfer 'broadcasting and marketing responsibilities of the 2008, 2010 and 2012 Paralympic Games to the Organizing Committee of these Olympic and Paralympic Games' (IPC 2003, 1). Subsequently this agreement has been amended to run up until after the 2020 Tokyo games (IPC 2012). While agreements such as this eases financial concerns for the IPC, it may also force a restructuring of disability sport. The IOC demands that the Paralympic Games are restricted in size to 4300 athletes. Limiting the size of future Paralympic Games in the eyes of the IOC makes it a more manageable product to market.

The marketing of the Olympics and Paralympics as a single entity has however undermined the IPC's autonomy to use the Paralympic Games to educate the public about [dis]abled athletes[1] and disability issues more broadly (Howe 2012; Purdue and Howe 2012a). The erosion of this educational imperative is problematic because it collides with one of the IPC's explicit aims: the effective promotion of opportunities for people with disabilities to get involved in sport. Moreover, the IPC's dictum 'empower, inspire and achieve' (Purdue and Howe 2012b) suggests the Paralympic movement aims to emancipate its athletes in the hope that their performances will inspire others to great achievements.

For over a quarter of a century, the IPC and its network of national affiliates, has placed integration of the [dis]abled in sport firmly on the sporting agenda (Labanowich 1988; Steadward 1996; Vanlandewijck and Chappel 1996) and celebrated closer harmony with the IOC (Howe 2008). To date, this process has been widely accepted as a positive step. However, there has been little critical reflection upon its impact. It is our belief that there is also an assumption, by policy-makers and the public alike, that Paralympic sport is synonymous with the spectrum of disability sport opportunities and this is hindering the expansion of participation and the idea of equality in sport for [dis]abled people.

This paper offers a culturally driven interpretation of human rights and stresses their value in understanding issues related to social justice and the value of sports participation for [dis]abled athletes. Beginning with an outline of Olympic and Paralympic ethos, this paper then turns its attention to the concepts of integration. We then highlight how a human rights lens, aided by a capabilities focus, can be used to illuminate a better understanding of 'sport for all' and the utility of this movement as an educational tool for policy-makers and the public alike. This education, we believe is conditional upon an expansion of opportunities for people with disabilities to engage in any form of sport or physical activity.

Paralympic ethos

Paralympism is an ideology celebrated by the IPC that has been developed in an attempt to establish a universal ethos that extends beyond the Paralympic Games in much the same manner that Olympism has transcended the more established Olympic Games (Howe 2008). Some scholars working within the field of disability sport have argued that a philosophy of Paralympism is not needed because the discrimination of individuals regardless of ability is against the principle tenets of Olympism and therefore this philosophy is appropriate for the Paralympic movement (Landry 1995; Wolff, Torres, and Hums 2008). Clearly there are examples of harmony between Paralympism and Olympism. The motto of the Barcelona 92 IX Paralympic Games 'Sport without limits' resonates with Olympism. Also the IOC's definition of Olympism is believed by some to reflect the centrality of the Paralympic Movement. The fundamental principles of the Olympic movement enshrined in the *Olympic Charter* (IOC 2015) suggest that

> Olympism is a philosophy of life, exalting and combining in a balanced whole the qualities of body, will and mind. Blending sport with culture and education, Olympism seeks to create a way of life based on the joy of effort, the educational value of good example and respect for universal fundamental ethical principles.

It further suggests

> The goal of Olympism is to place sport at the service of the harmonious development of man, with a view to promoting a peaceful society concerned with the preservation of human dignity.

Taking this at face value, 'the expression "Paralympism" appears to be somewhat superfluous, pleonastic; "Olympism" is sufficient … it says it all'. (Landry 1995, 5). In fact during the 1956 Olympic Games 'the International Olympic Committee awarded the Fearnley Cup to the organisers of the International Stoke Mandeville Games [the antecedent of the Paralympics] for "outstanding achievement in the service of Olympic ideals"'(Goodman 1986, 157). According to Parry 'Olympism is a social philosophy which emphasizes the role of sport in world development, international understanding, peaceful co-existence, and social and moral education'. (2004, 1). As a result, compliance with it can add virtue to the Paralympic movement. However, since the Paralympic movement possesses a distinctive cultural history and matching habitus (Howe 2008), it needs to establish a distinctive philosophy. There are also those who advocate simply the use of Olympism (Wolff, Torres, and Hums 2008) as a sign of the growing harmony between the Olympic and Paralympic Movement. In practice, however, both the Olympic and Paralympic games exclude the [dis]abled or to put it another way 'those who can't'. Yes, Olympism may be an inclusive ideology (Wolff, Torres, and Hums 2008) but the practice of high performance sport is not (Jones and Howe 2005). In this sense, when thinking of the equality of opportunities within sport implicit in a 'sport for all' approach both ideologies would fall short.

Almost three decades ago, Labanowich (1988) argued for the aglutination of the Paralympic Games into the Olympics based upon the number of countries and athletes contesting various sports within the Paralympic Games. While there may be some validity in this move we would argue that the essence of Paralympism is worth keeping separate (Howe 2008). In *The Fundamentals of the Philosophy of the Modern Olympics*, Courbertin, the 'father' of the Olympic Movement, highlights the degree to which an extremely exclusionary physical culture may be used as a vehicle to achieve sporting excellence when he states 'For a hundred men to take part in physical education, you must have fifty who go in for sport. For fifty to go in for sport, you must have twenty to specialise, you must have five who are capable of remarkable physical feats'. ([1935] 1956, 53). A place in the Olympic Games is only available to the best among the best. This is not a commonplace situation in Paralympic sport. From data collected in the context of Paralympic sport, it is clear that it is easier across the board to be selected than it is for the Olympic Games (Purdue and Howe 2012a, 2012b). This is the case because many of the classes of disabled athletes struggle to recruit enough athletes to hold an event as there must be 10 athletes on an event world ranking lists for individual sports to be contested at the Paralympic Games (Howe 2008). Even in the cases where there is exceedingly tough competition, notably class T54, the most 'able' of track wheelchair racers, access to technology may be a more determining factor than athletic ability. Of course, access to financial support is a factor in both able and [dis]able sport but there are no events cancelled at the Olympics due to a lack of competitors.

Although the Paralympic movement as a whole does not create a sporting aristocracy in the same extent as Coubertin believed the Olympics did, it has created its own identity. The establishment of the dictum 'empower, inspire and achieve' at the heart of Paralympism is distinct from the Olympic motto. In a sense, the Paralympic Games cannot follow Coubertin's vision of the cycle of Olympiad to provide the youth of any moment in time with the opportunity to compete in an international context. By stating that 'The Springtime of human life is found in the young adult who may be compared to a superb machine up and ready to enter, into full activity'. (Coubertin [1935] 1956, 53–54), Coubertin believed that the Olympics were an ideal environment for fostering the youth. Yet, many athletes who compete in the Paralympic Games are 'eligible' as a result of a traumatic occurrence in life which has no fixed time in the development of the individual. Rehabilitation following traumatic injury can be about creating a new identity equivalent to a re-birth (Seymour 1998). Opportunities to be engaged in sport, including at the high performance end of the spectrum, can play an important part in this process acclimatizing to a 'new' life. In other words Paralympians are generally older than Olympians and rehabilitation continues to be a feature of contemporary disability sport for the disabled.

While the IPC has distanced itself from any explicit discussion of Paralympism, relying instead on the dictum *Empower, Inspire, Achieve*, the vision of the movement is 'To enable para-athletes to achieve sporting excellence and inspire and excite the world'.[2] This vision is designed to create opportunities for athlete empowerment from the point that they enter the sport up to and including the Paralympic Games. It is a lofty goal but all too often the IPC is less concerned with the full participation of [dis]abled people within sport and society more generally And more concerned with replicating the spectacular success of the Olymic movement (see e.g. Howe 2008). As such the Paralympic movement like that of the Olympics 'all benefited from the benign myths of origin rooted in reverential attitudes toward the personal qualities of their respective founding fathers and the salvational doctrine they created'. (Hoberman 1995, 3). While de Coubertin is celebrated as the father of the Olympic movement, Ludwig Guttman a neurosurgeon of German heritage is seen as founding father of the Paralympic movement (Goodman 1986).

Much of the myth surrounding the Olympic movement is that the chivalric tendencies of the movement, the knightly ethos of officials and athletes alike 'was the precise negation of socialist rationality, solidarity, and the improvement of ordinary life for the greatest number'. (Hoberman 1995, 19). The first Paralympians fit this model albeit as wounded ex-servicemen (Goodman 1986; Guttman 1976; Howe 2012). Yet unlike 'Coubertin's original version of the idealized male action figure was the 'débrouillard', the dynamic 'go-getter' type (Hoberman 1995, 22) Paralympians have until recently be seen as charity cases (Howe 2008). As such it is not surprising that the Paralympic Games is seen as detrimental by the broader Disabled Persons movement (Purdue and Howe 2012b). Guttmann best summed this up in 1976 when he scored an own goal in his classic pronouncement '*Mens sana in corpore sano* (Healthy mind and healthy body) should read *Mens sana in corpore sano et invalido!*' (Healthy mind and healthy body or an infirm [weak or feeble] body) (Guttman 1976, 13). This statement highlights that the Paralympic Movement is in part about providing sporting opportunities for less than able bodies. There is of course a spectrum and hierarchy of ability within disability sport. Not everyone with a disability has the physical gifts to be a Paralympian. But there may also be those who have the physical gifts but whose impairment group is excluded from the movement for historical reasons (Howe 2008). According to Purdue and Howe:

> The impaired body, in all its different configurations, should not be treated as the social pariah of the elite sporting world which accommodates a range of able-bodies, be they tall, short, male, female, white, non-white, lean or so muscular to the extent they can be classified as clinically obese. The importance lies in seeing all bodies in the context of the sport in which they compete. All bodies possess limitations, even so called able bodies. It is important to appreciate elite disability sport on its own merits, just as sports fans do across the diverse spectrum of sporting practice that we have socially constructed overtime and engage with today. (2012a, 203)

In spite of these views, we still believe Paralympism personified in the dictum *Empower, Inspire, Achieve* is a goal worth pursuing. However, there seems to be a tendency to present the expansion of the Paralympic Games as the proof that the process of integration of [dis]abled people in sport is being achieved. It has to be emphasized however, that the Paralympic Games are, in many ways, an exclusionary phenomenon and therefore ineffective as the only banner for the widespread expansion of opportunities for [dis]abled people to be involved in sport. There is therefore a need to create and promote more diverse sporting opportunities for the [dis]abled than the Paralympics, if participation in sport is going to be expanded (Nixon 2007). We turn our focus now on the expansion of opportunities more widely. In doing so, we turn our attention to integration in sport, since as we have illustrated above the Paralympic movement is unsuitable to achieve this aim to its fullest extent.

Integration in sport

The integration of people with impairments within society has been seen over the past few decades as a marker of enlightened thinking and a sign of progress towards equality of opportunities to participate in society. The interdisciplinary field of disability studies has however been critical of the concept of integration since it implies to some that people with disabilities are required to change in order to join the mainstream (Northway 1997). Oliver (1996) has gone so far as to suggest that integration is based on concepts of normality. In other words, the concept of integration requires members of the disabled community to adopt an 'able' disposition in order to become members of the mainstream sporting community. Because of these shortcomings, Oliver dismisses integration as being heavily laden with policy rhetoric and sees the term inclusion as more appropriate due to its association with politics (Northway 1997; Oliver 1996). Inclusion, to some, means that members of the disability community have a choice of whether to fully embrace the mainstream community:

> [E]quality (defined as 'the participation and inclusion of all groups') may sometimes be best achieved by differential treatment. This does mean that if oppressed groups so choose they can opt for groups-specific recognition in policy and provision, since within an inclusive approach difference would be accepted or included as a natural part of the whole. (Northway 1997, 166)

Following these debates there has been a shift within the literature on disability from the dichotomy of integration/segregation to another where inclusion/exclusion are seen as a more politically appropriate way to advocate the acceptance of the [dis]abled. We advocate seeing integration as a literal intermixing that entails the culture of both groups adapting to a new cultural environment.

> Community integration is the acquiring of age, gender, and culture-appropriate roles, statuses and activities, including in(ter)dependence in decision making, and productive behaviours performed as part of multivariate relationships with family, friends, and others in natural community settings. (Dijkers 1999, 41)

In other words, integration is 'a multifaceted and difficult process, which although it could be defined at a policy level rhetoric, [is] much less easy to define in reality'. (Cole 2005, 341). The difficulty when evaluating the success of integration policies is that the balance between the philosophical position and the reality (in this case a cultural sport environment) is not always clear or evident. Simply exploring the policy landscape means that any interpretation is devoid of any explicit cultural influences, even though all policy is in fact a cultural artefact itself. This being said, the aim of integration, as we understand it, is to allow the [dis]abled to take a full and active role within society. The ideal would be

[a] world in which all human beings, regardless of impairment, age, gender, social class or minority ethnic status, can co-exist as equal members of the community, secure in the knowledge that their needs will be met and that their views will be recognised, respected and valued. It will be a very different world from the one in which we now live. (Oliver and Barnes 1998, 102)

In the context of sport, the Paralympic movement is often seen as a marker of a successful process of integration of people with disabilities. Yet, this utopian vision is hard to achieve. By its very nature, elite sport is selective as Bowen suggests 'Within professional sport, though, all but the super-able "suffer" from "exclusion or segregation"'. (2002, 71). In other words, the pursuit of excellence that is central to high performance sport, including the Paralympic Games is not an integrated environment. Therefore, it is problematic when the public and policy-makers use the Paralympic movement as a substitute for the disability sport. The act of including certain bodies in the Paralympic Games and excluding others (Howe 2008; Jones and Howe 2005) is in itself not a problem, as they are after all, the pinnacle of disability sport competition. However, this becomes paradoxical when Paralympics are used as synonymous with the whole spectrum of disability sport opportunities.

A successful level of integration is incompatible with the selective nature of elite sport. In order to fully understand the success or failure of integration within sport, it is important to begin to get a sense of the culture of disability sport. Exploring disability sports culture and the place of the Paralympic Games within this is essential to help articulate an agenda to increase participation (Howe 2008). More recent research highlighting the use of Paralympians as role models to enhance integration is problematic (Howe and Parker 2012; Purdue and Howe 2012b) in part because of the limited spectrum of acceptable embodiment within the Paralympic movement.

Given the limitations of using the Paralympic Games in promoting deeper levels of integration of people with disabilities in sporting structures, we turn to the concept of human rights to provide some clarity and enhance our quest for equality.

Human rights and [dis]ability sport

Conceptualization of human rights as the by-product of legislative social justice (Rawls 1971) will be explored in order to establish a framework to determine whether integration within the practice of sport can be seen to have been successful. Human rights are principles regularly used to highlight the wrong being done to an individual on the basis of an infringement of a basic need that is considered inherently 'natural'. The concept of 'natural rights' that should govern humanity comes originally from the work of philosopher John Locke in the seventeenth century (Locke [1689] 1970) and while human rights are not seen to be 'natural' today, there is a sense in the discourse on rights that there is something in all human societies leading us to believe in inherent basic rights (Donnelly 1985; Freeman 2002). However, philosophers remind us that a 'right' can only be achieved as the end result of a moral argument and not as a premise for the discussion in the first place. Following Harris,

when it is said that someone has a right to something, that just means that in all circumstances of the case she should not be hindered in or prevented from doing or achieving something. And if it is asked why she should not be hindered, the answer is *not* 'because she possesses something called a right which has been independently established or "discovered", but simply because there are good moral reasons why it is wrong to hinder her. (1985, xvi)

In other words, for the purpose of this paper, rights should not be seen as an object or a thing an individual possesses but as an entitlement that is the result of a moral or legal argument. As a result, the *Universal Declarations of Human Rights* of the United Nations (UN) was designed to highlight that all people should be treated with respect. This statute should not be seen as an answer to human rights violations but rather as a marker that they do occur. After all the UN is not a utopian body but a political one and since its Declaration was written there have been hundreds of examples of the gaps between the ideology associated with the establishment of universal human rights and the lived reality. As Freeman suggests, 'It is *politically* important that human rights have been codified in international and national law, but it is a mistake to believe that the legalization of human rights takes the concept of politics out'. (2002, 10).

UN human rights legislation is *not* intended to impose a legal obligation upon nation states but offer a set of guidelines that are seen as universally good behaviour. In other words, the *Universal Declaration of Human Rights* outlined what the UN felt were 'moral and political principles that could make a *prima facie* plausible claim to universality' (Freeman 2002, 36). The claims for universality are laid out in *Article 2* which states that we are all entitled to freedoms 'without distinction of any kind, such as race, colour, sex, language, religion, political or other opinion, national or social origin, property, birth or status'. To reinforce this statement, *Article 7* states that all are entitled to equal protection of the law without discrimination. While implementation of human rights was designed to eliminate human wrongs such as political oppression and racism, it is important that their implementation follows on from the development of a just society (Donnelly 1985). Societies continue to place a great deal of importance on human rights. The development of both the *Vienna Declaration* of 1993 on minority rights and the more recent *Convention on the Rights of Persons with Disabilities* of 2006 attest to the fact that human rights are not understood universally. In effect, rights exist in a hierarchy from local customs to national and international laws. As such it is normal for individuals or groups to seek resolution at the most local level before trying to resolve problems at the national or international level. Yet, it is the state (or rather those who signed up to these statutes) that has the obligation towards human rights which leave the way open for unseen violations in the corporate world for example or within the more private sphere of the family. Thus, it seems that despite being essential as an ethical barometer, the concept of human rights lack in practical currency.

In order to address these concerns, we turn to Martha Nussbaum who has developed a version of Amartya Sen's capabilities approach, proposing a list of 10 capabilities that are as universal as possible while being culturally sensitive to the quality of life of individuals (Malhotra 2008; Nussbaum 2006). Defending legal enforcement in terms of guaranteeing a minimum level of enjoyment of each one of these 10 capabilities, the list acts as a litmus test for the quality of life of individuals motivating moral action. As Nussbaum suggests

'[t]he capabilities approach is a political doctrine about basic entitlements, not a comprehensive moral doctrine. It does not even claim to be a complete political doctrine, since it simply specifies some necessary conditions for a decently just society, in the form of fundamental entitlements of all citizens'. (2006, 155)

Nussbaum (2006) uses the case of the disabled population in part because this segment of global society is absent from more conventional understandings of justice as triumphed by Rawls in his influential *The Theory of Justice* (1971). According to Nussbaum Rawlsian 'justice as fairness' is not appropriate for the achievement of social justice for marginalized groups, whereas a capabilities approach evaluates the individual in question in relation to fundamental capabilities such as living a full life, bodily health, freedom of movement and affiliation. Also included are abstract capabilities related to the senses of imagination and the capability for reason. (Nussbaum 2006, 76–78). 'Capability can be regarded as a combination of an individual's personal characteristics (such as age or physiological impairment), [a] basket of purchaseable goods [as a measure of their standard of living] and the individual's environment in the broadest sense' (Malhotra 2008, 85). In other words, a person's quality of life should be determined by the relationship between the physical and social environment and what their standard of living equates to in an individual context. As such the capabilities approach may help overcoming the lack of practical relevance of a human rights approach to equality since the unit of moral analysis is the individual.

The response by the UN to the polemic of various human rights groups against the claims of universalism and the problems associated with cultural imperialism was the establishment of the *Vienna Declaration* of 1993 that included a number of special categories, such as women, children, minorities, indigenous people, disabled persons, refugees, migrant workers, the extremely poor and the socially excluded. There is a need to recognize that these groups are more prone to human rights violations than the majority and they can get lost in the 'universality' of human rights that can so easily if not checked drift towards ideologically inappropriate cultural imperialism (Freeman 2002). To further solidify the case in 2006, the *Convention on the Rights of Persons with Disabilities* placed the spotlight on the disabled community and included *Article 30* which includes suggestions of the right to participate in cultural life including sport. The problem with disability-specific conventions is that it singles out 'the disabled' as a group that are in need of being helped. Many people with disabilities, including a high proportion of Paralympians do not require or accept their status as universally vulnerable people.

The documents revered and celebrated in some disability rights circles inherently lack the clout that disability activists often wish they had. For example, one of the capabilities Nussbaum highlights is the right to play and it is fair to assume we would all agree with that requirement for a good life. Yet, the simple act of playing is clearly distinct from codified professional sport such as the Paralympics. Even nations that enacted all UN human rights agreements have limited resources to police their implementation. Recent work by Friedman and Norman (2009) on legal issues surrounding the rights of Paralympians in receiving equal treatment, in terms of financial and medical support compared to Olympians within the United States, highlights that in terms of equality there is still a long way to go. What makes this position so unpalatable is that the tenets upon which the UN understands human rights are based are clearly inequitable.

MacIntyre (1999) reminds us, however, that *all* human beings are vulnerable and in fact we are dependent rational animals and this being the case we should as a species be more adaptable to a common good.

> [H]ow much is involved in allegiance to a conception of the *common good* that requires both the virtues of the independent practical reasoner and the virtues of acknowledged dependence. For this is a good common to the very young and to the very old, as well as to mature adults, to the paraplegic and to the mentally backward as well as to the athlete and to those engaged in intellectual enquiry, a good that has regard to every vulnerability to which our animal identity

and our animal nature, as well as our specifically human condition expose us.' (MacIntyre 1999, 165–166, empasis added)

It is in the pursuit of a common good that the *Universal Convention for Human Rights* and its various latter day 'offspring' were developed but clearly there are major problems with their implementation in practice. While the concept of human rights developed by the UN were created to limit the power of governments, the problem is that democracy by its very nature limits the rights of minorities (Freeman 2002). In a sense, human rights in individual nations need to be balanced with other values of social order.

Stammer (1999) suggests that we examine power relations and focus upon the role of institutions and social movements in the distribution of it rather than simply exploring the legal formalization of rights. In this respect, the IPC and the broader Paralympic Movement have a role to play through the development of a universalizing ethos. Unfortunately, of late, the Paralympic Movement has become commercialized which traditionally has been counterproductive with respect to human rights in much the same way as democracy was subverted by the will of those individuals with economic power. The problem is that '[t]he Universal Declaration is based on the assumption that individual human rights, including the prohibition of discrimination and the right to practice one's culture, are sufficient to protect cultural minorities'. (Freeman 2002, 114). This is problematic in so far as the political theory of liberal democracy has *not* been designed historically to solve the problems of cultural minorities such as the disabled in part because the classical construction of democracy presupposed culturally unified people. In the sports world, where we champion participation for all we know, there is great diversity and therefore individual differences need to be acknowledged and celebrated. This would lead us to the development of a much broader spectrum of sporting opportunities than currently existing today.

'Sport for all'

Despite its limitations, the concept of human rights appears to have salience when looking at the inequitable treatment of people within the realm of sport. United Nations Educational Scientific and Cultural Organisation (UNESCO) established the *International Charter of Physical Education and Sport* in 1978 which stated in *Article 1* that the practice of physical education and sport is a right for all. This charter, which was updated in 2015 to be more inclusive, ignited the emergence and development of the 'sport for all' movement. The relationship between human rights and sport is further reinforced by a key element within the *Olympic Charter* which means they are even believed to be of concern at the high performance end of the sporting spectrum. Due to the political currency of sport, and despite its limitation, the concept of human rights seems adequate to initiate a discussion of inequality of opportunity for people with disabilities to participate in sport.

Work by Kidd and Donnelly (2000) and Donnelly (2008) highlights the value of researching human rights issues as they relate to sport and see the actions of the UN as a good starting point from which to achieve 'Sport for all'. However, we must be mindful that the promotion of sport over traditional body cultures does not lead to decline in important traditions that may be just good for people's quality of life as the practice of sport. Therefore, the elevation of sport over other forms of physical education (used in the broadest sense) may not be considered a good thing.

Discussion

Traditionally scholars and political organizations such as the UN have turned to human rights to gain equitable treatment of marginalized populations. It is our contention, however, that a reliance upon state governments and international organisations such as the UN is a mistake because all too often the enforcement of legislation is problematic in that it relies upon marginalized individual to take large bureaucratic organization to task if rights have been violated. The act of drafting both the *Vienna Declaration* of 1993 and the more recent *Convention on the Rights of Persons with Disabilities* of 2006 and enacting them within national government is unlikely to facilitate a more integrated society. That being said these statutes have largely been a success in the West if we consider the capabilities approach triumphed by Nussbaum (2006) and focus on sporting participation which we believe adds to a person's *quality of life*.

> The capabilities paradigm is aligned with ideals of human development that gather significant and cross cultural international consensus. In many respects, this dovetails nicely with human rights philosophy with the added benefit that the focus on individual's life assessment acts as a potent weapon against discrimination. (Silva and Howe 2012, 38)

Access to Paralympic sporting provision is problematic for two reasons in terms of equality. Firstly the nature of high performance sport is such that some people will always be excluded due to a lack of ability (Bowen 2002; Jones and Howe 2005) and secondly the vast number of [dis]abled athletes are excluded from the Paralympic provision. As long as policy-makers assume Paralympic sport is [dis]ability sport, many of those with a desire to participate will not have the opportunity.

To the outsider, the inclusion of Paralympic Games within the matrix of the Olympic Festival may be seen as a statement of a progressive world view in tune with the need for adherence to human rights. However, a critical examination highlights that complete integration within sporting provision is problematic. As a result, we can see a heightened social division between the able and the [dis]abled. *Integration* or the intermixing of persons previously segregated has changed little in sport settings. Any real change will take a fundamental shift in social attitudes towards physical difference.

> Only when we acknowledge the near universality of disability and that all its dimensions (including the biomedical) are part of the social process by which the meanings of disability are negotiated, will it be possible fully to appreciate how general public policy can affect this issue. (Zola 1989, 420)

This interpretation should be considered by future policy-makers, nationally and internationally when they try to 'better' the world for marginalized populations such as the [dis]abled. We need to educate the public and policy-makers alike that Paralympic sport is not synonymous with the spectrum of [dis]ability sport opportunities. Until this is achieved, expansion of participation and the ideal of equality in sport for [dis]abled people is some way off. For far too long there has been an assumption that creating policy and legislation will lead to changes in practice. Remember 'sport for all' has been a battle cry for half a century this year – yet it is still a dream – it is time for us to make it a reality!

Notes

1. Throughout this paper we used the term '[dis]abled athlete' because for us there is a double bind in the context of what is commonly referred to as disability sport. Convention within disability studies would advocate adopting a person first approach. In other words, the term for some should be 'athletes with a disability'. Because society largely sees Paralympians as lacking ability, we turn the idea on its head encouraging our readers to exclude the [dis].
2. https://www.paralympic.org/the-ipc/about-us, viewed April 20, 2016.

Disclosure statement

No potential conflict of interest was reported by the authors.

References

Bowen, J. 2002. "The Americans with Disabilities Act and Its Application to Sport." *Journal of the Philosophy of Sport* 29: 66–74.

Cole, B. A. 2005. "Good Faith and Effort? Perspectives on Educational Inclusion." *Disability & Society* 20: 331–344.

Coubertin, P. [1935] 1956. "The Fundamentals of the Philosophy of the Modern Olympics." *Bulletin Du Comité International Olympique* 56: 52–54.

Dijkers, M. 1999. "Community Integration: Conceptual Issues and Measurement Approaches in Rehabilitation Research." *Journal of Rehabilitation Outcome Measurements* 3 (1): 39–49.

Donnelly, J. 1985. *The Concept of Human Rights*. London: Croom Helm.

Donnelly, P. 2008. "Sport and Human Rights1." *Sport in Society* 11 (4): 381–394.

Freeman, M. 2002. *Human Rights: An Interdisciplinary Approach*. London: Routledge.

Friedman, J. L., and G. C. Norman. 2009. "The Paralympics: Yet Another Missed Opportunity for Social Integration." *Boston University International Law Review* 27 (2): 345–366.

Goodman, S. 1986. *Spirit of Stoke Mandeville: The Story of Ludwig Guttmann*. London: Collins.

Guttman, L. 1976. *Textbook of Sport for the Disabled*. Aylesbury: HM&M.

Harris, J. 1985. *The Value of Life: An Introduction to Medical Ethics*. New York: Routledge.

Hoberman, J. 1995. "Toward a Theory of Olympic Internationalism." *Journal of Sports History* 22 (1): 1–37.

Howe, P. D. 2008. *The Cultural Politics of the Paralympic Movement: Through the Anthropological Lens*. London: Routledge.

Howe, P. D. 2012. "Children of a Lesser God: Paralympics and High-performance Sport." In *Watching the Olympics: Politics, Power and Representation*, edited by J. Sugden and A. Tomlinson, 165–181. London: Routledge.

Howe, P. D., and A. Parker. 2012. "Celebrating Imperfection: Sport, Disability and Celebrity Culture." *Celebrity Studies* 3 (3): 270–282.

IOC. 2015. Olympic Charter found at http://stillmed.olympic.org/Documents/olympic_charter_en.pdf

IPC. 2003. *The Paralympian: Newsletter of the International Paralympic Committee*. No 3. Bonn: International Paralympic Committee.

IPC. 2012. "IOC and IPC Extend Co-operation Agreement until 2020." https://www.paralympic.org/news/ioc-and-ipc-extend-co-operation-agreement-until-2020.

Jones, C., and P. D. Howe. 2005. "The Conceptual Boundaries of Sport for the Disabled: Classification and Athletic Performance." *Journal of Philosophy of Sport* 32: 133–146.

Kidd, B., and P. Donnelly. 2000. "Human Rights in Sport." *International Review for the Sociology of Sport* 35 (2): 131–148.

Labanowich, S. 1988. "A Case for the Integration of the Disabled into the Olympic Games." *Adapted Physical Activity Quarterly* 5: 263–272.

Landry, F. 1995. "Paralympic Games and Social Integration." In *The Key of Success: The Social, Sporting, Economic and Communications Impact of Barcelona '92*, edited by M. De Moragas Spâ, and M. Botella, 1–17. Bellaterra: Servei de Publicacions de la Universitat Autónoma de Barcelona.

Locke, J. [1689] 1970. *Two Treaties of Government*. Cambridge: Cambridge University Press.

MacIntyre, A. 1999. *Dependent Rational Animals: Why Human Beings Need the Virtues*. Chicago, IL: Open Court.

Malhotra, R. 2008. "Expanding the Frontiers of Justice: Reflections on the Theory of Capabilities, Disability Rights, and the Politics of Global Equality." *Socialism and Democracy* 22 (1): 83–100.

Nixon, H. L. 2007. "Constructing Diverse Sports Opportunities for People with Disabilities." *Journal of Sport and Social Issues* 31 (4): 417–433.

Northway, R. 1997. "Integration and Inclusion: Illusion or Progress in Services for Disabled People?" *Social Policy and Administration* 31 (2): 157–172.

Nussbaum, M. C. 2006. *Frontiers of Justice: Disability, Nationality, Species Membership*. London: Belknap Harvard.

Oliver, M. 1996. *Understanding Disability: From Theory to Practice*. Basingstoke: Macmillian.

Oliver, M., and C. Barnes. 1998. *Social Policy and Disabled People: From Exclusion to Inclusion*. London: Longman.

Parry, J. 2004. "Olympism and Its Ethic." Paper presented at the 44th International Session of the International Olympic Academy, May/June, Olympia.

Purdue, D. E. J., and P. D. Howe. 2012a. "See the Sport, Not the Disability: Exploring the Paralympic Paradox." *Qualitative Research in Sport, Exercise and Health* 4 (2): 189–205.

Purdue, D. E. J., and P. D. Howe. 2012b. "Empower, Inspire, Achieve: (Dis)Empowerment and the Paralympic Games." *Disability & Society* 27 (7): 903–916.

Rawls, J. 1971. *The Theory of Justice*. Cambridge, MA: Harvard University Press.

Seymour, W. 1998. *Remaking the Body*. London: Routledge.

Silva, C. F., and P. D. Howe. 2012. "Difference, Adapted Physical Activity and Human Development: Potential Contribution of Capabilities Approach." *Adapted Physical Activity Quarterly* 29 (1): 25–43.

Stammer, N. 1999. "Social Movements the Social Construction of Human Rights." *Human Rights Quarterly* 21 (4): 980–1008.

Steadward, R. 1996. "Integration and Sport in the Paralympic Movement." *Sport Science Review* 5: 26–41.

Vanlandewijck, Y. C., and R. J. Chappel. 1996. "Integration and Classification Issues in Competitive Sports for Athletes with Disabilities." *Sport Science Review* 5: 65–88.

Wolff, E. A., C. Torres, and M. A. Hums. 2008. "Olympism and the Olympic Athlete with a Disability." In *The Paralympics: Elite Sport or Side Show?*, edited by O. Schantz and K. Gilbert, 167–175. Maidenhead: Meyer & Meyer.

Zola, I. K. 1989. "Towards the Necessary Universalizing of Disability Policy." *The Milbank Memorial Fund Quarterly* 67 (Supplement 2): 401–428.

About inclusive participation in sport: cultural desirability and technical obstacles

Alexy Valet

ABSTRACT

What does it mean full participation of people with disabilities in 'sports for all'? Beyond the right of access, the right of sharing can enrich the quality of participation in sport, overcoming segregation. But how can be guaranteed an 'inclusive participation' that avoids the double risk of 'normalizing' integration or 'charitable' integration? Beyond 'being among the others' or even 'doing with the others', people with disabilities should also have the possibility to 'be valued by the others' through the real recognition of their participation in this shared sport experience. This is not only a cultural shift, but also a technical challenge, especially to fill the persistent gap between the inclusive rhetoric and the inclusive practices really available to the people. We will explore then the key issue of the technicality of inclusive participation in sport, showing the interest of applying the principles of design for all to the architecture of sports rules.

Preamble

This paper is largely extracted from a research project carried out for over six years through an ethnological investigation that studied the unusual case called 'Baskin' (a form of inclusive basketball) which was developed in Italy in the early 2000s to allow the joint participation of the so-called 'able-bodied' players and of players with disabilities (Valet 2013).

Let us start simply with a general observation. The world which we all live in is often claimed to be more and more driven by a participative culture. While this can be partly true, this world cannot so easily claimed to be dominated by an inclusive culture. Even if there are many initiatives promoting this cultural ideal, at an experimental stage or sometimes more deeply rooted in institutions, it must be still recognized that we live in a society where diversity often continues to inspire mistrust and suspicion, or to generate different kinds of selective and exclusive hierarchies. In this world, getting social recognition requires proofs of excellence, performance and results, because being first, fast and famous, being reactive and productive, arriving before the others means being worthy. Therefore, in this dominant cultural universe, there are also those who inevitably arrive last, behind the others, those who are slower or less productive, less efficient, less 'excellent' ... all this of course in relation to certain normative standards.

Although the complexity of the world always contains heterogeneous social situations and different cultural dynamics, this first unequivocal global picture sets the scene in which the issue of full participation of people with disabilities within sport is meaningful. In fact, it could be argued firstly that sport is a paradigmatic field of society, since it reflects this world of winners and losers, tending to legitimate that weakness and fragility can be crushed, because strength and speed should be celebrated. It could be admitted secondly that disability, as emblematic category of otherness, testifies a fragility that is continuously emphasized or even produced by the 'ableist' culture and rhetoric of performance, as pointed out in disability studies.

So, what can full participation actually mean in the sport field, and especially in 'sports for all'?

Introduction

The concept of 'participation' can be closely connected to the concept of 'inclusion', as it clearly appears in the by now famous *Index for Inclusion* (Booth, Ainscow, and Kingston 2002), even if both terms 'are not synonymous', as Patrick Fougeyrollas reminds (2010). *More inclusion* means *more participation*, quantitatively and qualitatively; while *more participation* does not always mean *more inclusion*, because segregated participation is possible. In fact, Fougeyrollas specifies that an inclusive situation may be considered 'as quality indicator of the environmental factors determining the quality of social participation of populations with diversified personal features'. Therefore, referring to the idea of an 'inclusive society' (Gardou 2012), inclusion is a cultural matrix facilitating a democratic and humanizing social participation, through supporting settings that become more responsive to the diversity of people's backgrounds, interests, experience, knowledge and skills. Besides, Henri-Jacques Stiker (2001, 35) talks about inclusiveness in terms of 'participative integration' associated to a culture of 'republican and democratic fraternity'. Then he specifies, as if there was the risk of remaining just a good intention, that this idea 'should be inscribed in laws and in apparatuses [through a] long technical road', which consists in giving a technical foundation to this idea of inclusiveness, in order to ensure the process of its effective implementation.

In any case, social participation is the wider concept, which can incorporate sporting participation – either in an inclusive or a segregated version. Close to the concept of 'social engagement', social participation can be defined in general terms as 'the extent to which an individual participates in a broad range of social roles and relationships' (Avison, McLeod, and Pescosolido 2007). In this perspective, key elements of social participation include activity – *doing something* – interaction – *at least two people need to be involved in this activity* – social exchange – *the activity involves giving or receiving something from others* – and lack of compulsion – *there is no outside agent forcing an individual to engage in the activity* (Prohaska, Anderson, and Binstock 2012). In the field of disability, social partici-pation takes the same meaning, while questioning who 'the others' should be and insisting on the idea of free choice. Indeed, it can be also linked to the notion of *community-based integration* on one side – avoiding or reducing effects of segregation's dynamics – and to the *Independent Living Movement* on the other side – affirming the claim of self-advocacy (Fougeyrollas 2010).

Likewise, 'participation' is a key concept in the Convention on the Rights of Persons with Disabilities (CRPD) (UN 2006)[1] and in the International Classification of Functioning, Disability and Health (WHO 2001).[2] If we refer to the medical model of disability, 'participation' can represent a way to reduce the social consequences of being disabled; while in the social model, 'participation' and 'disability' can even be presented as opposite concepts, because in that case disability would refer to a limitation of participation in social life due to an environment which is maladjusted to the individuals. Without entering directly in this specific debate, we will argue in favour of the general epistemological position of Gilbert Simondon that allows us – we believe – to go beyond this opposition. But overall, we consider that *social participation* can definitely contribute to impact positively the quality of life of all individuals, with and without disabilities, and that policies promoting social participation – under certain conditions – can contribute to create a caring and resilient community, or, in other words, a more inclusive society.

Although we will never reduce the social participation to the sporting participation, as well as we will never reduce the latter to a participation exclusively spent on the sports ground during a competition, because we are convinced that the essential of social life occurs mainly apart from this delimitated space and time, we choose, however, to focus on this symbolic form of participation of individuals with and without disabilities, within the reduced and artificial context of a team sports match. Indeed, we would like to propose to consider this specific situation as a technical dispositive invented and built by humans, and at the same time as a symbolic dispositive representing an interesting metaphor of society. Sport can represent a democratic fiction that codifies the collective relationships thanks to an architecture of rules specially thought for that. The rules regulate the relationship between teammates (cooperation) and between opponents (competition), and also regulate the evaluation of everybody's participation, through an objective assessment of the results produced by all practitioners.

Now, what will guide our reasoning here is the sporting participation of all, in the case of great heterogeneity of abilities. And we will see that many cultural and technical difficulties have to be challenged, before reaching the possibility itself to apply the principles of 'design for all' (Barnes 2011) to a sport, allowing a shared participation between individuals with and without disabilities. Indeed, if the offer of sporting activities to people with disabilities was structured during the twentieth century by the struggle for the 'right of access', this dynamics is gaining in complexity in the latest twentieth century and in the beginning of twenty-first century around a new struggle, which adds the 'right of sharing' and the 'right of choice' (Valet 2015). Yet, even if the inclusive culture is gaining ground within sport, a technical concern for redefining the architecture of rules of inclusive sports still seems to be required in order not to remain just in a rhetoric stage and to avoid the double risk of 'normalizing' or 'charitable' integration (Valet 2013).

Contextualizing and conceptualizing 'inclusive participation'

Contextualizing 'inclusive participation' in sport

We choose to address the sporting participation by putting at the centre the more general issue of individual and collective life quality, according to a holistic approach of human life, which has multiple scientific roots, as, for instance, the Human ecology theory

(Bronfenbrenner 1979). Participation may appear initially as an end, but it can in fact be directed or manipulated in multiple ways, to serve various purposes. Following the approach defended by Silva and Howe (2012; and in this volume), we choose an ethically oriented approach to conceive participation as a means to serve 'human development', individually and collectively, according to the *capabilities framework* of Amartya Sen applied to the specific field of adapted physical activity. By keeping in mind this global formulation of life quality, we want to better situate the sporting participation and its potential role in a wider life project, through a global overview on the multiple forms of social participation of people with disabilities, representing many actual challenges in different fields:

- *Education* (by accessing a school life, by sharing it with others and by making choices within a personal trajectory going from kindergarten to university or vocational training);
- *Work* (by accessing a professional life, by sharing it with others and by making choices within a personal trajectory which respects skills and aspirations);
- *Free time* (by accessing free time activities, by sharing them with others and by making choices among a range of valuable options within fields like sport, theatre or other cultural activities and artistic events);
- *Citizenship* (by getting actively involved in participative democracy, through assuming responsibilities in associative life and other civic or politic engagements);
- *Personal relationships* (by having the possibility, like any others, to live a self-regulated dependency to relatives, to develop friendships, to experience love life and sexual life).

The structure itself of the CRPD provides a good indicator to contextualize the role of sport in the life of people with disabilities: among its 50 articles, 1 is specifically dedicated to 'Participation in cultural life, recreation, leisure and sport' – a fact, which underlines the idea that the sporting participation is only one single modality of social participation. This is not at all to minimize the effects that sport has on life, but rather to facilitate the permanent awareness that the sporting participation only partly feeds a deeper desire of human development, namely that of social participation. This helps to remind all sport actors – teachers, instructors, representatives – of the critical principle that behind athletes there are always individuals, in all their complexity.

Nevertheless, the sport field can be considered as a paradigmatic field in social life. It gives us the opportunity to analyse the participation of people with disabilities in a particular context which incorporates one of the main obstacles of participation in our society, as common as hard to challenge: *competition*. Indeed, the promotion of participation of people with disabilities in our society usually forces to explore two different strategies, both seeking to avoid the unfair situations generated within the tricky context of competition. The first strategy is simply to eliminate and replace the competitive environment with a more individualized or cooperative setting, recognizing that there are many different modalities to creatively express one's own potential beyond the mere competitive performance, an approach that can also facilitate participation in a more inclusive situation. The second strategy is to accept to keep competition, on the condition that it is limited to a separate participation, within segregated ability groups. Both strategies can be pursued in sport at large: the first one through didactic activities in Physical Education (PE) or through different cooperative games and creative physical activities, within more or less formalized contexts; the second one either through the same above-mentioned contexts or most of the time through codified sport disciplines.

For our part, in this paper we would like to explore a third strategy, challenging two usual dangers of the competitive logic: *standardization* and *segregation*. In other words, on one side this strategy is likely to go beyond the normative culture which implicitly promotes the 'survival of the fittest', and, on the other side, to go beyond the only right to access to a separate sporting participation in segregated practices, thanks to the possibility for all to live a shared competitive experience in some 'inclusive sports'. Let us point out the historical dynamics allowing the emergence of this strategy. After being excluded from participation in many spheres of social life, people with disabilities could *access* a special education system, and some of them could progressively access new emerging sports specifically built for their ability's profile (like wheelchair basketball since Gutmann's experiments). This paradigm shift from 'exclusion' to 'specialization' led to the institutionalization of the disability sports movement, in parallel to the regular sports movement (Ruffié and Férez 2013). While this opening of sport to increasingly diversified recipients refers to an undeniable *democratization process*, this welcome to new audiences was achieved primarily through a *communitarian model* of participation, because people with disabilities had the opportunity to practice sport only 'among themselves', forming a special category compared to the sporting 'ableist' standards. In fact, nowadays, we sometimes refer to this kind of opportunity as a segregating tendency, since participants are likely to have no other choice than being involved in a separate activity, as if they were assigned to live 'among themselves'. Since participants are grouped according to their abilities or their medical diagnosis, these segregated situations deprive everyone of the freedom to choose with whom to share their life experiences and what form of participation they want to be involved in, even in *free time activities* like sports.

That is why we can sum up stating that the inclusive participation implies a culture which respects the 'right of access' to overcome the exclusion, the 'right of sharing' to overcome the segregation and the 'right of choice' to overcome the welfarism. These three complementary rights determine the quantity and quality of participation. We think this focus on 'inclusive participation' in sport can bring interesting insights because combining competition and inclusion is precisely one of the most difficult challenges in the dominant sport culture as well as in our society.

Conceptualizing 'inclusive participation' from Simondon's epistemology

Taking inspiration from the epistemology of Gilbert Simondon, we can say that *participation* can encourage the human 'individuation' of people, thus simultaneously their biological, psychic and social formation (Barthélémy 2014). Moreover, we propose to associate *social participation* to the 'transindividual' dimension of human realities. The latter – beyond the merely inter-individual dimension – reflects the transversal movement across the limits of the interior (psychic: 'I') and the exterior (collective: 'we'), through an associated medium – symbolic and technical – which connects both (Combes 1999). Actually, inspired by Simondon's concept, Bernard Stiegler talks about 'transindividuation', socializing its use within the Ars Industrialis working group, whose vocabulary explains this as follows: 'The social at large is produced by transindividuation, that is to say through the participation within associated environments where meanings are shaped (the meaning is between or through the beings)' (Stiegler and Petit 2013).[3]

Why do we refer to Gilbert Simondon's philosophy about participation of people with disabilities? Because, according to this author, the reality of *being* is fundamentally linked to the reality of *doing* (in an extended meaning). Being is a process of becoming, not a state; and it is an operative and relational process. Then the individuals are simply defined by their process of 'individuation'. This 'ontogenesis of individuals' displaces the question of human essence to that of 'constitutive relation'. Gaston Bachelard already called for this shift that considers *being* less a substance than a relation: *according to his view, far from the idea that the being illuminates the relation, it is the relation that illuminates the being.* But Simondon goes further, by insisting also on the operative 'ontogenesis of individuals' (Barthélémy 2014), because relations are always mediated by practices and objects (symbolic and technical). So the practices between individuals precisely feed *their being*. In other words, as a singular node of relationships, each person is essentially a relational matrix whose life is a complex, dynamic and operative process, directly depending on its associated environment.

Consequently, the quality of social participation determines the quality of individuation of each person, with or without disabilities, and thus one's 'human development' according to the 'capabilities' approach. Reciprocally, since the individual and the collective are fundamentally linked by their 'mutual and constitutive co-individuations' (Combes 1999), the individual human development – through social participation – favours the building of a collective which is more sensitive to the contribution of all, leading thus to a participative democracy generating a collective human development. Let us just precise that *participation* needs to be 'ethically reasonable' to guarantee the mutual human development of the individual and the collective, as underlined by the ethically normative approach of 'capabilities' (Silva and Howe 2012).

This epistemological precision on 'transindividual' concept and on a 'relational ontology' is especially important when it comes to discuss about the participation of people with disabilities, because it critically questions the classical view on the individual autonomy – as the smallest unit of social life – and on the individualistic ethic of independence. In this new theoretical framework which makes place to the *relationship* – as the smallest unit of social life – and to the ethic of 'self-regulated dependency' (Goodwin 2009) or more generally to the ethic of interdependence (Gilligan 1982),[4] the individual fragility has to be thought as a social potential,[5] that the collective can realize or not. If so, the collective can transform the fragility into a cultural resource, by building a more empathic community that learns to value and takes advantage of the participation and contribution of all.

Besides, the Vocabulary of Ars Industrialis indicates that 'transindividuation is the transformation of the "I" by the "we" and the "we" by the "I", and in the same movement the trans-formation of the technico-symbolic environment which makes it possible for the different "I" to meet each other as a "we"' (Stiegler and Petit 2013).[6] Therefore, a second interest in getting inspired by Simondon's philosophy emerges more and more clearly. Indeed, beyond the value of his ontological approach to discuss the *participation* of people with disabilities, we want to underline the key concept of 'transindividuation' to discuss also the specific issue of *inclusion,* by asking a critical question: who is the 'we'? Is it a particular 'we', that is to say a special group, or is it a more universal 'we', humanity?

Finally, the concept of transindividuation suggests a last critical consideration that is going to become decisive below. Building an inclusive culture (symbolic level) can connect the 'I' in an unified 'we', but this requires the related invention of inclusive practices (technical level) to embody this culture in action. Actually, academics do not fail to distinguish, on the one hand, the discourses on inclusive culture that are growing up in our society, including the sphere of sport, and, on the other hand, the actual practices embodying these words that do not necessarily grow at the same rate. Indeed, when it comes to turn into real activities the desire to develop inclusive participation in sport, a persistent distance between saying and doing can be highlighted (De Pauw and Gavron 2005; Thomas and Smith 2009). Now, if the issue is to fill the gap between rhetoric and practices, the transindividual perspective helps us to conceive the 'inclusive participation' not merely as a cultural challenge but as a technical one. Similar to Jesus, Sanchez (2005) when he suggests thinking 'the accessibilisation' as both a cultural and a practical support for mainstreaming, we also propose to associate these two dimensions, cultural and technical, by recognizing their reciprocal causality, but also by giving its full value to the technical dimension which is often underestimated.

Indeed, by considering the technical architecture of the activities as a key factor in determining the quality of participation in sport, we will examine the way the inclusive culture can crystallize in codified sporting practices shared by all participants. Through the analysis of the technical difficulties to develop this kind of inclusive participation, we will explore different cultural meanings of participation of persons with and without disabilities in sport.

The technicality of 'inclusive participation' in sport

Taking off the barriers to participation one by one ... towards inclusive settings

The 14th World Conference on Sport For All, held in Beijing in 2011, stated: 'Sport For All is a movement promoting the Olympic ideal that sport is a human right for all individuals regardless of race, social class, ability or sex'. But concerning people with disabilities, what right does it talk about? Is it only a right to 'access' or also a right to 'share'? Indeed, even if 'access' and 'accessibility' are often the privileged terms in the institutional speeches, the question remains the same: are we talking about an access limited to 'separate activities' or also about an access extended to 'shared activities', too? *Who is the 'we'*, as we were asking above? This distinction suggests to interrogate the *nature of participation* in sporting activities for people with disabilities. If access is not guaranteed, participation is not possible. If access is guaranteed, participation is possible, but it can be implemented in a segregated or inclusive way. Actually, if the right of sharing is not guaranteed, then inclusion is not an available option for people with disabilities and the right of choosing the nature of their participation vanishes.

Moreover, beyond the interest to clarify step by step the interconnections between these three rights, as we're going to propose, we would like to underline the ambiguity of what 'sharing' a common experience means, by soliciting the conceptual distinction suggested over 30 years ago by theorists in special education between three types and levels of 'integration' (Söder 1980): the 'physical integration' that requires *to be among the others*; the 'functional integration' that means *to do with the others*; and the 'social integration' that consists in *becoming valued by the others*. While the first level is not too difficult to achieve, the second level is a bit more complicated to implement, but the third level (incorporating both first levels) remains the highest cultural and technical challenge, largely yet to be met.

Indeed, this distinction will prove expedient for discerning different levels of participation quality for people with disabilities in mainstream settings.

(1) We can agree with the idea that accessibility is a key condition of participation. But then we must interrogate the very *nature of accessibility* on which the quality of participation depends. The only concern on physical accessibility of installations and equipment does not guarantee a full participation, because the activities provided in these accessible venues can be inaccessible, due to the inadequate requested tasks. Therefore, the practical question is: once inside the gym, what activities are provided and for whom? A shift to a wider conception of accessibility is required, towards a material and immaterial accessibility. In the field of sport, it appears necessary to take into account also the politics of sport organizations and the techno-pedagogical architecture of the activities themselves. This is the central question of the design of sporting disciplines.

(2) We have to recognize that enormous efforts have been already done during twentieth century, concerning the design of sporting disciplines for people with disabilities in order to allow them an accessible participation, through the invention of special sports. But then, even after having solved the problem of accessibility in terms of sporting infrastructures and design of the activities provided – at least for people who have no severe impairments –, it must be recognized that we have not even totally reached the first level of inclusiveness described above, yet: the 'physical integration' allowing the individuals with disabilities to 'be among the others'. Indeed, this co-presence is only a possibility depending on the hosting politics of local sport organizations, because the latter can be specialized in particular sport activities for a special public only, for example, with disabilities. Even in case of a mainstream club – which has decided politically to open its doors to the participation of everyone – the activities proposed are often still specific to different categories of participants (with or without disabilities). Because of a timetable distributing the different workouts over several time slots for the different groups of participants, we still may refer to 'separate activity' among the options of the 'inclusion spectrum' (Black and Williamson 2011). So 'being among the others' still should be an explicit political and cultural choice.

(3) Let us say that the politics of local sport organizations can facilitate the 'physical integration' of people with disabilities 'among the others', by creating favourable conditions for all participants to meet each other in the social life of the club; this means having more chance to eventually share some informal moments, not through the sport practice itself but 'around' it, usually outside the sports ground or the gym. Besides, this posture seems to be the one that emerges implicitly from the policies towards the participation of people with disabilities evoking 'mainstream' sports venues or organizations. Nevertheless, without providing further explanation, this position does not give any guarantee to people with and without disabilities to live really 'mainstreaming' sports experiences and to share sport emotions in the same activities (at the same time and in the same space). That is why at a more committed level, a sport club can also decide explicitly to host in 'mainstream' activities all interested participants regardless of their abilities, seeking to bring together people with and without disabilities in the same sports

ground or the same gym. In that last case, the sport club cannot anymore be concerned only with the 'physical integration' (being together), promoting just a joint presence in the same space and at the same time; in fact, the concern of 'functional integration' (doing together) emerges as well, promoting a joint participation. By encouraging the participation of people with disabilities in 'mainstream' sports *organizations,* but also in 'mainstream' sport *activities,* we can admit that this sport politics is the most committed position towards inclusive participation that emerges in the CRPD (article 30), if we leave aside, here, the important question of 'self-advocacy' of people with disabilities.

(4) Below, we argue that this stage is the most tricky one. Indeed, in contrast to an inclusive participation, it can be admitted that the most spontaneous and easy participation PE in sport occurs when there is some homogeneity of abilities among participants, because the relative uniformity of their respective skills does not impose to be concerned as much about a diversification of the tasks or about a specific pedagogical mediation for some group members. But what does it come to pass if a club seeks the 'functional integration'?

Challenging the barriers to a quality inclusive participation: the key issue of sport design

As we have already mentioned above, beyond the inclusion rhetoric, to put into action the inclusion principles within sport, and especially in team sports, it is very important to be deeply aware of the practical difficulties that represents the reconciliation attempt between sporting participation and heterogeneity of capacities. In this regard, it is necessary to exit from a priori normative considerations, such as the supposed positivity of inclusive settings, by practically evaluating the actual effects on the lives of those concerned.

Instead of wondering if sporting logic harms inclusion, Nigel Thomas and Andy Smith wonder conversely to what extent the inclusion harms sport or, more exactly, to what extent the current application of inclusive policies generates an adverse impact on individual sporting participation of the disabled population (Thomas and Smith 2009). Therefore, they provide a review of literature on this issue, focusing in particular on PE and sport at school. Thomas and Smith clearly warn against the risk of 'unplanned outcomes' of inclusion policies, especially when young disabled people are required to 'fit into' existing curricula.

> Inclusion has been uncritically accepted and considered as an unambiguously good and desirable policy response designed to bring about, among other things, more equitable and positive experience of PE and school sports for all pupils, but particularly those with disabilities and SEN'. However 'the first point to note in this regard is [...] the failure of social policies [...] to achieve their declared objectives, and to have outcomes that were unplanned and which may even be the opposite of what was intended. [...] In contrast to the expectations of policy-makers and government ministers, the emphasis on inclusion appears to have had the effect of further alienating some pupils (particularly those with more severe needs) from others. (Thomas and Smith 2009, 113–114)

We can summarize the analysis of the authors about these unplanned effects through their recognition of a weakening of both quantity and quality of participation of pupils with disabilities in PE and in sport at school, when they are involved in inclusive settings compared to the special school sector, and even more if pupils have severe impairments or if the activities are competitive team sports. Indeed, beyond a lower involvement, it can be observed as well a perverted participation quality because the 'same opportunities' offered to all tend to be 'more unequal' for those whose profile of abilities is far from the norm.

To face the difficulties of this 'joint participation' in sporting mainstream settings, especially in competitive team sports, we can identify three paradigmatic strategies (as ideal-type models), which determine every time a different quality of participative experience.

(1) The first way of proceeding, which is usually not an explicit strategy, is selecting only few athletes with disabilities, those who are 'able enough' to be integrated in a mainstream activity and to compete in such group of participants, because their sporting skills are not so far from the standard. Using sport competition as a proof of 'ableism', the cultural challenge here is to go over the preconception associated to the medical diagnosis of some disabled individuals, limiting this critical questioning to the ones who have the lightest impairments compared to the norm and who can really compete with able-bodied athletes on a fair base. In that case, the right of sharing and the full participation in sport for all is allowed for disabled people on condition to fit to the sporting requirements of mainstream activities. Few of them may claim 'to be among others', 'to do with others' and even 'to be valued by others', sportingly speaking, because they are *like others* or *'comparable' to others*. Is it a question of 'merit' for those who can (who are able enough) and 'demerit' for those who cannot (who are too disabled)? To avoid the sacrifice of sporting competition on the altar of 'inclusive participation', is it admitted that some peoples with disabilities should be sacrificed on the altar of a standardized sport excellence? Is there no risk to fall into the danger of a 'normalizing integration' (Valet 2013)?

(2) The second way, which usually needs an explicit strategy, is supplying personal support to people with disabilities to encourage their participation in mainstream activities. The required sporting skills remain more or less the same, even if the general approach is more flexible. But, if participants with disabilities cannot satisfy these requirements, they are helped by assistants. For that reason, the competition is not as emphasized as in the 'normalizing integration' because it must be *facilitated* to all. This personal support is offered by specifically trained staff, volunteers or other players accepting to act as volunteers; and it is usually proportional to the level of disability. The cultural challenge is simply to recognize the moral necessity of embracing human diversity in sport by denying the exclusion of the weakest and, on the contrary, by making space to their fragility through a protection system that allows them to participate. In that case, the right of sharing and the participation in sport for all is allowed for people with disabilities, provided that they are given enough support in quantity and quality. All of them may claim 'to be among others', 'to do with others' and in a special way 'to be valued by others', because the *few others* are those who accept to be the supporting intermediates. Is it a question of 'generosity' or 'compassionate welfarism'? To avoid the sacrifice of 'inclusive participation' on the altar of sporting selective process, is it admitted that some participants without disabilities should be sacrificed – sportingly speaking – on the altar of 'assistantship'? Is there no risk to fall into the danger of a 'charitable integration' (Valet 2013)

(3) The third way, which is still rarely explored even if it is gaining ground, suggests to bring back at the centre the key issue of activity's design, questioning to what extent the rules of sport disciplines themselves can also represent a barrier to shared accessibility and inclusive participation. This leads at the same time to understand how the rules could represent, on the contrary, the technical potential to overcome this kind of barrier, giving access for all to a common sport experience, valuing the specific skills of individuals with disabilities – whatever the nature or level of impairment – and facilitating a 'fully shared participation' in competitive team sports. The cultural challenge here is to overcome the double risk of 'normalization' and 'commiseration' which represent in our view the two paradigmatic dangers of whatever sporting experience within inclusive settings at large, namely when there is a minimum of heterogeneity of abilities in the group of participants (with or without disability presence). As we suggested above, a shift is required, from a concern for physical accessibility to mainstream sports venues to a deeper and broader concern for pedagogical accessibility to mainstreaming sport activities, by moving from the design renewal of the sport infrastructures to that of the sport activities themselves, with their architecture of rules. In that case, the right of sharing and the participation in 'sport for all' can be allowed for people with disabilities, provided that the cultural challenge is transformed into a technical challenge, developing a pedagogical engineering process focused on the activity itself, so that everybody can really claim 'to be among others', 'to do with others' and even 'to be valued by others'.

It must be considered that the architecture of rules of each sport, resulting from a pedagogical engineering process, constitutes the potential 'inclusive technicality' of sport participation. Researches that focus on this specific question are not yet numerous, and existing practices are even more rare. However, we can mention Baskin ('Inclusive Basketball') that well illustrates this third strategy, and has actually inspired this paper (Valet 2013).

Conclusion

The possibility to choose a sporting activity is an important dimension of social participation and quality of life of disabled people as any other person. Article 30 of the Convention on the Rights of Persons with Disabilities (CRPD), focused on 'cultural life, recreation, leisure and sport', underlines in its paragraph 5 the need to promote the right of participation of disabled people to 'disability-specific sporting activities' (designed especially for them), but also the need to 'encourage and promote their participation [...] in mainstream sporting activities'. Nevertheless, this last reference to 'mainstream sporting activities' is ambiguous: is it about sporting activities whose local organizational context is open to all, or sporting activities whose practice itself is open to all? Does the CRPD mean that the proposal of a joint participation in any sport is only a matter of good will of the local organizations?

As indicated by Thomas (2011) in the Summary Report to the European Commission called *All Sport for All: Perspectives of Sport for People with a Disability in Europe*, 'research suggests that while mainstreaming has been central to sport policy for disabled people, it has not necessarily – thus far at least – been successful and may need further dialogue between all agencies to establish which models are most likely to work'. We have argued that the persistent gap between inclusive rhetoric and inclusive practice can be partly understood by the undervalued technical challenge of an activity-centred approach. Indeed, while many other factors are usually taken into account in the sport policies promoting the inclusive participation of people with disabilities, we note that the 'design for all' of the sporting activities is an almost forgotten question. However, the pedagogical technicality of each activity – its internal logic (Parlebas 1991) – may be a key issue in our view, as technical support for materializing the social and cultural phenomenon of inclusion.

Actually, when it comes to the issue of sporting public policies that promote the mainstreaming of people with disabilities, the main identified challenges are limited to the training of personnel involved, the quality of support offered and the accessibility of infrastructures (Thomas 2011), and sometimes also the institutional integration between the specialized and ordinary sports governing bodies (Sorensen and Kahrs 2006). But in these only terms, we can easily understand that even the most fervent policies on inclusion for disabled people would hardly be able to put into action a real inclusive participation if the offered sporting activities are not themselves really 'designed for all'. Marcellini 2005) confirms that an innovative engineering process would be necessary to practically achieve the joint participation in sport practices.

That's why we personally think that using 'mainstream' term is ambivalent – similar to the use of 'normalization' until a recent past – especially talking about sporting activities, the dominant design of which is still largely consistent with a hegemonic model of sport that tends, if not to exclusion or segregation, to a selective integration ('normalization') or a philanthropist integration ('charity'). Because, as we have seen, 'being among the others' or even 'doing with the others' is not enough to guarantee a full inclusive participation in sport. Still the 'physical integration' and the 'functional integration' should be completed by the possibility for people with disabilities to 'be valued by the others' through the recognition of the value of their participation in a shared sport experience. That's why we believe that it is still preferable to talk explicitly about 'sports designed for all', 'inclusive sports', or even 'generalized sports', rather than 'mainstream sporting activities'. This would give to 'Design for all' or 'Universal Design' (Article 2 of the CRPD) the status of an applied concept, and not just an abstract one linked to a general statement of intent.

The idea of sports designed for all suggests that humanity cannot conceive sport anymore in terms of a sacred object which can't be modified and which suits only to an elected population. It is not anymore people who must be adapted to the already existing sports, but the sports system which should be designed to suit to the people, moving from the requirement of an ergonomic design of human beings, to the one of an ergonomic design of sports and society. We have argued that this shift is not only a cultural challenge, but also a technical one. The architecture of rules of sports designed for all should provide a new performance assessment system, objectively based on the different personal abilities. So, within sport, are we sure that the rules should be the same for all, in name of justice? On the contrary, if people are different, then the rules should precisely not be the same for all, in name of equity. Valuing the relative performance (and not the absolute one) promotes a new idea of justice and fairness in sport and it suggests to change from a privileged heroism to a more merited, pluralist and democratic one. Baskin may be an interesting example of a codified inclusive sport, likely to reflect this paradigmatic renewal of the democratic project within sport, based on equity (Valet 2013).

In conclusion, even if the literature already addresses in a certain way this issue of accessibilizing sporting activities in terms of inclusive design, it is mostly to highlight the necessary professional skills to adapt all the local activities to each singular person and to each contingent situation (Black and Williamson 2011; Fitzgerald 2009; Garel 2007). In this perspective, the most important points seem to be the adaptation theory (Sherill 2003), the principle of pedagogical flexibility and the didactic craft logic that characterize the Adapted Physical Activity and its 'epistemology of singularity' (Pépin 2005). But the situation is very different when it comes to the building of a common sporting culture, at a global scale, since the question of the universal design of new codified sports emerges. In fact, beyond the Olympic Games and the Paralympic Games, what about the symbolic and technical building of the 'All'ympic Games' (Valet 2015)?

Notes

1. 'Full and effective participation and inclusion in society' is one of the eight guiding principles of the Convention.
2. 'Participation' is one of the three main components of the systemic conceptual approach of ICF: 'body functions and structure', 'activities and participation' and 'personal and environmental factors'.
3. See also: http://arsindustrialis.org/transindividuation (our translation).
4. Linked to the ethic of care, Carol Gilligan proposed the principle of *interdependence*, rather than that of *rules*, as the basis of morality.
5. To deepen this point, we have proposed elsewhere to refer to a 'cross-border epistemology of fragility' (Gardou and Valet 2014).
6. See also: http://arsindustrialis.org/transindividuation (our translation).

Disclosure statement

No potential conflict of interest was reported by the author.

References

Avison, W. R., J. D. McLeod, and B. A. Pescosolido. 2007. *Mental Health, Social Mirror*. London: Springer.
Barnes, C. 2011. "Understanding Disability and the Importance of Design for all." *Journal of Accessibility and Design for All -JACCES* 1 (1): 55–80.
Barthélémy, J.-H. 2014. *Simondon*. Paris: Les Belles Lettres.
Black, K., and D. Williamson. 2011. "Designing Inclusive Physical Activities and Games." In *Design for Sport*, edited by A. Cereijo-Roibas, E. Stamatakis and K. Black, 195–223. Farnham: Gower.
Booth, T., M. Ainscow, and D. Kingston. 2002. *Index for Inclusion: Developing Play, Learning and Participation in Early Years and Childcare*. Bristol: Centre for Studies on Inclusive Education. http://www.eenet.org.uk/resources/docs/Index%20EY%20English.pdf.
Bronfenbrenner, U. 1979. *The Ecology of Human Development: Experiments by Nature and Design*. Cambridge, MA: Harvard University Press.
Combes, M. 1999. *Simondon, Individu et collectivité: Pour une philosophie du transindividuel*. [Simondon, the Individual and the Collective: For a Philosophy of the Transindividual]. Paris: Presses Universitaires de France.
De Pauw, K. P., and S. J. Gavron. 2005. *Disability Sport*. Leeds: Human Kinetics.
Fitzgerald, H., ed. 2009. *Disability and Youth Sport*. London: Routledge.

SPORT AND DISABILITY

Fougeyrollas, P. 2010. "Social Participation". In *International Encyclopedia of Rehabilitation*, edited by J. H.Stone, and M. Blouin. Center for International Rehabilitation Research Information and Exchange (CIRRIE). http://cirrie.buffalo.edu/encyclopedia/en/article/335/.

Gardou, C. 2012. *La société inclusive: parlons-en!* [Inclusive Society: Let's Talk About It!]. Toulouse: Erès.

Gardou, C., and A. Valet. 2014. "La recherche sur le handicap : légitimité d'un savoir de l'intérieur" [Disability Research: The Legitimacy of an Inside Knowledge]. In *Épistémologie du corps savant. Tome1 Le chercheur et la description scientifique du réel* [Epistemology of the Knowing Body. Volume 1: The Researcher and the Scientific Description of Reality], edited by M.Quidu. 111–134. Paris: L'Harmattan.

Garel, J.-P. 2007. "Accessibiliser les pratiques sportives" [Accessibilizing Sports Practices]. In *Désinsulariser le handicap. Quelles ruptures pour quelles mutations culturelles ?* [De-isolating Disability. What Ruptures for What Cultural Shifts?], edited by C.Gardou, and D.Poizat, 223–231. Toulouse: Erès.

Gilligan, C. 1982. *In A Different Voice*. Cambridge: Harvard University Press.

Goodwin, D. L. 2009. "Self-regulated Dependency: Ethical Reflections on Interdependence and Help in Adapted Physical Activity." In *Ethics, Dis/ability and Sports*, edited by E. Jespersen and M. McNamee, 86–98. Abingdon: Routledge.

Marcellini, A. 2005. "Un sport de haut niveau accessible? Jeux séparés, jeux parallèles et jeux à handicap." [An Accessible High-Level Sport? About Separate Games, Parallel Games and Games with Handicap Systems] *Reliance* 15 (1): 48–54.

Marcellini, A. 2007. "Inspirer la 'mixité sportive'" [Inspiring 'Sporting Mixity']. In *Désinsulariser le handicap. Quelles ruptures pour quelles mutations culturelles ?* [De-isolating Disability. What Ruptures for What Cultural Shifts?], edited by C.Gardou, and D.Poizat, 233–240. Toulouse: Erès.

Parlebas, P. 1991. "Didactique et logique interne des APS." [Didactics and Internal Logics of Sport Activities] *Revue EPS* 228: 9–14.

Pépin, C. 2005. "Activités Physiques Adaptées. Une épistémologie des singularités". In *Dossier Handicaper : Education corporelle et handicap (Eduquer 11)*, edited by Marcellini, Anne, 87–99. Paris: L'Harmattan.

Prohaska, T. R., L. A. Anderson, and R. H. Binstock. 2012. *Public Health for an Aging Society*. Baltimore, MD: JHU Press.

Ruffié, S., and S. Férez, eds. 2013. *L'institutionnalisation du mouvement handisport (1954–2008). Tome 1: Corps, Sport, Handicaps* [The Institutionalization of the Disabled Sports Movement (1954–2008). Volume 1: Body, Sport, Disabilities]. Paris: Téraèdre.

Sanchez, J. 2005. "L'accessibilisation, support concret et symbolique de l'intégration" [The Accessibilisation: Concrete and Symbolic Support of Integration]. In *Handicap et environnement* [Disability and Environment], edited by J.-F. Ravaud and F. Lofaso, 33–47. Paris: Frison-Roche.

Sherill, C. 2003. *Adapted Physical Activity, Recreation, and Sport: Crossdisciplinary and Lifespan*. New York: McGraw-Hill Higher Education.

Silva, C. F., and D. Howe. 2012. "Human Development and Capabilities Approach: Does APA Need It?" In Dossier Playing Sports with a Disability: Adapted Physical Activity (APA), edited by C. Boursier, and H. Benoit. *La nouvelle revue de l'adaptation et de la scolarisation* 58 (July), 37–46. Suresne: INS HEA.

Söder, M. 1980. "School integration of mentally retarded – analysis of concepts, research and research needs". In *Research and development concerning integration of handicapped pupils into the ordinary school system*, edited by The National Swedish Board of Education, 1–30. Stockholm: NBE.

Sorensen, M., and N. Kahrs. 2006. "Integration of Disability Sport in the Norwegian Sport Organizations: Lessons Learned." *Adapted Physical Activity Quarterly* 23 (2): 184–202.

Stiegler, B., and V. Petit. 2013. *Pharmacologie du Front National, suivi du Vocabulaire d'Ars Industrialis* [Pharmacology of the National Front, followed by Vocabulary of Ars Industrialis]. Mesnil-sur-l'Estrée: Flammarion.

Stiker, H.-J. 2001. "De l'exposition des infirmes à la classification des handicaps: Quelle éthique?" [From the Exhibition of Infirms To the Classification of Disabilities: What Ethics?]. In *Une nouvelle approche de la différence: Comment repenser le 'handicap'* [A New Approach to the Difference: How to Rethink the 'Disability'], edited by R. De Riedmatten, 23–36. Geneva: Médecine et Hygiène.

Thomas, N. 2011. *All for Sport for All: Perspectives of Sport for People with a Disability in Europe.* Reporting Factsheet. Disability Sport Policies. Lyon: European Observatoire of Sport and Employment.

Thomas, N., and A. Smith. 2009. *Disability, Sport and Society. An introduction.* Abingdon: Routledge.

Valet, A. 2013. "Sport, inclusion, innovation. Le cas italien du Baskin (2001–2013)" [Sport, Inclusion, Innovation. The Italian Case of Baskin (2001–2013)]. Doctoral diss., Université Claude Bernard Lyon 1. December 09. http://www.theses.fr/2013LYO10318.

Valet, A. 2015. "Sport et handicap: du droit d'accès au droit de partage. Le cas du Baskin" [Sport and Disability: From the Right of Access to the Right of Sharing. The Case of Baskin]. In *Dossier 'Le bonheur est dans le sport'* [Happiness is in Sport], edited by M. Meziani. *Revue Juridique et Economique du Sport* 151: 21–22.

Forgotten bodies – an examination of physical education from the perspective of ableism

Martin Giese and Sebastian Ruin

ABSTRACT

Contemporary social interpretations of the body are multifaceted, and in some cases paradoxical. Looking at the field of sport, there exists a global trend for (normalized) physical self-optimization on the one hand, and the struggle to achieve acceptance of (bodily) diversity triggered by the societal claims for inclusion on the other hand. Thus, this theoretical paper seeks to subject social practices in the area of sport (with a main focus on Physical Education in schools in Germany) to critical reflection especially in the light of inclusive ideals, using the perspective of ableism. The meaning of the body in Physical Education in Germany is examined in an explorative and hermeneutic manner. The observations make clear that there are numerous barriers facing the project of inclusion at all levels. In addition to obvious problematic implications in sport, the examinations reveal that conceptual and curricular approaches also imply exclusionary potentials that increasingly shift the focus onto the individual and his or her self-determined and self-reflected movements in the world.

The body in contemporary Western societies – paradoxical interpretations

Even though our everyday world seems to be becoming ever more disembodied as well as increasingly diffuse, the body has paradoxically been thrust more and more into the focus of individual members of our contemporary Western societies (Gugutzer 2015). The particular bodily practices that have their origin in the context of sport have taken on greater significance in a broader social context. In addition to the ever-expanding role that sport plays in the entertainment industry (Barrow 2013) and the close give and take between trends in sport and popular culture (Alkemeyer and Schmidt 2003) the most striking development has been the worldwide fitness boom. As fitness becomes a 'lifestyle', it exerts more influence on the everyday habits of an ever-wider swath of the general population (Andreasson and Johansson 2014). The growing popularity of phenomena that have a tendency to technologize the body such as 'human enhancement' (Allouche et al. 2015) and 'self-tracking' (Frandsen and Lomborg 2016) can also be attributed to the explosive growth of the fitness movement. Increasingly, the moulding of the individual body seems to have become a project that concerns itself with the formation of an identity (Shilling 2012). To a certain extent, these are processes of discursive formation, presumably through socially constructed, seemingly self-evident norms (Foucault 1977), such as the body images and fitness ideals propagated in the media (Duncan 1994) or normative concepts dictating the sort of movements that are proper in a sports setting (these could be traced back to aesthetic considerations or more often to a desire to increase effectiveness) (e.g. Jaric and Markovic 2004).

People whose bodies[1] do not conform to these ideals – possibly as a result of their own free choice but also due to a particular physical disposition – are at risk of being excluded to some extent because they do not conform with the normative expectations of society. Against the trend of physical self-optimization, their bodies are in danger of being forgotten or failing to meet the 'benchmark of humanity' (Overboe 1999, 24). They are denied the status of being *fully human*. Parallel to these developments, there are now increasingly vocal demands – as can be seen in the various debates surrounding equal opportunity and an inclusive society (i.a. Nussbaum 2006) – that being a global society, we should make it possible for groups, such as persons with disabilities, who have been the subject of frequent discrimination, to participate more widely in society at large (e.g. UN 2006). This in turn means that we will be confronted with interpretations of the body that are sometimes incompatible with ingrained societal norms. Bodies that had by and large been marginalized or did not conform to the norm have now been recognized as having equal rights and thus equal value. This is especially significant for persons with disabilities – in particular as a result of the UN Convention on the Rights of Persons with Disabilities (CRPD) (UN 2006). However, the same is equally true for other discriminated groups such as those based on ethnicity, gender or sexual orientation (i.a. Booth, Ainscow, and Kingston 2002). The main point of interest relating to these efforts, as far as the body is concerned, is the basic tenet that all bodies should be accepted on their own terms and treated equally – this also includes bodies that may be perceived as strange, different or also those that have special needs or are especially fragile.

Therefore, the common practices in the area of sport, which are, as touched on above, in many ways entangled with implicit normative expectations, should be reflected critically. This might be an important step to encourage full participation in the cultural phenomenon of sport. Hence this paper examines in a hermeneutic and explorative manner the role and the understanding of the body in the field of sport. To do so, the external perspective of ableism is used as a critical perspective to look on empirical outcomes of existing exemplary studies on the body in this field. Mainly this paper thereby focuses on Germany as a country with a strong emphasis on segregation as for example a glance at the German educational system demonstrates (Amrhein and Booth 2014).

The body in physical education – the tension between efforts to promote inclusion and exclusionary mechanisms

Although sport is without a doubt a field that encompasses a complex range of activities, the following will primarily focus on the examination of sport in educational environments, in particular in the school setting. After all, these settings can be said to play a central role in wider efforts to create an inclusive society (Ainscow and Miles 2009). If one understands school to be a social institution that carries out societally organized socialization (Fend 1975), it becomes obvious why this is a setting where it is possible to set societal change into motion. This is surely not only true for cognitive aspects – which are, most of the time, the primary association that comes to mind when discussing learning at school – but it is also equally applicable to interpretations and experiences of the body. Following Merleau-Ponty ([1945] 2011) it is even possible to argue that it is only possible for a human being to participate in the world through being and having a body. Thus, Physical Education (PE) takes on a special role within the school curriculum in efforts to promote inclusion, and due to this subject's close connection to the body – at least as it is taught in the German tradition – PE is considered one of the fundamental building blocks of a holistic school education (Laging 2005). The human body here has always been considered as a basic aspect of school education – as an unavoidable part of every educational process (Meinberg 2011). The fact that human beings are anchored in the world through their body, which is both a carrier and producer of meaning, is traditionally used to justify PE processes (see e.g. Grupe 1984). Therefore the body – at least in Germany – plays a central role in the actual changes towards an inclusive educational system.

Although progress has been uneven in different countries, international efforts to promote inclusive education system have meant that the societal changes regarding the body outlined above have become even more relevant. On the one hand, school as a social institution must – in addition to expanding students' knowledge and competencies – transmit socially relevant values and norms to the next generation; this could include a constructive accepting attitude to (physical) diversity or disability (Booth, Ainscow, and Kingston, 2002). On the other hand, the individual actors that make up the institution (students, instructors, etc.) bring their own value systems that have resulted from their own process of socialization with them into the school setting, thus implicitly shaping the institution – often this remains hidden below the surface and is not subject to a process of critical reflection. However, this is a possible avenue for the entry of societally conditioned norms about the body (e.g. norms relating to sport outside of school contexts and movement culture). And these norms, which may imply discriminatory attitudes, are therefore often antithetical to inclusive ideals. Reconciling these two opposing world views poses significant challenges (Booth et al. 2002; UN 2006). In addition these sort of normative expectations may also be replicated or amplified through pedagogical traditions, curricular objectives and most of all by the way that individual teachers structure their lessons. Bodies that do not conform to the normative categories and do not possess the abilities deemed necessary (in a normative framework) as a prerequisite for accessibility may be in danger of being 'forgotten' in this setting.

In an international comparison, the German school system can be seen as a tradition that has placed a particularly strong emphasis on segregation (Amrhein and Booth 2014). As such, the transition to an inclusive school system in Germany must work against an extremely strong bias towards the status quo (Reich 2012b), which makes the process in Germany a very interesting case for academic study. In representative surveys, both teachers and parents have been found to hold quite critical attitudes to inclusion if it affects their immediate environment (e.g. Heyl and Seifried 2014; TNS Emnid 2014). However, the central issue with these surveys – as well as the wider academic discourse on inclusion – is that the structures and organization of the German school system are principally concerned with boosting students' performance on cognitive dimensions – rarely the body. This tendency to neglect the body can perhaps be seen as emblematic of the hegemony of the rational in the sense of the Cartesian mind-body dualism, which has been so instrumental in shaping our intellectual history right into the modern era (Meuser 2004). And thus the German pedagogical tradition as a whole – despite the existence of a PE tradition that can be traced back to the work of philanthropists in the nineteenth century (Krüger 1993) – has until now shown little if any interest in tackling issues connected with the body (Reich 2012a). And when this does occur, the (physical) education is, even to this day, an extension of the ideal of *kalokagathia* extolled by classical Greek writers (cf. Giese 2016), which claims that human existence is characterized by 'a unity of mind and body as well as the basic principle of balance in a person's education' [*mens sana in corpore sano*] (Grupe 1993). Along with this comes the implicit assumption that 'certain moral qualities are connected' to the practice of such an ideal (Weiler 2003).[2] A serious examination of the meaning of the body in (inclusive) school settings – in particular in the context of vulnerability, dependence or insufficiency – is for the most part still a desideratum.

With this in mind, we will examine the meaning of the body in PE at schools in Germany on three levels in the following section. We will apply the perspective from ableism in our hermeneutic and explorative analysis to help us reflect on and break out of exclusionary, discriminatory and prejudicial bodily practices. After a brief discussion of ableism, the hermeneutic reflections on the meaning of the body follow. These are broken down into the level of teaching methodology and conceptual framework, the level of educational policy and curriculum and the level of the classroom and the people directly involved in instruction.

Ableism

Traditionally, imperfection has had no place in the pedagogy of PE. This thesis also explicitly includes the area of so-called 'rehabilitation sports' or 'disabled sports', which serve to maintain the status quo stabilizing the system, (also) functioning as a vehicle for discrimination and exclusion. So-called 'disabled sports' become most interesting precisely at the point where they undermine the intrinsic logic of performance and enhancement in sport:

> And we are not only the high-toned wheelchair athletes seen in recent television ads but the gangly, pudgy, lumpy, and bumpy of us, declaring that shame will no longer structure our wardrobe or our discourse. We are everywhere these days, wheeling and loping down the street, tapping our canes, sucking on our breathing tubes, following our guide dogs, puffing and sipping on the mouth sticks that propel our motorized chairs. (Linton 1998, 3)

So ableism is used to reflect and deconstruct hidden barriers to inclusion. It is here that ableism can make a significant contribution by allowing us to gain a new perspective that transcends superficial phenomena. This specific viewpoint will make it possible to reflect on barriers to inclusion that are intrinsic to the field on a structural level. In this sense, ableism enables us to access the grammar of exclusionary processes. With this in mind, romanticized body images are problematic. They do not take into consideration the fundamental dependency, poverty and fragility of the human condition and repeat the narrative that the sculpting of the body through training is a path towards a metaphorical paradise. In order to highlight the discriminatory potential of such images, the following section will take a closer look at ableism, a vein in disability studies that, as will be shown, is particularly suited to raising awareness of implausible or illegitimate attributions of abilities in a sport pedagogic context.

The starting point for this line of argument is that, from the perspective of ableism, disability is located in the intersubjective and social *attribution of abilities* and not seen as something different form the norm. This approach questions the assumption that a person's abilities must be understood as an individual category. Individual abilities are also understood as socially conditioned and culturally impregnated external attributions.

> It is essential to problematize and criticize [...] irrational, injurious, cruel and implausible conceptions of ability (and thus disability) that are intimately linked with concepts of meritocracy, performance-based distributive justice and, in general, all social models based on ideals of liberalism that, in the guise of neoliberalism, have pushed all of the contradictions of this political and anthropologic theory of the individual nature of ability to its limits: the winner takes all. (Buchner, Pfahl, and Traue 2015, 1)

Here it is important to consider that these invisible institutionalized attributions of 'abilities do not seek to describe an ontological but rather a *relational* quantity that is tied to the social position of the observer and thus shaped by ideology' (Buchner et al. 2015, 2). In this respect, the view of ableism is always a sociocultural one as long as the causes can be located in central attributions of abilities coming out of a neoliberal social order that requires the production of healthy and productive workers to maintain the invisible logic of the system:

> Phantasms of perfect bodies, ableistic prototypes, as they can also be found in the construction of neoliberal fitness ideals, serve therefore to develop a corporal standard. To produce such a normative matrix it is necessary to have a constructive external, a negative template, which can be consulted by individuals as a set of criteria for sorting into 'normal' and 'not normal'. (Buchner et al. 2015, 3)

This approach makes clear that it can no longer be enough to think about and reflect on disability from the perspective of the individual, rather it is much more about looking at the situation as intersubjective, scientific and social production mechanisms and achievement imperatives, which have the potential to profoundly affect every individual in every stage in life and also in an explicitly threatening manner.

> Assignments of abilities must be judged as illegitimate if they lead to acts of cruelty [...] or injustice [...] or they are the results of acts of cruelty or injustice. Assignments of abilities are cruel if they lead to illegitimate violence [...] against people, for whom these abilities are temporarily or permanently denied. Assignments of abilities must be deemed unjust if the access to qualification systems is blocked. (Buchner et al. 2015, 6)

Thus, ableism opens up the possibility to adopt an analytical perspective that, in the context of sports pedagogy, seems to be particularly suited to – in the sense of the above quotation – turning our gaze to unjust assignments of abilities with regard to the body, allowing us to reflect on their discriminatory and exclusionary potential. Naturally, the point here is not to fundamentally challenge or even reject the often necessary and legitimate assignment of abilities. The goal is rather to promote the sensitization to and disruption of illegitimate assignments of value. The above discussion should have made sufficiently clear that ableism can be located in the context of a radical critique, which provides the appropriate analytical and descriptive instruments for analysis that can help to sensitize us to body ideals that are as romantic as they are discriminatory.

Teaching methodology and conceptual framework

Building on the perspective on conceptions of the body in the area of PE in schools presented in the previous sections, we will now examine this on the level of teaching methodology and conceptual framework. In the discourses on teaching methodology conducted here, the ultimate aim is to come to an agreement on the goals, methods and content of how PE should be, whereby fundamental issues concerning what meaning should be assigned to body in school PE programmes can be handled implicitly. Correspondingly, we will provide a sketch of the current discourse in Germany, which even to this day includes questionable approaches to teaching methodology, and evaluate this from the perspective of ableism.

Towards the end of the 1960s, extracurricular sports were becoming more popular and began to exert more influence on PE in schools; they became an important benchmark for achievement. The subject in school was charged with preparing students for the societal norms and expectations that were operative in the popular and competitive sports outside of the school context (Kurz 1993). This new programme of reform brought about a large number of new approaches to sport pedagogy that can be taken together as the *pragmatic qualification* approach (Prohl 2010). From the 1970s until the mid-1990s, these approaches dominated sports pedagogy in Germany and are still influential today. To a greater or lesser extent, such PE classes have the goal of achieving purposeful and rational enhancement of the physical performance of young people using evidence-based methods from exercise science (Ruin 2015). Their bodies are for the most part reduced to functional objects and used 'consciously as a means to an end' (Söll 2000, 6). Using systematic exercises, normalized skills are taught. Often in these types of PE courses, the bodies of young people are subjected to an inflexible performance standard to which they must conform (Ruin 2015). Last but not least, the focus on the societal expectations for extracurricular sports and the associated body ideals comes extremely close to a normalization of bodies (Foucault 1977). The individuality of the students (and their bodies) has a tendency to be seen as an error that should be corrected.

The ableistic view on this teaching methodology clearly states that this is an example of illegitimate assignments because the educational potential or achievement of the individual, among other factors, is linked to the ability to be able to reproduce normative skills. In this model, imperfect or insufficient bodies are – to return to the metaphor of forgotten bodies – simply ignored. Naturally, there are people (including those with disabilities) who do not possess these skills, and they will not only be denied the chance to succeed in such educational settings but will also be silently labelled per se as incapable of being educated.

Motivated by the wide-range of criticism of extracurricular competitive and high-performance sport (instrumentalisation of the body, doping, commercialisation, etc.), a countermovement to the pragmatic qualification model began to form in the 1970s in West Germany: the *critical emancipatory* approach (Prohl 2010). Although it is often in conflict with the pragmatic qualification school, this line of discourse is still a significant voice today. Here it is not the social context of sport that is the crucial benchmark, but rather these (certainly more diverse) approaches advocate for a form of PE in which pedagogic concerns take centre stage (Prohl 2010). Building on earlier approaches (i.a. Grupe 1984) these new methods refer to concepts from anthropology, which are combined with historical and sociological viewpoints. Thus, for example, it is not possible to establish a general, abstract meaning of sport activity, but rather the meaning as well as the essence of sport is only performed in the interpretation of the media and signs that are representative of this activity (Ehni 1977). As such, the facticity of young people's specific 'everyday reality' must be accepted in PE, but at the same time the 'pattern' of this everyday reality must be laid bare (Ehni 1977). The main focus is, therefore, not on teaching different sports and physical skills, but rather leading the students towards a mature and preferably autonomous relationship to sports and movement. One relevant point here is the exposure of complexes of meaning relating to the social phenomenon of sport that have until now been largely accepted without critical reflection in the field. Here too the goal is to encourage a deeper examination of the body. The person is seen as an 'active designer' and a 'subject of his or her own doing' and is emphatically not reduced to the 'object of his or her life circumstances' (Funke 1991, 15).

In this direction in sports pedagogy, the (autonomously moving) body as a medium of experience and expression is the focal point, where it is also possible at the same time to encourage critical reflection on instrumental functionalist tendencies to co-opt the body in the context of sports (Ruin 2015). Even though this approach includes a moment of (self-) reflection that accompanies the educational process, and these reflections are without a doubt in accordance with the assumptions of classical educational theory, this approach nevertheless will also exhibit a potential for discrimination in the case of persons with disabilities: the first major issue seems to be that here too there is a fundamental unspoken assumption that the individual is able to move autonomously and purposefully and that he or she can, at will, access a functioning body that is largely unrestricted in its ability to move. On a fundamental level, we are dealing with a romanticizing '[p]hantasms of perfect bodies, ableistic prototypes' (Buchner et al. 2015, 3). In addition, educational achievement is linked to a highly developed capacity for abstraction and reflection. In ableistic terms, the *ability* to be educated is inherently coupled with the *ability* to reflect. Because of this, persons with mental disabilities or a behavioural disorder might for example not be able to engage in the working relationship that would be necessary because of internal conflicts within the person and would thus experience unspoken discrimination and exclusion. Ableism makes clear in this context that the responsibility for stigmatisation, exclusion and disability cannot be ascribed to the individual; these are instead first actively generated by the discursive body image.

Over the course of heated discussions on the direction and legitimacy of German sport pedagogy in the second half of the 1990s, many in the field began to increasingly see the need to mediate between individual and social demands; the goal was to reconcile the two opposing camps (see above) with one another. This was an effort to stay true to the pedagogic concept of 'Educational' PE (*erziehender Sportunterricht*) whose central motivation is a double mission (encouraging the students' development through movement, play and sport while simultaneously integrating the cultural aspects of movement, play and sports). 'Educational' PE was originally proposed in the state-wide curriculum reform in the German state of North Rhine Westphalia, and it gradually began to take hold in a large number of curricula thereby making a lasting contribution the theoretical discourse on teaching methodology. Up to the present day, this is considered to be the prevailing didactic concept (Stibbe 2011). The next section will examine in more detail how the body is understood in 'Educational' PE in the context of the curricular discourse.

Educational policy and curriculum

While didactic concepts presented in the previous section took the form of recommendations, educational policy and curriculum, in the form of state-mandated standards, set out in detail how PE should be structured in the schools. These standards (curricula) arise out of the charged relationship between educational policy and teaching methodology. On the one hand, they are an expression of educational policy standards and accordingly must be legitimized (Aschebrock and Stibbe 2007). On the other hand, they are for the most part oriented to the pedagogic and didactic discourses that are current at the time (Krick and Prohl 2006). Curricula for PE classes document the institutional standards against the backdrop of the zeitgeist in educational policy, sport pedagogy and society as a whole.

The pragmatic qualification model (see above) that dominated teaching methodology for almost a decade also gave rise to a 'pragmatic action-oriented' phase in curriculum development that left its mark on the vast majority of West German curricula in the 1980s and 1990s (even continuing to influence some until around the turn of the century) (Aschebrock and Stibbe 2007). Ruin documented some cases where there is an increased focus on enhancing performance and the body is then understood as a functional object that is to be disciplined (Ruin 2015). Due to the emphasis of topics based on extracurricular sports, the imperative is to shape the students' bodies to conform to the requirements of particular sports. This implicitly transports an idealized normative expectation of a healthy, defect- free, fully functioning body capable of performing (athletically) at a high level. The type of PE curriculum propagated here seems to be in many ways a body-focused process of normalization.

As already mentioned, the introduction of 'Educational' PE in the curriculum around the turn of the century marked the beginning of a new phase in curriculum development in which athletic and pedagogic concerns tended to be given equal weight (Aschebrock and Stibbe 2007). In this context, new interpretations regarding the body become apparent, as analyses by Ruin have revealed (Ruin 2015). With the focus now on an autonomous subject who takes responsibility to educate him- or herself, PE today should encourage the student to engage in a process of experience and reflection that consciously seeks to counteract the notion of the body as an object to be disciplined and normalized. More often the pedagogic efforts highlight self-guided initiation of and reflection on how to deal with bodily experiences, bodily expression and sensual perception, which once again underlines the high cognitive demands that were problematized above. Although this approach seeks to reconcile competing view on didactic methods, it becomes clear that when viewed through the lens of ableism on the level of the grammar of exclusionary mechanisms that, among other issues, needs of persons with disabilities are also not addressed here and the concept of the human being and his or her physical constitution as metaphor for paradise is further replicated. Education as a process of self-formation remained dominant as an act of self-reflection and continued to ignore the real circumstances of the subject. It was especially this project of perfecting, enhancing competencies and 'higher education' that caused people (from sociocultural and economically disadvantaged backgrounds and those with disabilities) to fail. (Stinkes 2008, 87)

At this point, subjecting this to an ableistic analysis would mean focusing less on the material substrate of the education process and instead taking a closer look at grammatical mechanisms that gave rise to it. Here self-determination should not be understood as autonomy that is tied to complex cognitive structures and processes, which often do require a capacity for quite extensive rational and reflexive thinking that can hardly be expected from many people. From an anthropological point of view, self-determination seeks to recognize that humans are able and wish to understand, evaluate as well as live their life in a specific way. (Zirfas 2012, 80)

Thus, 'Educational' PE must also be seen as having an exclusionary potential because its basic theoretical assumptions also reproduce the romanticized bodily phantasms silently without critical reflection or critical (self-)distance. Conversely, it is important to look critically at what the inherent body images mean for the bodies that do not possess the intended abilities. This is not a purely academic question. The previous discussion has already made clear that the so-called 'affected' persons will be denied access to educational facilities and excluded from school education, and the principal goal of promoting inclusion as well as the CRPD will come to nothing – a failure that brings with it dire consequences for persons with disabilities.

As a reaction to Germany's unexpectedly poor performance in international comparative studies on academic performance, the political pressure from the educational establishment became ever greater in Germany (and elsewhere) to introduce graded, standardized and competency-oriented curricula. Almost all federal states in Germany yielded under this pressure in their PE curricula (Ruin and Stibbe 2014). The competency-oriented PE curricula currently in use must therefore be understood as a result of a political agenda rather than an expression of the discourse on didactic methods (Stibbe 2013). Mandatory, standardized competencies that students are expected to achieve – mostly with normative performance expectations – are the focus of these condensed curricula. There is little in terms of concrete advice on how to structure the actual lesson. The general goals still include numerous references to 'Educational' PE, but in the end this is not taken into account in the rigid performance standards at the centre of these curricula (Ruin and Stibbe, 2014). The body is thus again cast as an object that has a strong potential for optimization, and should be optimized, as was already the case in the curricula during the pragmatic action-oriented phase. The main focus is on teaching a more functional understanding of skills that allow the students to do specific types of sports with a tendency towards an increased focus on boosting performance (Ruin 2015). Apparently, young people's bodies should be made to approximate the normative expectations of a high-performance, healthy and fit body (Ruin 2014).

If we return to our initial goal that, given the increasing awareness of inclusion or the provisions of the CRPD, now is the time to finally grant bodies that may be considered strange and different the access to PE in schools that they are entitled to, ableistic analyses show that the teaching methodology in PE as well as the curriculum seem to be more suited to body images and bodily practices that harbour an exclusionary, discriminatory and inhibitory potential when it comes to persons with disabilities. The present generation of competency-oriented curricula, which – also in relation to the body – implicitly transport a neoliberal fantasy of efficiency and feasibility (Thiele 2008), seem to further aggravate this tendency, a blatant contradiction of the intended long-term goals of fostering a just society that respects the needs of marginalized and discriminated groups of people.

Actors at the classroom level

In addition to conceptual and curriculum considerations, the particular notions of the body that guide the actions of specific actors within schools are of great relevance to this investigation. Here particular focus is put on the teaching staff since it is them who ultimately deliver the lessons. Although the teachers can undoubtedly be influenced by teaching methodology, the conceptual framework, as well as educational policy and curriculum, it can equally be assumed that they will bring certain individual attitudes and dispositions, acquired either through the socialization process they have gone through (in their professional environment), or possibly also via other preconceived assumptions that they may have, which are not necessarily in harmony with the ideas inherent in teaching methodology or curricular considerations. Furthermore, in the subject of PE, the de facto quasi-traditional position regarding extracurricular, high-performance and competitive sport widely disseminated in the media (see above) has since the 1970s also become particularly relevant for teachers. Against this backdrop, many teachers' notion of 'sport' as an object (to teach) is presumably substantially determined by their own active history of participation in sport (Reinartz and Schierz 2007). This could very well be accompanied by a tendency towards performance and comparison-oriented norms.

An interview study conducted by Meier and Ruin with 48 PE teachers in various different types of schools suggests that PE teachers tend to adopt more of a functional view of the body (see Meier and Ruin 2015). Here the body is often seen as akin to a 'tool' utilized by its owner to perform sport. From this perspective, PE devotes its efforts to training and optimising this tool. In the case of most teachers, this interpretation also goes hand in hand with normative expectations about how the body should move, what is the ideal bodily constitution and above all what constitutes a 'healthy' body – children and teenagers with disabilities are for example in many cases deemed 'sick' and their adverse deviations from the norm are presented by teachers as a problem (Meier and Ruin 2015). Nevertheless, the study also makes clear that there are teachers who perceive the body as something far beyond simply a functional object. For these teachers, PE is about encouraging individual experiences of the body and reflection thereupon that foster the development of the student's personality. Emotional and communicative aspects that extend beyond the domain of sport are also given significant time and attention. In addition, a definite orientation to individual abilities and needs of students seems to take place. These teachers – increasingly women, armed with experience in teaching heterogeneous groups of students – were however in the minority of the subjects surveyed (Meier and Ruin 2015).

What has hitherto been the critical nature of the attitude adopted towards people with disabilities seems thus also to be reflected in the stance of the actors involved. Subliminal, invisible and illegitimate attributions of abilities are not only manifest themselves in the teaching methodology or educational policy settings, these are also, not at all surprisingly, subliminally brought to bear through the actors who operate in the pedagogic environments described.

Conclusion

Starting from the paradoxical contemporary social interpretations of the body this investigation has sought to subject the increasingly questionable social practices in the area of sport to critical reflection especially in light of inclusive ideals of encouraging full participation for all people in the cultural phenomenon of sport. In particular the rift between normalized physical self-optimization, on the one hand, and the struggle to achieve acceptance of (bodily) diversity, on the other hand, seems to be impossible to bridge. The main focus of this investigation was the area of PE in schools.

The critical reflections presented make clear that there are numerous barriers facing the project of inclusion in the area of PE in schools (as far as the level of the body is concerned). First and foremost are the obvious traditional implications in sport, which assume that all people are endowed with the same potential to enhance physical performance by appropriately training the body. In sport pedagogy settings, where these implications are still at work even to this day, this means that a great number of persons with disabilities are deemed unfit for education if they do not meet the existing physical normative expectations. These sorts of implications can be noticed on the level of teaching methodology and the conceptual framework of PE – in particular in the prominent approaches advocated by the *pragmatic qualification* school – as well as on the level of educational policy and individual programmes in numerous curricula. It is hardly surprising that this has a ripple effect all the way down to the level of individual actors in the classroom. Thus, it appears that PE teachers also have a general tendency to instrumentalize the body. Those holding this basic attitude tend to focus on deficits when dealing with persons whose bodies deviate from the norm. This is without a doubt an obstacle for full and equal participation for all young people in PE at school. Even without drawing on the perspective of ableism, these circumstances have already been subject to critical reflection in sports pedagogy. It has recently been suggested that the expansive and all-encompassing tendency of the neoliberal project is particularly to blame for the current state of affairs; educational policy has become infused with neoliberal thought, where decisions have been reduced to a process of efficient generation of human capital (Macdonald 2011; Ruin 2014).

Moreover, the theoretical perspective of ableism can be useful in revealing that conceptual and curricular approaches also harbour exclusionary potentials that increasingly shift the focus onto the individual and his or her self-determined and self-reflected movement in the world. The *critical-emancipatory* approach to pedagogy as well as 'Educational' PE have been widely represented in curricula and are two of the principal currents in education that play a central role in this context. On the surface, these approaches seem to be well suited to the project of inclusion due to their emphasis on individuality (Tiemann 2012); however, they are based on the fundamental anthropological assumptions of humans that move under their own control and have the capacity to reflect on themselves, which – as the article shows – also excludes certain people. Those who are not able to reflect on themselves and their own movement to the degree required will be 'forgotten', just as those who are not able to achieve the envisioned range of experience of movement due to purely physical restrictions or also because of psychological or cognitive dispositions. In the present discourse on sport pedagogy in Germany, these sort of critical moments have until now, however, often been overshadowed by the more superficial imperative to focus on inclusive education (Giese 2016).

Although the approach is somewhat different, the so-called 'rehabilitation sport' as well as the so-called 'disabled sport' reveal themselves to be a similar sort of paradox. From the perspective of ableism, these movements can be seen as playing conservative, system-stabilizing roles, and the so-called disability sport is, when all is said and done, only in the spotlight when – to the detriment of the stated goal of proclaiming the participatory nature of the event, which clearly goes down well in the media – it succumbs to the logic of high-performance and continual enhancement intrinsic to sport. Presumably, this does little to encourage a truly equitable participation in sport.

Surely, one area that gives us reason to be optimistic about the outlook for active participation in PE at school can be found in the analysis of the actors at the classroom level. In the process of planning lessons and setting learning objectives, some PE teachers do indeed adapt these to the individual abilities and skills, as well as to the needs of their classes. Successfully designing such lessons includes, among other things, engaging in a process of negotiation with the learner. At present this, however, means that teachers in

Germany must often consciously ignore curricular standards and work contrary to commonly accepted lines of discourse on teaching methodology. This is, however, likely not just a problem in Germany.

From the evidence presented above, it is clear that in the context of inclusion in sport pedagogy settings – possibly indeed for sport in general as a cultural phenomenon – there is a need for an entirely new theoretical basis. Efforts to achieve an inclusive environment in this area would do well to try to identify a suitable new theoretical basis and to engage in a process of self-reflection that goes deeper than has been the case up to now. Without a doubt, ableism can be helpful in this process – sensitizing us to hidden and subliminal barriers to inclusion. Only by involving all the stakeholders can we eventually hope to escape the (sport pedagogic) trap, in which some bodies will be 'forgotten'.

Notes

1. Similar issues also exist in areas unconnected to the body (one only needs to think of psychological or mental phenomena). However, the focus of this article has been deliberately limited to the bodily aspects.
2. This is all the more extraordinary as Weiler (2003) has shown that this image of humanity had already been used by Aristotle to legitimize the exclusion of slaves, barbarians and women from the category of human beings and that from the beginning onward 'a sort of inversion of the *kalokagathia* ideal existed, namely that ugly human beings were considered to be evil and dangerous'.

Disclosure statement

No potential conflict of interest was reported by the authors.

ORCID

Martin Giese http://orcid.org/0000-0002-5621-9429

References

Ainscow, M., and S. Miles. 2009. *Developing Inclusive Education Systems. How Can We Move Policies Forward?* http://www.ibe.unesco.org/fileadmin/user_upload/COPs/News_documents/2009/0907Beirut/DevelopingInclusive_Education_Systems.pdf.

Alkemeyer, T., and R. Schmidt. 2003. "Habitus and Self. Irritations of Body Hexis in Popular Culture." In *Bodys Set for the Match*, edited by T. Alkemeyer, B. Boschert, R. Schmidt, and G. Gebauer, 77–102. Konstanz: UVK.

Allouche, S., S. Bateman, J. Gayon, J. Goffette, and M. Marzano, eds. 2015. *Inquiring Into Human Enhancement. Interdisciplinary and International Perspectives*. Basingstoke: Palgrave Macmillan.

Amrhein, B., and T. Booth. 2014. "An Interview with Prof. Tony Booth: Developing Inclusion – A Continous Process." In *Teaching Methodology Inclusive. Searching didactical Guidelines for Treating Diversity in Schools*, edited by B. Amrhein, and M. Dziak-Mahler, 25–29. Münster: Waxmann.

Andreasson, J., and T. Johansson. 2014. "The Fitness Revolution. Historical Transformations in the Global Gym and Fitness Culture." *Sport Science Review XXIII* 3–4: 91–112.

Aschebrock, H., and G. Stibbe. 2007. *Curricula Sport. Basics of the Research of Curricula Sport*. Baltmannsweiler: Schneider.

Barrow, G. 2013. "Not Just a Game: The Impact of Sports on U.S. Economy." *emsi [Economic Modeling specialists Intl.]*. http://www.economicmodeling.com/2013/07/09/not-just-a-game-the-impact-of-sports-on-u-s-economy/.

Booth, T., M. Ainscow, and D. Kingston. 2002. *Index for Inclusion: Developing Play, Learning and Participation in Early Years and Childcare*. Bristol: Centre for Studies on Inclusive Education. http://www.eenet.org.uk/resources/docs/Index%20EY%20English.pdf.

Buchner, T., L. Pfahl, and B. Traue. 2015. "On the Critic of Abilities: Ablism as a New Research Perspective of the Disability Studies and its Partners." *Zeitschrift für Inklusion* 2. http://www.inklusion-online.net/index.php/inklusion-online/article/view/273/256.

Duncan, M. C. 1994. "The Politics of Women's Body Images and Practices: Foucault, The Panopticon, and Shape Magazine." *Journal of Sport and Social Issues* 18 (1): 48–65.

Ehni, H. 1977. *Sports and Physical Education. Didactic Analysis and Examples from the School Practice*. Schorndorf: Hofmann.

Fend, H. 1975. "Societal Prerequisites and Consequences of Reforming Curricula Out of the Perspective of Theories of Socialization." In *Handbook Curricula*, edited by K. Frey, 92–103. München: Piper.

Foucault, M. 1977. *Discipline and Punish. The Birth of the Prison*. New York: Vintage Books.

Frandsen, K., and S. Lomborg. 2016. "Self-tracking as Communication." *Information, Communication & Society* 19 (7): 1015–1027.

Funke, J. 1991. "Open Lessons – Teach Further Open." *Sportpädagogik* 15 (2): 12–18.

Giese, M. 2016. "Critical Considerations on an Anthropological Foundation." *Sportwissenschaft* 46 (2): 102–109.

Grupe, O. 1984. *Bases of Sport Pedagogy. Body, Movement and Experience in Sports*. Schorndorf: Hofmann.

Grupe, O. 1993. "An Olympic Image of Humanity and Olympic Education." In *Aspects of Sport Pedagogy: Contributions to the Pedagogical Discourse on Sport*, edited by R. Prohl, 31–38. Schorndorf: Hofmann.

Gugutzer, R. 2015. *Sociology of Body*. Bielefeld: Transcript.

Heyl, V., and S. Seifried. 2014. "'Inclusion? Anyway, Everyone's in Favour For It!?' Research on Attitudes Towards Inclusion." In *Inclusive Education: Findings and Concepts of Teaching Methodology and Special Education*, edited by S. Trumpa, S. Seifried, E.-K. Franz, and T. Klauß, 47–60. Weinheim: Beltz.

Jaric, S., and G. Markovic. 2004. "Movement Performance and Body Size: The Relationship for Different Groups of Tests." *European Journal of Applied Physiology* 92: 139–149.

Krick, F., and R. Prohl. 2006. "Curricula and Curricula Research – Programmatically Basics of Physical Education." In *DSB-SPRINT-Study. A Study on the Situation of School Sports in Germany*, edited by Deutscher Sportbund, 19–52. Aachen: Meyer & Meyer.

Krüger, M. 1993. *Introduction in the History of Physical Education and Sports. Part 2: PE in the 19th Century*. Schorndorf: Hofmann.

Kurz, D. 1993. *Physical Education in the Federal Republic of Germany. Eras of a Teaching Methodology*. Bielefeld: University of Bielefeld.

Laging, R. 2005. "Movement and Body Education." In *Theoretical Basics on Physical education*, edited by J. Bietz, R. Laging, and M. Roscher, 159–179. Baltmannsweiler: Schneider.

Linton, S. 1998. *Claiming Disability. Knowledge and Identity* (Cultural front). New York: New York University Press.

Macdonald, D. 2011. "Like a Fish in Water: Physical Education Policy and Practice in the Era of Neoliberal Globalization." *Quest* 63, 36–45.

Meier, S., and S. Ruin. 2015. "Is There a Change Needed? Body and Performance in the Context of Inclusive PE." In *Inclusion as a Challenge, Task und Chance for PE in Schools*, edited by S. Meier and S. Ruin, 81–99. Berlin: Logos.

Meinberg, E. 2011. *Bodily Education in the Technical Civilisation. About Treating the Body*. Berlin: Lit.

Merleau-Ponty, M. [1945] 2011. *Phenomenology of Perception*. London: Routledge.

Meuser, M. 2004. "Between 'Body Oblivion' and 'Body Boom': Sociology on the Body." *Sport and Society* 1 (3), 197–218.

Nussbaum, M. C. 2006. *Frontiers of Justice. Disability Nationality Species Membership*. Cambridge, MA: Belknap Press of Harvard University Press.

Overboe, J. 1999. "'Difference in Itself': Validating Disabled People's Lived Experience." *Body & Society* 5 (4): 17–29.

Prohl, R. 2010. *Ground Plan of Sport Pedagogy*. Wiebelsheim: Limpert.

Reich, K. 2012a. *Equality of Opportunitiess and Forms of Capital. Social and Individual Chances in Times of Capitalisation*. Wiesbaden: Springer.

Reich, K. 2012b. *Inclusion and Eductional Justice*. Weinheim: Beltz.

Reinartz, V., and M. Schierz. 2007. "Biography Work as a Contribution to Professionalisation of PE Teachers? Justifications, Concepts, Limits." In *Profession PE-teacher. Personality and Competencies of the PE-teacher*, edited by W.-D. Miethling, and P. Gieß-Stüber, 39–55. Baltmannsweiler: Schneider.

Ruin, S. 2014. "Fitter, Healthier, More Able to Work – On the Narrowing of the Body Image in Physical Education Curricula in the Process of Competence Orientation." *Zeitschrift für Sportpädagogische Forschung* 2 (2): 77–92.

Ruin, S. 2015. *Body Images in PE-concepts – An Examination Out of the Perspective of the Sociology of the Body*. Berlin: Logos.

Ruin, S., and G. Stibbe. 2014. "The Educational and Rearing Aspects of Curricula Oriented Toward Competence." *Sportunterricht* 63 (6), 168–173.

Shilling, C. 2012. *The Body and Social Theory*. London: Sage.

Söll, W. 2000. "The Sport-concept in Past and Present." *Sportunterricht* 49 (1), 4–8.

Stibbe, G. 2011. "Standards, Competencies and Curricula in Physical Education – An Introduction." In *Standards, Competences and Curricula*, edited by G. Stibbe, 11–15. Schorndorf: Hofmann.

Stibbe, G. 2013. "For Spectrum Sport Didactic Positions – A Conceptual Trend Report." In *Didactic Concepts for Physical Educations*, edited by H. Aschebrock and G. Stibbe, 19–52. Aachen: Meyer & Meyer.

Stinkes, U. 2008. "Education in Response to the Need and Coecrion to Lead His Life." In *People with Complex Disabilities*, edited by B. Fornefeld, 82–107. Munich: Reinhardt.

Thiele, J. 2008. "'Enlightment, What Else?' – Developments in Physical Education and its Future Against the Background of Neoliberal Monopolization of the Educational System." *Spectrum der Sportwissenschaften* 20 (2): 59–74.

Tiemann, H. 2012. "Diversity in Physical Education – Challenges and Enrichments." *Sportunterricht* 61 (6): 168–172.

TNS Emnid, ed. 2014. *3. Jako-O Education Study. Parents Judge Schools in Germany*. Short abstract. https://cdn.jako-o.de/content/LP/3bildungsstudie/PDF/Kurzzusammenfassung_Bildungsstudie_JAKO-O_100914.pdf.

UN (United Nations). 2006. *Convention on the Rights of Persons with Disabilities*. New York: UN.

Weiler, I. 2003. "The Greek Athlete – Modell of a Timeless Male Anthropogenetitc? Reflections on the Antique Physiognomy." In *Images of Humanity in Sports*, edited by M. Krüger, 51–83. Schorndorf: Hofmann.

Zirfas, J. 2012. "An Pedagogy Anthropology of Disability." In *Ethics in Special Education*, edited by V. Moser and D. Horster, 75–89. Stuttgart: Kohlhammer.

Social participation of people with disabilities in boxing and capoeira: a comparative ethnographic multi-sited focus

Martial Meziani

ABSTRACT

This research focuses on the social participation of people with disabilities practising capoeira in Brazil and boxing in France. From a multi-sited ethnographic research, we observed that disability did not prevent social participation. On the one hand, capoeira and boxing are based on cultural values through which vulnerability and alterity are seen positively. On the other hand, the degree of socio-political participation is higher in boxing, because disabled boxers have had to stand up for disability rights in order to be officially recognized within the federal boxing system. Conversely, in capoeira, disabled capoeiristas have to follow the path of the master to be accepted, which gives them position for potential increase in the social participation of disabled people.

In this paper, we study the social participation of people with disabilities practicing capoeira in Brazil and boxing in France, from a comparative ethnographic multi-sited focus. In other words, we use several ethnographic cases to understand the social statute of people with disabilities in these two sports. For the last 20 years, the social participation of people with disabilities has been an increasingly important issue in contemporary societies. We want to examine the practical consequences of the emergence of this issue in the context of sports.

New social and moral injunctions of inclusion emerged and became the main ideology in the field of education (UNESCO 1994, 2010). With inclusion, the environment has to be designed for everyone, and especially for people with disabilities (WHO 2001; UN 2006). In this context, France in 2005 and Brazil in 2008 passed laws to promote the human rights of people with disabilities. These legal changes had significant impacts on sports with strong educational values, such as boxing and capoeira.

In the following, we focus on the role of disabled boxers and capoeiristas in their own participation to climb up the social ladder of each activity. To do this, we have to understand the social and cultural contexts of these sports. In this sense, with the emergence and extension of the concept of social participation, we can observe that sport has changed its social function, particularly in public policies. Sport is not only an educational space, it has also turned into a privileged tool for social inclusion (Council of European Union

2010). We therefore have to analyse how disabled people participate actively in the world of sport. Can they practice sport with the same freedom as other practitioners? If so, do they take decisions for their own social participation? Are they included in groups with non-disabled persons? If they are, can they fully participate? How is it possible? To answer these questions, we tried to understand how disabled people participate 'in the ring', but also at the organizational level. Indeed, if people with disabilities manage to participate at this level, they could have the power to change the practices and social meanings of sport.

This paper is divided into three parts. In the first part, we will present the social context and theoretical framework. Even though authors conceptualized an inclusion scale for every type of practice, it also appears, as in the school system (Michailakis and Reich 2009), that active participation is determined by sociological dimensions. In other words, social participation is determined by cultural values, possible careers and social norms. In the second part, we will discuss methodological aspects. We will explain why we chose to compare capoeira and boxing. Although capoeira and boxing are considered as fighting practices and educational activities, they are structured in significantly different ways. In the third part, we will present findings to discuss the different forms of active participation in several boxing gyms and capoeira academies where observations have been carried out. This social participation alters the social meaning of each activity. In this sense, one's position in the social hierarchy is determined by compliance with specific standards. Even though there is no stigmatization, a process of normalization is underway which leads disabled boxers and capoeiristas to learn to respect norms and cultural values.

Theoretical framework and context

The issue of social participation questions the social function of sport in contemporary societies. Through the concepts of inclusion and participation, public policies and social mobilizations question the educational function of sport. Indeed, from the point of view of public policies, considering that sport has to promote social inclusion, leads us to think of sport as an institution of social affiliation (Castel 1995), which implies that we consider sport from a structuralist perspective (Elias and Dunning 1986; Guttman 2004). It also implies that we consider sport in its political dimensions (Gasparini 2008). Yet, these perspectives are not sufficient for us to understand the social changes in the daily life for social actors, be they disabled or not. For this reason, we chose to focus our approach on a microsociological perspective. However, to understand social stakeholders, we have to understand the context of emergence of the issue of social participation in boxing in France, and in capoeira in Brazil. Indeed, the French Boxing Federation (FFB) created the *handiboxe* licence, to support boxers with disabilities, following the national movement for people with disabilities, even though there had been individual and local initiatives for 25 years beforehand. The *handiboxe* is a specific licence in FFB for people with disabilities, which authorizes specific competitions for them.

In capoeira, any federation coerces social actors. Through contracts between municipalities, associations for disabled persons and groups of capoeira, local initiatives have multiplied in order to create inclusive classes. It is understandable that these social actors try to comply with political expectations.

However, studies about sport for people with disabilities raise the question of the social function of sport. For some, sport is a way of developing forms of collective mobilizations

(Murphy 2001), contributing to try to change the image of disability, even though stigmatization goes on (Schantz and Gilbert 2012). Sport clubs, which involve people with disabilities have also been studied as a way to build a new social identity (Marcellini 2005). Recent studies have shown that, with the emergence of inclusive ideals, the social function tends to change social function of sport. From now on, social representations will change, by promoting interactions between persons with and without disabilities through sport activities (Meziani 2015; Valet 2015). Several authors have designed a scale for inclusion in sports (Black 2011; Black and Stevenson 2011; Black and Williamson 2011; Stevenson 2009; see also Kiuppis in this volume). In this perspective, authors divide physical activity into five types: separate practices (Paralympic sports), parallel practices (sport for all with separate activities), reverse integration practice (such as wheelchair basketball, see Mojtahedi and Katsui in this volume), open practices (such as dance) and modified practices (such as *Baskin*, see Valet in this volume). From this standpoint, capoeira can be seen as an open practice because the activity does not need to be modified to be practised by individuals with and without disabilities on the same playground. *Handiboxe* is a reverse integration practice, as we will later see.

In our study, we should not underestimate the importance of social organization, as political decisions are taken in the context of the institutional system. To fully participate, people with disabilities therefore have to fit into this hierarchy. Thus, decision-makers and coaches determine the degree of social participation of people with disabilities. In this sense, if a disabled athlete plays a major role in the organizational hierarchy, he/she acquires the legitimacy to transform his/her sport. In this perspective, the main point is not to know whether people with disabilities can take part in the same sport or not, but to be aware of their position in the social system. The fact that capoeira and boxing instructors may have disabilities themselves also reveals the degree of acceptability of disability in capoeira and boxing. Furthermore, social hierarchy is not solely built on specific physical capacities. In boxing, careers of coach and of fighters are separated. A boxer does not need to fight at a high level to become coach. In capoeira, the mastery of the game (*jogo*) is based on the ability to adapt one's behaviour to the context of the game, not only on acrobatics or agility.

If people with disabilities have a position in the social hierarchy, they will develop their capabilities. They will also be able to spread the idea that people with disabilities have the necessary skills to lead a group regardless of the social identity of each member of the group. We decided to address the issue of social participation from a socio-political point of view, according to which obtaining statuses in the social hierarchy reveal the real degree of active participation. In this perspective, we understand sport as a human activity, in which secondary socialization and the process of professionalization exist (Berger and Luckmann 1966). This approach allows us to tackle what lies behind the scene of sport interactions. Indeed, the initiatives for people with disabilities that we have observed have been constructed by the persons themselves, especially in boxing. Conversely, in capoeira these initiatives stem from Physical Education teachers, who are masters of capoeira. These situations could be surprising, as UNESCO recognized capoeira as an activity promoting social inclusion for a large diversity of populations (UNESCO 2014). Furthermore, we observed that several people with disabilities benefited from an important symbolic position.

How is it that in boxing, initiatives were made by people with disabilities whereas in capoeira, the same type of actions were initiated by non-disabled masters? In our case, it seems that disability does not have the same symbolic meaning for boxers and capoeiristas.

For this reason, we based our theoretical framework on the theory of liminality (Murphy 2001; Stiker 2005). From this point of view, the competition system produces successive forms of exclusion, while social diversity promotes inclusion. In this sense, we can argue that masters of capoeira symbolically include disability, while boxing coaches include people with disabilities in the federal system. At the same time, the federal system produces symbolic exclusions from the mainstream system, with the creation of specific classifications. Conversely, masters with disabilities tend to not be excluded, but considered at the same level as anyone.

Methodology and objects of comparison

From a methodological point of view, we chose multi-sited ethnography (Marcus 1995; Cefaï et al. 2010; Falzon 2012) to study social participation. It enables us to collect qualitative data in different contexts and to analyse them according to an inductive approach. In boxing, the observations were conducted in five gyms in the north of France over one year and a half. These observations were supplemented by formal interviews with six trainers, five students, then three with the creators of *handiboxe*. Although the observations were first conducted near Paris, it appeared necessary to carry out observations outside of Paris, so as to understand the origin of *handiboxe*. For this reason, we interviewed key stakeholders who created this new type of boxing. In capoeira, after two initial years of study (Meziani 2010, 2012), data collection was made in four groups in the south-east of Brazil, for three months. The observations were supplemented by three formal interviews of students with disabilities and many informal discussions with four teachers. Even though a federal system has been built in Brazil, the large majority of capoeira groups ignore it.

For analysis, we focused not only on practical methods and social organization, but also on symbolic and cultural values to understand the role of disability in each activity. Through this approach, we were able to spot differences and similarities between the two activities. We chose to focus our study in France and in Brazil, because in each country, capoeira and boxing have a similar position. Indeed, capoeira in Brazil is known as a famous activity, as boxing in France. Furthermore, each activity in this national context accepts cultural and social diversity (Beauchez 2010).

Main differences and similarities between capoeira and boxing

The first difference between boxing and capoeira lies in their social organization. On the one hand, boxing has a federal system structure, which is in charge of regulating the practices, competitions and vocational trainings of the coaches. On the other hand, though a hierarchical structure exists in capoeira, its development is locally based. Thus, even though there is a federal organization in the region where the observations have been made, such an organization does not exist in the rest of the country. Above all, masters keep their power and do not delegate it to a collective organization such as a federation. This lack of power is explained by a local federal leader: 'I would like to have a useful job'. The overall situation tends to strengthen the power of masters. This situation is largely due to their refusal, for several generations, to submit their action to the Brazilian State, which tried to impose its power on capoeira (Gaudin 2009). Thus, boxing and capoeira are organized differently, especially because capoeira is legitimized by cultural representations. Indeed, capoeira is seen as *the* Brazilian sport. In that respect, contrary to boxing, masters do not need to federate their practice to legitimize it.

The second main difference between boxing and capoeira is based on the type of game. While boxing is a symmetric duel, with a winner and a score system, capoeira is a paradoxical game (Parlebas 1999; Meziani 2010). The game – as capoeiristas call it – is founded on an approach where activity stands between fighting and dancing, or a fight hidden under a pretence of dancing. In other words, motor synchronization techniques are combined with fighting skills. It explains why the game is possible without adjustments between men and women, adults and kids, disabled and non-disabled people. The most important thing consists in working out an interaction though which the two players will be able to play together. In our research, we observe that local policy-makers tried to use capoeira to develop social inclusion.

An important similarity between the two activities lies in their cultural representation. In the United States, 'the black boxer' became a cultural figure, at times when black people were ostracized by the mainstream society (Wacquant 2000; Philonenko 2002; Trémoulinas 2008). Nowadays, boxing in France is a common space for intercultural encounters (Beauchez 2010), so that the culture of boxing maintains specific ties with marginalized populations. Capoeira is known as an Afro-Brazilian physical activity, created during slavery in Brazil. Myths around the history of capoeira are usually disseminated by songs and music. They tell stories of how slaves and outlaws fought slave oppression: this culture nourishes a special relationship with the otherness, glorifying figures of marginality. Finally, each activity gives to the marginality and to the otherness social positive values.

If these elements summarized above enable us to understand differences and similarities between boxing and capoeira, they also help us formulate hypotheses about the specific status of the social participation of people with disabilities, and particularly about differences in participation in boxing and capoeira. The fact that capoeira is less regulated and follows an inclusive logic could suggest a more important active participation. Nevertheless, less regulation means that masters of capoeira are endowed with more power. More regulation in boxing, on the contrary, implies less power for the central stakeholders. The latter, within a federal system, has to comply with national laws, particularly so as boxing is not an open practice like capoeira. In the same way, under the federal regulation, boxing trainers can have a career as local leader or coach without having had a high-level career in the past. Conversely, in capoeira, to become master, apprentices have to be recognized as very good players, even though the rules are less constraining than in boxing. The particular relationship to otherness in each activity explains the role of disabled people. Indeed, masters of capoeira can continue to develop the idea that they fight every kind of oppression, as they often repeat about racism. In boxing, even though the boxing ring is still seen as a place of masculinity, boxers have developed specific awareness. Indeed, the very nature of their sport implies that they risk serious injuries. They have subsequently developed an acute awareness of human vulnerability.

Activities promoting active participation for all?

These general considerations about capoeira and boxing enable us to understand how the active participation of disabled people works. In this third part, we will present our findings, showing the similarities, in a first part, and the differences, in a second part, between capoeira and boxing.

Erasing stigma, long-term commitment and creating strong links

In boxing and in capoeira, if disabled people who attend classes want to have the ability to become central social stakeholders, they have to commit for a long time, like the other apprentices. We could consider that the social participation of disabled people is determined by their will to follow a specific path, which means a 'career' in the sense of Howard Becker (1963) and Erving Goffman (1961). In each activity, we met disabled athletes who used to be coaches or masters. For example, Steeve[1] holds an official certification from the French State and the FFB. With it, he can teach professional non-disabled boxers, even though he has a degenerative disease and is a wheelchair user. Along with other disabled colleagues, he created the *handiboxe*. More specifically, he invented the classification system to organize competitions. In capoeira, several masters have disabilities, but one graduate student (equivalent of black belt in judo) who has a specific role. Danilo, who has autism, is 40 years old. Even if he is not a leader, he participates in public demonstrations and other important events. Furthermore, his own participation to these events sheds lights on activity's ability to accept social diversity. In other words, his participation is granted at the symbolic level, because he gives a positive image of capoeira. In boxing, Steeve can participate at the practical level, even though he never led a high-level career. Beyond this, disabled athletes have reached this position because they developed strong connections. For example, Steeve has developed a friendship with Pierre, a famous French coach. Pierre has trained a woman who won a professional world championship. Steeve became friends with her too. These connections allowed him to get federal support in order to create the *handiboxe* licence.

This ability to develop links within a specific community is related to another dimension: the deletion of stigma (Meziani 2014). Thus, Jonathan, a young 22-year-old boxer with a dystrophy on the right hand, feared professional boxers' reactions when they would see his impairment during the first class. But during the third class, his mentor told him: 'If you don't take your hand out of your pocket, I will hit you!' Jonathan took his dystrophic hand out of his pocket. The boxers' reactions surprised the young man. As Jonathan recalls:

> Everybody said: 'but, we didn't know! It's huge! That's great! You are brave!' From this moment on, the disabled boxer became the 'darling' of the club.

In capoeira, we can observe a similar process based on another principle. Disabled apprentice players have to learn to face and deal with the different forms of rejection from non-disabled peers. In such a situation, a disabled player said during the semi-structured interview: 'they don't realize it. They are not aware, but it doesn't matter'. Thus, the apprentice player does not have the right to show he could be hurt. He has to remain stoic when he faces rejections. This principle is related to the *habitus* of capoeiristas. Indeed, during their apprenticeship they have to learn to be quiet and relaxed, particularly when they face adversity and violence. As this apprentice capoeirista had no overreactions, he became a master's favourite. Finally, both in capoeira and boxing, we have met with three common dimensions. First, there is a structural possibility, for various reasons, for disabled persons to be recognized as boxers and capoeiristas. This recognition is important to enter the social or symbolical hierarchy. Finally, they have the power to actively participate.

We have also noted a process of deletion of stigma. Even if this process permits social participation, all disabled apprentice players will not be part of the hierarchy. Indeed, to be part of this process, master and coach have to detect specific abilities, as it is the case for non-disabled people.

The third common dimension enabling social participation is the personal ability of disabled athletes to develop bonds. This skill is related to the two other skills and seems to be reinforced when they are recognized by coaches and masters.

However, although we noted common points in the possibilities to develop social participation in both activities, we also noticed significant differences in the process of socialization. Finally, to be recognized, disabled boxers, have to make use of institutional innovation to find their own place in the federal system. In capoeira, recognition is at first symbolic. As for disabled capoeiristas, they are already affiliated, they have not developed innovation, but they are ultimately less powerful than disabled boxers.

In boxing, advantage is given to institutional innovation

In the world of boxing, the participation of disabled people existed until 2008, but only in an informal way, in gyms where coaches accepted disability. Regarding access to competition, it was possible if the impairment did not contravene official boxing rules. The category of mental disability is still related to the risks of brain injuries. Professional boxers are aware of this risk when they go to the ring, and they are afraid that a person who has a mental disability will not control his/her own strength.

But, since 2008, the creation of the *handiboxe* licence has changed the practice. From a general point of view, this licence appeared in a context where sport has a new social function: developing the social inclusion of marginalized populations. We can understand the symbolic importance of this licence, but we can also argue that this licence stems from disabled boxers and coaches. To succeed, they had to fight against part of the federal system.

Ultimately, they created the licence and specific classification system to compete. Nowadays, three categories exist: physical, motor and mental impairments. For two years, a working group has been designing the licence and classification system. Even though there were non-disabled coaches, it appears that Pierre and Steeve, the disabled boxing coaches, maintained stranglehold in the group, despite conflicts with other coaches.

The inventor of wheelchair boxing

Before being affiliated to the FFB, Steeve started in a French kickboxing gym. He also learned the *canne de combat*.[2] He explains that 'the boxing I taught to people with disabilities looked like boxing and not like kickboxing, as they were in wheelchairs. Therefore, I became a member of a boxing gym'. This change can be understood as a strategy. Indeed, if French kickboxing gyms have welcomed disabled people for a long time, the federal system never intended to institutionalize local and informal initiatives. Steeve moved to a boxing gym in order to improve his opportunities to develop wheelchair boxing. He explains his will to develop this project as a wish to pass on his knowledge. This wish derived from the frustration not to compete:

> As I could not compete, I thought taking care of people would be a good job. And the things is, I like bringing things with people, I really do.' Independently from the type of practice, he noted that people looked at him with different eyes: 'In the gym [...] there was no prejudice. I trained and I received advice taking into account my disability.

Nowadays, after several years of learning and teaching, boxing is an essential part of his life. Indeed, it has offered him precious memories:

I lived great moments as a trainer or a boxer. I boxed with […] famous boxers. […] With my particular practice, I experienced intense moments with great champions. No matter I never achieved high level, I am a prize-winner of memories, of beautiful memories.' His initiative was rooted in an original idea: 'I was the only disabled boxer and I always had a social awareness […] So I thought, why not create a system where everybody could box? […] First, I told my gym […] I would start the project with Pierre. He immediately jumped in. We went on until we reached the federal level.

Since this moment, national competitions have been organized every year. This alliance with Pierre has enabled Steeve to build a network in the federal system, so that there are now several proxies to develop *handiboxe* in other French regions.

Abolition of rules, maintaining equality of opportunities and political vision
To succeed in this project, Steeve was conscious that it was necessary to include federal values in his own objective. This consciousness derived from a first failed experience with the *canne de combat*:

I developed wheelchair *canne de combat* […] some people opposed the idea, others agreed […] How can there be fights between people in wheelchairs and non-disabled people? With my idea, non-disabled people stands. We don't need to put standing men in wheelchairs. That's great! So, I keep struggling for my invention to be recognized, but some people were against it.

Steeve wants to develop a mixed practice. In fact, he tries to abolish classifications in the sport system. For him, equality of opportunity would be respected, but specialists of *canne de combat* do not want their sport to be perceived as a 'disabled sport'. This failure shows another reason why the FFB chose to develop *handiboxe*. The FFB seems to be more of an institutional space for innovation, than the French kickboxing or *canne de combat* federations. However, the classification system of *handiboxe* invented by Steeve takes his experience into account:

This is a classification where we separate three kinds of disability: physical, motor and mental. […] Later, [during the competition] we try to 'balance' impairments. We don't want to differentiate individuals too much. It was more related to the motor potential than to weight categories, which we did not use.

These adjustments have been made to respect the boxing culture partly based on equality of opportunity. For *canne de combat*, institutional opposition comes from the fact that equality of opportunity can be reached without regulatory adaptation. Steeve's interest is related to this equalization without adaptation: the victory of a disabled people against a non-disabled people will prove the merit of the first one. In a sense, Steeve wants to reverse the cultural hierarchy in which adaptations stigmatize disabled people. At the same time, the institutionalization of *handiboxe* was only possible because these rules have been specifically adapted to separate disabled and non-disabled people. In the same vision of social diversity, Steeve – as many other non-disabled and disabled boxers we've met – does not approve of the separation between disabled and non-disabled people. He opposes specialized federations:

If there is a disabled person in my classes, the French disabled sport federation immediately wants us to take a license in their own federal system. I'm against this idea. Any practitioner must provide a medical certificate allowing them to practice. I won't take a specific license for them. If I did this, it would be discrimination.

This anti-discriminatory stance is developing in sports classes despite the adjustments:

Disabled people can train when they want, all week long. Moreover, there are specific classes for them that, often, non-disabled people attend […] at the end of the class, everybody trains together [without distinction].

Finally, this institutional innovation will be disseminated even in gyms with a local tradition based on the training of professional boxers. Thus, Thibaut, a former 40-year-old professional boxer, tries to use *handiboxe* for his own professional retraining. In the same logic, the gym started opening specific classes for children with autism or Down's syndrome. But at the same time, Thibaut criticizes the principle of competition for this population:

> Something has been forgotten during the national competition. Some practitioners with Down's syndrome were hit in the face. I've always prohibited this. [...] [But] that's the beginning of *handiboxe*. For sure, it implies conflicts and tensions.

Even though he tries to organize part of his own work slightly aside, the most important for him is to belong to the movement that includes *handiboxe*. In this perspective, he trains Jonathan, a young 22-year-old student, and puts the young man with a dystrophy of the right hand in the limelight. For example, during an international event, Thibaut organized a *handiboxe* demonstration in front of 500 people. After the show, Jonathan explained how proud he was to have participated in this exhibition.

A boxer like the others?

Beyond this pride, Jonathan has been practicing boxing for three years. Although he did not follow the same path as Steeve, we can note a similarity with the disabled coach. Indeed, Jonathan has an important past as a sportsman:

> Yes, I used to practice golf with dad, every Sunday. I also practiced tennis and football in a sport-study program. [...] I played football in a club. One day, I was noticed. [...] It was a day when I was in great shape. I scored several goals. [...] [The recruiters] thought I was brave enough to play with non-disabled people.

After being recruited, he played at Paris-Saint-Germain's training centre for two years. He says he stopped seeing his family and friends, and also because he did not think he would have a future in this path. Julien is a man with disabilities, but he is foremost a sportsman. He also developed special skills for tennis:

> The most difficult was to serve, but I soon found a solution, as I am resourceful enough. [...] I had the tennis racket in the left hand and the ball was blocked between my right arm and the sieve. [...] My services were good.

Ultimately, Jonathan adapted the gesture to his impairment, quite like Steeve. He also created a practical innovation. During the semi-structured interview, Julien explained that he considered he had a classical background. For example, he always attended mainstream schools. More generally, 'I don't want to impose my disability'. Jonathan's discourse is opposed to the actions of Steeve who tries to impose the issue of disability to the federal system of boxing. However, even though Jonathan does not want to impose his disability, he has the possibility to actively participate in the development of *handiboxe*. As we have already explained, Thibaut made Jonathan show his dystrophy of the right hand. From this moment on, Julien became the gym's mascot. This moment is clearly a moment of reversal of stigma, but it is also the first step for Julien on his journey to be accepted and become popular in the gym. Through this discovery, Julien became brave, in his own eyes as in the eyes of all professional boxers in the club. In this perspective, we can conclude that for boxing, the capacity to forge strong links is a major individual skill. The second major skill is the capacity to innovate. Indeed, Steeve and Jonathan have been accepted because they developed specific abilities during their training. Finally, in boxing, to enable people with disabilities to actively participate, one has to develop specific abilities. In capoeira, masters require abilities to face and overcome the different forms of rejection.

In capoeira, social participation on the playground

In capoeira, the emergence of inclusion has changed many practices. Before this time, disabled masters were trained in mainstream classes, there was no division. With the obligation to make the Brazilian society more inclusive, local policy-makers and association leaders signed contracts with masters to create inclusive classes where non-disabled and disabled people would be equally welcomed. Although the former type of classes still exists, from this moment on, the majority of disabled people have been attending 'inclusive classes'. Thus, though more people with disability can practise outside of their special institution, they will have less possibilities to actively participate. As special educators manage the inclusive classes along with masters, they impose new practices, where capoeira is just used for the well-being of people with disabilities. Therefore, people living in special institutions try to develop a different way to participate.

In inclusive classes, a differentiated participation

In a first class, inclusive classes look like an awareness-raising campaign by experimentation. Soninho, a 55-year-old master, teaches young non-disabled people, between 5 and 12 years old, and disabled people from a special institution. This course enables young people to practise with disabled people. In this perspective, Soninho tries to develop social diversity among the two groups. For example, there are many games between members of each group. In this context, disabled capoeiristas give to the class a new dimension. During one of them, in the games between capoeiristas, the interactions were particularly violent. This violence from the people with disabilities was not expressed against the younger apprentice players, but against Soninho and the older non-disabled players. Alberto, 45 years old, the shortest apprentice player of the course, tried many times to knock his master off, with aggressive techniques. Other disabled apprentice players tried to impose their way of playing onto the oldest non-disabled apprentice players of the group. At the same time, with the youngest ones, they did not express aggressiveness and took care of them. All along the observation sessions, when a player knocked another off, the people with disabilities were pleased and applauded. The day when Alberto tried to knock Soninho off, the latter did not hesitate to knock Alberto back. Then, all disabled capoeiristas shouted: 'Knock him off! Knock him off! Knock him off!' while clapping hands at the same pace. Some non-disabled capoeiristas pretended to hit as Soninho had just before. Shortly later, Alberto was amused when he saw that one of the young apprentice players seemed frightened. When he played with him, he carried on until the fear was soothed. Later, other disabled players began to display synchronized circular movements so as to change the atmosphere of the circle, particularly with non-disabled apprentices wearing an adult belt. This way, disabled capoeiristas could express their emotions and feelings. At the same time, it was not a kind of catharsis, because they expressed their frustrations in a responsible way, taking good care of the younger ones.

For these apprentice players, this freedom of expression only seems to be possible on the playground. Indeed, they never participate in the most important events of the capoeira group. They never make decisions about their own participation in the adult classes, although they are all adults. This constrained social participation is shown even more clearly by the social hierarchy. Soninho explains:

They get the same belts [as the non-disabled people], but we know their capacities. Anyway, they never pass the most important belts.

To conclude, inclusive classes enable disabled people to practise capoeira with non-disabled people, though with a limited level of social participation. In another inclusive class, a female professor apologized because her sister – who had a mental disability – had followed the classes given by two masters. The master answered that there was no problem, whereas participating without asking permission would have normally been an immediate cause of exclusion from the capoeira academy, following an explicit rule. This tolerance shows how disabled apprentice players are considered. They are not taken seriously, because nothing is expected from them. However, when disabled apprentice players attend mainstream courses, expectations increase if they want to climb up the ladder of social hierarchy.

A normative expectation to integrate the symbolic hierarchy

During a *batizado*,[3] Danilo tried to impose many things to the others – where they should sit or which behaviour was suitable, for instance. As a graduate student, it is his role to check compliance with the norms, but he was also aggressive and angry. His master showed him he was dissatisfied with this attitude. At the end of the event, one professor and two apprentice players scoffed at him, just before Danilo once again tried to impose his point of view. When the teacher showed an acrobatic movement, Danilo reacted by saying: 'It's not properly done!' Challenging him, the teacher answered back: 'Come on! Do it! Show me!'

Danilo was very surprised by the answer and his three opponents laughed. This teasing has to be understood in a more general context. First, during classes, Danilo tried to perform other acrobatic movements, encouraged by the master. Secondly, as he is a graduate student, the other teachers expected him to behave like a leader. The teasing can be understood as a reminder of his expected role in the group. Expectations that are of the utmost important: Danilo participates to demonstrations to highlight the acceptance of diversity in capoeira. He therefore bears the responsibility of an important potentiality at the symbolic level to attract new disabled apprentice players.

Conclusion

In this research about the social participation of people with disabilities in capoeira and boxing, we demonstrated that this social issue is not a mere matter of imposing new norms. Indeed, the ideal of inclusive society suggests a new kind of socialization process without social barrier. However, implementing the principle of inclusion has different consequences.

Firstly, we saw how the federal system of boxing accepted disability by developing new practice methods. This gives disabled boxers an additional possibility to have a socio-political participation inside the Olympic federation. In capoeira, the inclusion ideal imposed new ways of teaching where the goal is not to train apprentice players anymore. The objective is now to change mindsets about disability. Interesting as initiative might be, we must stress that it also implies a lower degree of participation among people with disabilities.

Secondly, capoeira and boxing are specific activities in which human vulnerability and otherness differently are welcomed. In this sense, we can understand why we have noticed many initiatives in favour of people with disabilities, for many years in each activity. Through initiatives, some disabled people were able to become masters or trainers.

However – and this is the third point – this social affiliation of some disabled apprentice players is only possible when the latter develop specific skills. They must have to build strong links with their peers. This explains why, in capoeira, the main difference between two disabled apprentice players is the link developed with the group master. In boxing, the invention of *handiboxe* would not have been possible without the network developed by Steeve. Finally, we can argue that social participation rests on individual abilities. To give an example, not all people with disabilities will have the ability to face the risk of rejection or to have a political vision on individual aptitudes. Note also that these aptitudes are not shared widely among non-disabled people either. In a sense, we can conclude that the active participation of disabled people in capoeira and boxing is a reality, but that this reality does not suppress another reality, namely, that the social worlds of bowing and capoeira remain based on selection. Ultimately, masters and trainers continue to decide who is entitled to actively participate. Hence, the crucial importance of reaching a significant position in the social hierarchy.

Notes

1. All the names have been changed to ensure anonymity.
2. The *canne de combat* means in French 'martial art', in which fighters use a cane.
3. A *batizado* is a ceremony in which capoeiristas of one group will change graduation together.

Disclosure statement

No potential conflict of interest was reported by the author.

References

Beauchez, J. 2010. "Quand les boxeurs 'mettent les gants': le sparring et les limites de l'institution du combattant." http://www.ethnographiques.org/2010/Beauchez.

Becker, H. 1963. *Outsiders: Studies in the Sociology of Deviance*. New York: The Free Press.

Berger, P. L., and S. T. Luckmann. 1966. *The Social Construction of Reality. A Treatise in the Sociology of Knowledge*. New York: Anchor Books.

Black, K. 2011. "Coaching Disabled Children." In *Coaching Children in Sport*, edited by I. Stafford, 197–211. London: Routledge.

Black, K., and P. Stevenson. 2011. *The inclusion club*. http://theinclusionclub.com/.

Black, K., and D. Williamson. 2011. "Designing inclusive physical activities and games." In *Design for sport*, edited by A. Cereijo-Roibas, E. Stamatakis, and K. Black, 195–223. Farnham: Gower.

Brazil. 2008. *Política Nacional de Educação Especial na Perspectiva da Educação Inclusiva*. http://portal.mec.gov.br/seesp/arquivos/pdf/politica.pdf.

Castel, R. 1995. *Les Métamorphoses de la question sociale* [Changes of social issue]. Paris: Fayard.

Cefaï, D., P. Costey, E. Gardella, C. Gayet-Viaud, P. Gonzalez, E. Leménér, and C. Terzi, eds. 2010. *L'Engagement ethnographique*. Paris: Éditions de l'EHESS.

Council of European Union. 2010. "Council conclusions of 18 November 2010 on the Role of Sport as a Source of and a Driver for Active Social Inclusion." *Official Journal of European Union* C326: 5–8.

Elias, N., and E. Dunning. 1986. *Quest for Excitement: Sport and Leisure in the Civilizing Process*. Oxford: Blackwell.

Falzon, M.-A. 2012. *Multi-sited Ethnography: Theory, Praxis and Locality in Contemporary Research*. Farnham: Ashgate Publishing Limited.

France. 2005. *LOI n° 2005-102 du 11 février 2005 pour l'égalité des droits et des chances, la participation et la citoyenneté des personnes handicapées*. http://www.legifrance.gouv.fr/affichTexte. do?cidTexte=JORFTEXT000000809647&categorieLien=id.

Gasparini, W. 2008. "L'intégration par le sport?" *Sociétés contemporaines* 69: 7–23.10.3917/soco.069.0007

Gaudin, B. 2009. "Les maîtres de capoeira et le marché de l'enseignement." *Actes de la recherche en sciences sociales* 179 (4): 52–61.

Goffman, E. 1961. *Asylums: Essays on the Condition of the Social Situation of Mental Patients and Other Inmates*. New York: Doubleday Anchor.

Guttman, A. 2004. *From Ritual to Record: the Nature of Modern Sports*. New York: Columbia University Press.

Marcellini, A. 2005. *Des vies en fauteuil... Usages du sport dans les processus de déstigmatisation et d'intégration sociale*. Paris: CTNERHI.

Marcus, G. 1995. "Ethnography in/of the World System: The Emergence of Multi-sited Ethnography." *Annual Review of Anthropology* 24: 95–117.

Meziani, M. 2010. "La capoeira: ni lutte, ni danse. Proposition de définition." *International Journal of Sport Science and Physical Education* 89: 43–50.

Meziani, M. 2012. "Capoeira Angola et Regional. Entre tradition et modernité." *L'Ethnographie* 5: 81–93.

Meziani, M. 2014. "Normes et mises en scène de la déficience. De l'effacement du stigmate dans la boxe et la capoeira." In *Les porteurs de stigmates. Entre expériences intimes, contraintes institutionnelles et expressions*, edited by C. Dargère and S. Héas, 249–260. Paris: L'Harmattan.

Meziani, M. 2015. *Excellence corporelle et handicap. Boxe en France, capoeira au Brésil*. Suresnes: INS HEA/Champ social.

Michailakis, D., and W. Reich. 2009. "Dilemmas of inclusive education." *Alter. European Journal of disability research* 3 (1): 24–44.

Murphy, R. 2001. *The Body Silent*. New York: Norton.

Parlebas, P. 1999. *Jeux, sports et sociétés. Lexique de praxéologie motrice*. Paris: INSEP.

Philonenko, A. 2002. *Histoire de la boxe*. Paris: Bartillat.

Schantz, O., and K. Gilbert, eds. 2012. *Heroes or Zeros? The Media's Perceptions of Paralympic Sport*. Champaign: Common Ground Publishing.

Stevenson, P. 2009. "The Pedagogy of Inclusive Youth Sport: Working Towards Real Solutions." In *Disability and Youth Sport*, edited by H. Fitzgerald, 119–131. London: Routledge.

Stiker, H. J. 2005. *Corps infirmes et sociétés, Essais d'anthropologie historique*. Paris: Dunod.

Trémoulinas, A. 2008. "Sport et relations raciales. Le cas des sports américains." *Revue française de sociologie* 49 (1): 169–196.

UN (United Nations). 2006. *Convention on the Rights of Persons with Disabilities*. New York: UN. http://www.un.org/disabilities/convention/conventionfull.shtml.

UNESCO. 1994. *The Salamanca statement and framework for action on special needs education*. Paris: UNESCO. http://www.unesco.org/education/pdf/SALAMA_E.PDF.

UNESCO. 2010. "The Inclusive Education." http://www.unesco.org/new/en/education/themes/strengthening-education-systems/inclusive-education/.

UNESCO. 2014. "Capoeira circle." http://www.unesco.org/culture/ich/en/RL/capoeira-circle-00892?RL=00892.

Valet, A. 2015. "Sport et handicap: du droit d'accès au droit de partage. Le cas du baskin." In *Activités physiques et sportives: le bonheur est dans le sport. Jurisport - Revue juridique et économique du sport*, edited by M. Meziani 151: 21–22. Paris.

Wacquant, L. 2000. *Corps et âme. Carnets ethnographiques d'un apprenti boxeur*. Marseille: Agone.

WHO (World Health Organization). 2001. *International Classification of Functioning, Disability and Health*. Geneva: WHO.

Epilogue

Cheri A. Blauwet

I am very pleased to write the epilogue for this book. As an athlete, advocate, and now leader within the Olympic and Paralympic movements, I have personally had the pleasure of watching the evolution of disability sport over many years. Before my very eyes, I have observed sport opportunities for people with disabilities evolve from being seen primarily as a method for medical rehabilitation or charity to now be considered a rights–based issue, as validated in the United Nations Convention on the Rights of Persons with Disabilities (UN-CRPD). With this evolution has also come increasing resources, as well as opportunities for participation at all levels from grassroots to elite. The growth of the disability sport movement has been rapid and impressive due to the hard work of many passionate and talented advocates such as those that have contributed to this volume.

Despite this success, we still have far to go, and much to learn regarding the optimal impact of disability sport to both empower the individual, and also to augment health outcomes and provide opportunities for increased longevity and quality of life for people with disabilities. Far too often, disability sport is seen as a "nice thing to do," rather than a tool that can truly move the needle in facilitating a healthier population. According to the 2011 WHO World Report on Disability, approximately 20% of our global population is individuals with disabilities. Yet, as society, we are far too complacent regarding the impact of sedentary lifestyles and chronic disease in this population. This must change, and disability sport must play a key role. Additionally, far too often we still find ourselves in an offensive role, explaining and arguing our way into opportunities to fully recreate, play, and compete alongside our peers. Full, true inclusion at all levels remains elusive – an aspiration yet to be achieved. Ultimately, we strive for an environment in which the topic of "disability sport" becomes simply – "sport" – given the seamless inclusion of people with disabilities at all levels.

To achieve this requires ongoing advocacy at all levels, from the highest levels of executive leadership down to the grassroots participation of people with disabilities in community sports events. To describe this succinctly, I often point to a concept that was developed by my husband and known disability sport scholar and advocate, Eli Wolff (see the Preface). This concept can be succinctly described as the following causality:

Invisible → Visible → Invisible

What do I mean by this? Within any minority-based movement, people are often initially hidden, or "invisible," due to overwhelming cultural stigma and lack of opportunities for full participation in society. In order to achieve access, people must become very vocal, or purposefully "visible," in order to stimulate recognition and changes to policies and structure that enable participation. Once visible for a period of time, there is then the opportunity to

EPILOGUE

establish relationships, build understanding, and create a framework for full participation. With these changes, people may again become "invisible" due to seamless integration in all aspects of society. Although this causality has applications for all rights-based movements, I think it is particularly germane to disability. We are currently in the "visible" portion of this spectrum, but have to achieve full inclusion, i.e. a desired form of "invisibility."

Thank you for taking the time to enjoy this volume. I hope that you will continue to teach, share, and advocate for the progress of disability sport, for the betterment of us all.

Index

1970s disability rights movement 93–94

able-bodied terminology 25–26
abolishing rules 173
accessibility: access to sport 45; ADA 94; participation condition 144
access to sport: ADA 94; affordability 45; deaf female limited 65; disability divide 45–46; discriminatory processes 46–47; duty-bearers lack of consultation with persons with disabilities 46; females with disabilities 65; government responsibility 45; IDEA 94; inaccessibility 45; international aid 46; sport for all moment 133; sporting participation of all 139; sustainability 45
ADA (Americans with Disabilities Act) 94
adapted physical activity 78
adaptive equipment: affordability 45; finding 33; STEP 16
adults other than teachers 110
affordability: access to sport 45
after-school programmes: sense of belonging 96
All Sport for All: Perspectives of Sport for People with a Disability in Europe 147
alternative settings of sport: integration continuum for sport participation 12
Americans with Disabilities Act (ADA) 94
Ammons, Dr. Donalda 69
Article 30 of CRPD 41
Article 30.5 of CRPD 1
assistance model: origins 108–109
athlete status 26
awareness: physical education faculty development from running a sports camp for children with VI 85

Bandura: self-efficacy theory 52–53
barriers: accessibility 45; affordability 45; communication 65; competition 140–141; DHHGW 69; discouragement 33–35; Eugenics 29–30; females with disabilities 65; financial costs 32; Global South right to sport 41–42; impairment factors 32–33; medical system

30–31; participation of people with disabilities 5; physical impairment 31; rules 147; social 31–32
Baumeister, R.F.: sense of belonging 93
Bendix, Reinhard: terms in different social contexts 5
Bertillon, David: Inclusion Spectrum 14
Black, Ken: Inclusion Spectrum 13–15
Blundell, M.: TAs Seven Cs model 106–107
body attractiveness: children with disabilities self-efficacy 58
bonding: enabling social participation 172
boxing: abilities to overcome rejection 174–175; bonding 172; building strong links with peers 177; capoeira comparison 169–170; career path 171; creation of wheelchair boxing 172–173; deletion of stigma 171; developing links within specific communities 171; expectations 176; handiboxe licence social function 172; welcoming human vulnerability and otherness 176
Brighton Declaration on Women and Sport 71
BUP (psychiatry for Children and Young People): children with disabilities self-efficacy study 53–55; ADHD diagnosis 58; body attractiveness 58–59; CY-PSPP 55–56; leader competence development 61; participation levels in activities 59–60; physical condition connection with self-efficacy 60; quick rewards 61; regularly physical active effect 57–58; selection 57; toning down competition element 61; trying out activity intervention 54–55

CA (Camp Abilities) 78
'Calling for the Global Sport Community to Promote the Rights of Persons with Disabilities in Accordance with CRPD' IDA statement 1–2
camp programmes: sense of belonging outcome 93; types 92
capoeira: bonding 172; boxing comparison 169–170; building strong links with peers 177; deletion of stigma 171; developing links within specific communities 171; expectations

INDEX

176; inclusive classes 175–176; initiatives to creative inclusive classes 167; symbolic level participation 171; UNESCO recognition of promoting social inclusion 168; welcoming human vulnerability and otherness 176

career path of social participation 171

CDT (Critical Disability Theory) 22; Medical/Social Model distinction 25; perspectives 24

Chair in Inclusive Physical Education, Sport, Fitness and Recreation at IT, Tralee terminology definitions 7–9

challenging experiences with similar peers 99

Chang, Cindy: disabled people's need to to exercise 30

Children and Youth Physical Self-Perception Profile (CY-PSPP) 53–56

children's sport camps: participant outcomes 78

children with disabilities self-efficacy: ADHD diagnosis 58; body attractiveness 58–59; CY-PSPP 55–56; leader competence development 61; participation levels in activities 59–60; physical condition connection 60; quick rewards 61; regularly physically active effect 57–58; selection 57; study description 53–55; toning down competition element 61

citizenship: social participation 140

classroom inclusion see IE

collaboration: TAs 117

Collins, Patricia: intersectionality 28

coming home: summer camps 98

commercialization: Paralympics 133

communication barriers 65–67

communitarian model 141

communities of practice 115–116

community-based integration 138

compensatory normalization 110

competitiveness: inclusive participation in sport 140–141

compliment stereotypes 27

concealing disabilities 95–96

confidence 51

consulting with persons with disabilities in issues regarding them 46

Convention on the Rights of Persons with Disabilities see CRPD

costs: fitness 32

Courbertin: *The Fundamentals of the Philosophy of the Modern Olympics* 127

Crenshaw, Kimberlé: intersectionality 28

crippled terminology 25

Critical Disability Theory see CDT

CRPD (Convention on the Rights of Persons with Disabilities) 1, 131; Article 30 41; Article 30.5 1; Olympic Movement 2; participation 139; role of sport in life of people with disabilities 140

CY-PSPP (Children and Youth Physical Self-Perception Profile) 53–56

Davis, L.: normalizing discourse 109

Deaflympics: definition 64; eligibility 66; female participation 68; first Winter 67–68; funding 69; gender statistics 68; history 67–69; ICSD 66; interpreting services 69; Olympic Movement 2; sign communication 67; Summer 66; Winter 66; women in leadership positions 69

Deaf or Hard-of-Hearing girls and women see DHHGW

Deaf or Hard-of-Hearing see DHH

deaf sporting community: challenges 65; Deaflympics 64; invisibility 65–66; world records 67

de Bendequz, Maria Dolores Rjas of Venezuela: first deaf woman and Latin American to be elected to ICSD 69

Deficit Model 25, 108

democratization process 141

dependency: educational 109; origins of assistance model 108–109

design for all 148

developing links within specific communities 171

DfES (Special Educational Needs and Disabilities Act) 109

DHH (Deaf or Hard-of-Hearing): communication needs 67; Deaflympics participation 68; leadership positions 69

DHHGW (Deaf or Hard-of-Hearing girls and women) 65, 69; barriers 69; Deaflympics participation 68; discrimination 65; double discrimination 65; interpreting services 69; participation and leadership opportunities survey 70; reasons for lack of participation 71

disability: awareness 85; definition 8; discrimination 27; divide 45–46; terminology 25–26

Disability Rights Movement 23–24, 91–94

disability sport activity 14

disabled people *versus* people with disabilities 6–7

disabled terminology 26

disabling hearing loss 65

discouragement: inclusion challenges 33–35

discrimination 27; access to sport 46–47; deaf women 65; females with disabilities 65; intersection of gender and disability 65; school settings 95; specialized services 94

double discrimination: females with disabilities 65

Dresse, Antoine: International Silent Games 67

duty-bearers: consultation with persons with disabilities 46

education inclusion see IE

EIPET (European Inclusive Physical Education Training) 8–9

Empower, Inspire, Achieve 127–129

equality: Paralympics 134; social participation 173

INDEX

equipment: affordability 45; finding 33; STEP 16
essentially excludable 29–30
Ethiopia access to sport 42–43; affordability
 45; disability divide 45–46; discriminatory
 processes 46–47; duty-bearers lack of
 consultation with persons with disabilities 46;
 Ethiopian National Paralympic Committee 42;
 government responsibility 45; inaccessibility
 45; international aid dependence 46;
 participant characteristics 43–44; Sport Policy
 of Federal Democratic Republic of Ethiopia
 42; sustainability 45; wheelchair basketball
 integration 42–43
Ethiopian Basketball Federation 42
Ethiopian National Paralympic Committee 42
Eugenics 24–25; barrier to inclusion 29–30
European Inclusive Physical Education Training
 (EIPET) 8–9
exclusion: shift to specialization 141; sporting
 competitions 11–12
expectations: social participation 176

facilitating integration 146
faculty member's professional development
 from running sports camp for children
 and youth with VI 79, 82; case study
 design 78; data analysis 80; data collection
 79–80; effects on students 77; empowering
 participants 85; high learning expectations
 85–86; participants 79; pre-service teacher
 attitudes 86; research 77, 83–84; service
 64–65, 77, 84–85; teaching role 77, 81–83;
 trustworthiness 81
females with disabilities 65
FFB (French Boxing Federation) 167; handiboxe
 licence 167; institutionalization of handiboxe
 173–174
FIBA (International Basketball Federation):
 Ethiopian Basketball Federation 42
fitness 24–25; costs 32; discouragement
 33–35; Eugenics-influenced barriers 29–30;
 impairment factors 32–33; medical system
 barriers 30–31; self-expression 36; social
 barriers 31–32; supportive factors 35–36
Fitter Families contests 24
Fougeyrollas, Patricks: inclusion *versus*
 participation 138
Fox, K.R.: physical self-esteem 62
free time: social participation 140
French Boxing Federation *see* FFB
friendship development 96–97; summer camps
 99–100
functional integration 143; inclusive participation
 in sport 145
*The Fundamentals of the Philosophy of the Modern
 Olympics* 127
funding: Deaflympics 69; Global South disability
 sports 46

Garland-Thomson 23–24
gender: access to sport 47; Deaflympics statistics
 68; intersection with disability 65; role
 reinforcement 36; TAs 114; *see also* DHHGW
Gesler, W.M.: therapeutic landscape 98
Gill, C.J.: coming home 98
global self-esteem: children with disabilities self-
 efficacy 57
Global South: disability sport funding 46; right to
 sport barriers 41–42
Golden, Marilyn: disability discrimination 27
government responsibilities: access to sport 45
Groff, D.J.: identity exploration 98
Guidelines for Inclusion 10
Guttman, Ludwig: Paralympic movement 128

Habilitation Centre children with disabilities
 self-efficacy study 53–55; ADHD diagnosis
 58; body attractiveness 58–59; CY-PSPP
 55–56; leader competence development 61;
 participation levels in activities 59–60; physical
 condition connection with self-efficacy 60;
 quick rewards 61; regularly physically active
 effect 57–58; selection 57; toning down
 competition element 61; trying out activity
 intervention 54–55
handiboxe licence 167; creation 171;
 institutionalization 173–174; social function 172
Harris, J.: rights 130–131
Heidi 29–30
heroic narrative 108
hierarchy: disability groups 46–47
Hollywood movies: social isolation reinforcement
 29–30
humanistic approach 108–109
human rights: *Convention on the Rights of Persons
 with Disabilities* 131; entitlement 131; natural
 rights 130; policing UN agreements 132;
 sport for all 133; *Universal Declarations of
 Human Rights* 131; universalism 132; *Vienna
 Declaration* of 1993 131; vulnerability of
 human beings 132–133

IBE (International Bureau of Education):
 inclusion 4
ICF (International Classification of Functioning,
 Disability and Health) 8
ICSD (International Committee of Sports for the
 Deaf) 64; Deaflympics gender participation
 statistics 68; DHHGW needs 71; governing
 Deaflympics 66; IOC recognition 66;
 membership 67; objectives 66–67
IDA (International Disability Alliance): 'Calling
 for the Global Sport Community to Promote
 the Rights of Persons with Disabilities in
 Accordance with CRPD' 1–2
IDEA (Individuals with Disabilities Education
 Act) 91, 94

INDEX

identity exploration: summer camps 98
IE (Inclusive Education) 4; benefits 94–95; deficit model of disability 108; dependency and passivity 109; fostering sense of belonging 96; inclusion debates 10; inclusion in regular classrooms 94–95; inclusion in sport comparison 5–6; mainstream secondary schools 109–110; meeting normal social perception 95; negative outcomes 95; new 10; one-size-fits all standard 94; origins of assistance model 108–109; PE 114–115; peer role models 96; sense of belonging 96; schools as alienating institutions 94; social participation 140; support staff naming 110; weaknesses 95; *see also* TAs
impairment: barriers 31–33; hierarchy of disability groups 46–47; inability and deficiency 108; injury risks 33; severity 32
inaccessibility: access to sport 45
inclusion: camouflages the social inequalities 97; connection with participation 138; definition 94; Disability Rights Movement 23–24; intent 94; masking and emphasizing participant differences 97; meeting normal social perception 95; negative outcomes 97; one-size-fits all standard 94; as participative integration 138; PE 114–115; scale 168; social inequalities 96; sport versus education comparison 5–6
Inclusion Spectrum 11; introduction 13; modalities of practice 14–15; types of physical activity 14
inclusive camp settings 92: camouflages social inequalities 97; negative outcomes 97; unstructured time 98
Inclusive Education *see* IE
inclusive participation in sport 139–141; accessibility 144; adverse impact on individual sporting participation 145; competition barrier 140–141; design for all 148; functional integration 145; inclusion scale 168; individuation 141–142; integration levels 143; mainstream activities 144–145; physical integration 144; quality of participative experience 146–147; relational ontology 142; role of sport in life of people with disabilities 140; rules as barrier 147; Simon don's epistemology 141–143; social participation forms 140; sports designed for all 148; standardization and segregation 141; transindividuation 142–143
inclusive summer camps: friendship development 96–97
Index for Inclusion 138
individualizing: physical activity 60
Individuals with Disabilities Education Act (IDEA) 91, 94
individuation of people 141–142

informal social opportunities: summer camps 100
injury risks: impairment vulnerabilities 33
institutionalization: handiboxe 173–174
instructional assistants 110
integration 129–130; community-based 138; facilitating 146; inclusive participation in sport 143; normalizing 146; participative 138
integration continuum for sport participation: alternative settings 12–13; revisions 13–14
internalized oppression 26–27
international aid: access to sport 46
International Basketball Federation (FIBA) 42
International Bureau of Education (IBE) 4
International Charter of Physical Education and Sport 133
International Classification of Functioning, Disability and Health (ICF) 8
International Committee of Sports for the Deaf *see* ICSD
International Conference on Education: inclusion 4
International Disability Alliance (IDA) 1–2
International Paralympic Committee (IPC) 125
International Silent Games 67 *see also* Deaflympics
interpreting services for DHH 69
intersectionality 27–28
intimate sharing 96
invalid terminology 25
invisible disabilities: concealing disability and passing as nondisabled 95–96
IOC (International Olympic Committee): agreement with IPC 125; ICSD recognition 66; Olympic Charter 2 126, 133
IPC (International Paralympic Committee) 125–129

Jeanes: sports development continuum 11–12
Jordan, Jerald M. 65–66
justice as fairness 132

Kleiber, D.A.: identity exploration 98

Labanowich, S.: agglutination of Paralympic Games into the Olympics 127
language: re framing oppressive 35
Lankshear, Colin: literacy in reform conceptions 9
learning experiences: summer camps 99
Leary, M.R.: sense of belonging 93
leaving no one behind 41
Le Clair: disability definition 8
literacy in reform conceptions 9
Lloyd, C.: compensatory normalization 110
Locke, J.: natural rights 130

INDEX

MacIntyre, A.: vulnerability of human beings 132–133
Magee: sports development continuum 11–12
mainstreaming 144–147
mainstream secondary school inclusion 109–110
Malion:
Malion, Ida: TAs evolution from independent tutor to collaborative partner 114; teaming 117
Marston, R.: university faculty teaching, research, and service roles 77
meaning of words 5
media representation: Deaflympics 69; triumph over adversity 108
Medical Model 25; barriers to inclusion 30–31; cured of disability to attain fit body 29; participation 139
medical summer camp programmes 92
membership: ICSD 67
Million Dollar Baby 30
modalities of practice: inclusion spectrum 14–15
modified activity activities 15
Morris, Estelle: mum's army 107
motivations: quick rewards 61
mum's army 107
Murderball 23–24

National Recreation and Park Association: inclusion practices 91
natural rights 130
NCPE (National Curriculum for Physical Education) 114–115
negative outcomes: inclusive camp settings 97; school settings 95
New Inclusive Education 10
non-teaching staff 110
normalizing: discourse 109; integration 146
normal social perceptions 95–96
Novak, A.: disability divide 45–46
Nussbaum, Martha: 10 universal capabilities 131; Rawlsian justice as fairness 132

Oliver, M.: integration based on normality 129
Olympics: IOC Olympic Charter 2, 126, 133; marketing with Paralympics as single entity 126; Movement 2
Olympism 127
open activity 15
oppression: deaf women 65; internalized 26–27; language 36
outcomes of running sport camp for children and youth with VI on adapted physical activity faculty roles 79, 85; high learning expectations 85–86; research 83–94; service 84–85; teaching 81–82
overcoming disability stereotype 27

paraeducators 110
parallel activities 14
Paralympics: commercialization 133; Empower, Inspire, Achieve 127–129; equality 134; integration within sport 129–130; marketing with Olympics as single entity 126; Olympic Movement 2; paralympism methods 126–129; policing UN human rights agreements 132
paralympism 126–129
paraprofessional 110
participation in sports: competition barrier 140–141; competitiveness 140–141; connection with inclusion 138; CRPD 139; integration 138; quality of life 134; role of sport in life of people with disabilities 140; *see also* barriers
participative culture 137
passing as nondisabled 95–96
passivity 109
Patrick O'Hearn Elementary School inclusion practices 95
peer role models: inclusive classrooms 96; summer camps 99–100
PE (Physical Education) inclusion: disabled student participation 114–115; Seven Cs model 106–107; TAs 117
Penney, D.: privileging of PE games and marginalized activities 115
People First language 6
people with disabilities *versus* disabled people 6–7
personal relationships: social participation 140
perspectives: CDT 24
physical activity: adapted 78; individualizing 60; types 14, 168
Physical and Health Education Canada: physical literacy definition 9
physical condition: children with disabilities self-efficacy 59; connection with self-efficacy 60
Physical Education *see* PE
physical impairments 31
physical integration 143–144
physical literacy: definition 9
physically challenged terminology 26
physical self-efficacy 53
physical self-esteem 52, 57
physical strength: children with disabilities self-efficacy 58
policing UN human rights agreements 132
positive messaging 37
positive outcomes: summer camp participation 97–98
professionalizing TAs 116
progressive realization 41

QPE (quality physical education) 6–9
quad rugby 23–24
quality of life 134

185

INDEX

quality of participative experience 146–147
questionnaires 79
quick rewards: children with disabilities self-efficacy 61

Raustorp, A.: physical self-efficacy 53
Rawls, J.: *The Theory of Justice* 132
reciprocity 96
reframing oppressive language 36
regularly active children and self-efficacy 57–58
Rehabilitation Act of 1973 91
relational ontology: inclusive participation in sport 142
relevant messaging 37
Rembris, Michael: athlete status 26
research mission 77
research theme: physical education faculty development from running a sports camp for children with VI 82–84
retarded terminology 25
right to participate in sports 40–41; Global South barriers 41–42
Right to Play 26
routine covering of teaching 107
Rubens-Alcais, Eugene: International Silent Games 67
rules: abolishing 173; barriers 147
running sport camp for children and youth on faculty: trustworthiness 79

Salamanca Statement and Framework for Action 10
Salmon, N.: negotiating stigma of disabilities 96
scale for inclusion 168
scanning bodies relaxation medication 33
SDGs (Sustainable Development Goals): right to participate in sports barrier 41
SDP IWG (Sport for Development and Peace International Working Group) 1, 40
segregation 141; inclusive participation in sport 141; summer camp programmes 92
self-efficacy of children with disabilities: ADHD diagnosis 58; body attractiveness 58–59; CY-PSPP 55–56; leader competence development 61; participation levels in activities 59–60; physical 53; physical condition connection 60; quick rewards 61; regularly physically active effect 57–58; selection 57; study description 53–55; toning down competition element 161
self-efficacy theory 52–53
self-esteem 51–52
self-expression 36
self-perceptions: TAs role 107
semi-structured interviews 80
SEND (special educational needs and disabilities) 106

sense of belonging 91–93; definition 93; dependent on social environment 94; fostering in school setting 96; friendship development 96–97; summer camp outcome 98
separate activities 14
service role: faculty 77; faculty members' professional development from running sports camp for children and youth with VI 83–85
Seven Cs model 106–107
severity of impairments 32
sign communication 67
Simondon, Gilbert: epistemology 141–142
social barriers 31–32, 96
social exclusion: Hollywood movie reinforcement 29–30; sporting competition 11–12
Social Model of Disability 25, 93–94
social participation: abilities to overcome rejection 174–175; abolishing rules 173; bonding 172; building strong links with peers 177; capoeira initiatives to creative inclusive classes 167; defined 138; deletion of stigma 171; developing links within specific communities 171; equal opportunities 173; expectations 176; forms 140; handiboxe licence 167, 172; hierarchy 168; inclusion scale 168; inclusive capoeira classes 175–176; institutionalization 173–174; integration 143; multi-sited ethnography 169; perceptions of normal 95–96; policy of inclusion 94; political vision 173; sense of belonging 94; socio-political 176; sport as institution of social affiliation 167; sporting participation 139; summer camps 100; transindividual dimensions of human realities 141; welcoming human vulnerability and otherness 176; will to follow specific path 171
Society for Disability Studies: people with disabilities terminology 7
socio-political participation 176
Spaaij, R.J.: sports development continuum 11–12
space: STEP 15
Space, Task, Equipment, and People (STEP) 15–16
Special Educational Needs and Disabilities Act (DfES) 109
special educational needs and disabilities (SEND) 106
specialized services: as discrimination 94
Special Olympics: Olympic Movement 2
specialty sport camps 92
sport: definition 8
sport camps for children with disabilities: participant outcomes 78
sport competence: children with disabilities self-efficacy 59

INDEX

sport for all 133, 148

Sport for Development and Peace International Working Group (SDP IWG) 1, 40

Sport Policy of Federal Democratic Republic of Ethiopia 42

sports development continuum 11–12

standardization 141

STEP (Space, Task, Equipment, and People) 15–16

stereotypes: canceling out medical knowledge 30; framed as compliments 27; gender role reinforcement 36; overcoming disabilities 27

sterilization programs 24–25

Stevenson, P.: inclusion spectrum modalities of practice 14–15

stigma of disability 96, 171

Stiker, Henri-Jacques: inclusiveness as participative integration 138

structured time: summer camps 98

summer camp programmes: types 92

summer camps for youth with disabilities: challenging experiences with similar peers 99; coming home 98; friendship development and role models 99–100; informal social opportunities 100; learning experiences 99; positive outcomes of participation 97–98; promoting segregation and alienation 98; sense of belonging outcome 98; structured/unstructured time 98; therapeutic landscape 98

Summer Deaflympics 66

super-crip 27, 35

supportive factors 35–36

support staff name 110

sustainability: access to sport 45

Sustainable Development Goals (SDGs) 41

TAs (teaching assistants) 106, 110; collaboration 117; communities of practice 115–116; contradictory demands 108; defining the role 112–113; empathy and compassion 118; gender-bias employment 114; growth and impact 112; humanistic approach 108–109; as mum's army 107; naming the profession 110; PE 117; professionalizing 116; role clarity 111; routine covering of teaching 107; self-perceptions of role 107; semi-teaching role 113–114; Seven Cs model 107; as substitute teachers 107

task: STEP 15

Taylor, Hudson: IOC Olympic Charter Principle 6 2

teaching: faculty behaviors and attitudes 77

Teaching, Rules, Equipment and Environment (TREE) 16

teaching assistants *see* TAs

teaching role: faculty members professional development from running sports camp for children and youth with VI 81–85

teaming 117

The Theory of Justice 132

therapeutic landscape 98

therapeutic summer camp programmes 92

Thomas: mainstreaming 147

Titchkowsky, T.: disability is essentially excludable 29

tragedy view 108

transindividuation 142–143

TREE (Teaching, Rules, Equipment and Environment) 16

trying out activity intervention 54–55

types: physical activity 14; summer camp programmes 92

UK: policy and practice agenda 108; Social Model 6–7; teacher shortages and heavy workload 107

UN: Decade of Disabled Persons 6; person-first terminology 6; *Universal Declarations of Human Rights* 131

UNESCO (United Nations Educational, Scientific, Cultural Organisation): Chair in Inclusive Physical Education, Sport, Fitness and Recreation at IT, Tralee terminology definitions 7–9; Charter on Physical Education, Physical Activity and Sport 2; education inclusion 4; Guidelines for Inclusion 10; *International Charter of Physical Education and Sport* 133; physical literacy definition 9; QPE definition 8–9; recognization of capoeira for promoting social inclusion 168

unique experiences: physical education faculty development from running a sports camp for children with VI 85

Universal Declarations of Human Rights 40–41, 131

UNOSDP (United Nations Office of Sport for Development and Peace) 1

unstructured time: summer camps 98

Van Rheenan, Derek: sport goalball 23

veterans: special political status 47

Vickerman: TAs Seven Cs model 106–107

Vienna Declaration of 1993 131

vulnerability: human beings 132–133

Walsh, D.: tying teaching, research, and service activities to youth sports camp 77

Ward, K.: faculty service role 77

Watson, M.: normalizing discourse 109

wheelchair basketball training camps in Ethiopia 42–43

INDEX

wheelchair boxing 172–173

WHO (World Health Organization): disability definition 8

Williamson, D.: inclusion spectrum modalities of practice 14–15

Winnick, J.P.: integration continuum for sport participation 12–13

Winter Deaflympics 66

Wittgenstein, Ludwig: meaning of words 5

WomenSport International *see* WSI

work: social participation 140

World Conference on Special Needs Education: inclusion at all levels of education systems worldwide 4

World Health Organization (WHO) 8

WRC (World Records Commission): deaf athletics 67

WSI (WomenSport International) 69–70; Task Force on Deaf and Hard of Hearing Girls and Women in Sport Survey 73–75

Milton Keynes UK
Ingram Content Group UK Ltd.
UKHW021840180324
439528UK00017B/131